Using Technology in the Library Workplace

LIBRARY SUPPORT STAFF HANDBOOKS

The Library Support Staff Handbook series is designed to meet the learning needs of both students in library support staff programs and library support staff working in libraries who want to increase their knowledge and skills.

The series was designed and is edited by Hali Keeler and Marie Shaw, both of whom teach in support staff programs and have managed libraries.

The content of each volume aligns to the competencies of the required and elective courses of the American Library Association-Allied Professional Association (ALA-APA) Library Support Staff Certification (LSSC) program. These books are both textbooks for library instructional programs and current resources for working library staff. Each book is available in both print and e-book versions.

Published books in the series include:

1. *Foundations of Library Services: An Introduction for Support Staff*
2. *Library Technology and Digital Resources: An Introduction for Support Staff*
3. *Cataloging Library Resources: An Introduction*
4. *Working with Library Collections: An Introduction for Support Staff*
5. *Communication and Teamwork: An Introduction for Support Staff*
6. *Supervision and Management: An Introduction for Support Staff*
7. *Foundations of Library Services: An Introduction for Support Staff, Second Edition*
8. *Using Technology in the Library Workplace: An Introduction for Support Staff*

Using Technology in the Library Workplace

An Introduction for Support Staff

Marie Keen Shaw

ROWMAN & LITTLEFIELD
Lanham • Boulder • New York • London

Published by Rowman & Littlefield
An imprint of The Rowman & Littlefield Publishing Group, Inc.
4501 Forbes Boulevard, Suite 200, Lanham, Maryland 20706
www.rowman.com

6 Tinworth Street, London SE11 5AL, United Kingdom

Copyright © 2021 by The Rowman & Littlefield Publishing Group, Inc.

All rights reserved. No part of this book may be reproduced in any form or by any electronic or mechanical means, including information storage and retrieval systems, without written permission from the publisher, except by a reviewer who may quote passages in a review.

British Library Cataloguing in Publication Information Available

Library of Congress Cataloging-in-Publication Data

Names: Shaw, Marie Keen, author.
Title: Using technology in the library workplace : an introduction for support staff / Marie Keen Shaw.
Description: Lanham : Rowman & Littlefield, [2021] | Series: Library support staff handbooks ; no. 8 | Includes bibliographical references and index. | Summary: "This text is written for the library support staff who are the backbone of technology success. Each chapter provides a practical overview of how the technology advances library services. With abundant examples of how to apply the technology in real situations, it is an essential handbook for students entering into the library profession"-- Provided by publisher.
Identifiers: LCCN 2021011729 (print) | LCCN 2021011730 (ebook) | ISBN 9781538145340 (cloth) | ISBN 9781538145357 (paperback) | ISBN 9781538145364 (ebook)
Subjects: LCSH: Libraries--Information technology--Handbooks, manuals, etc. | Libraries--Communication systems--Handbooks, manuals, etc. | Library technicians--Effect of technological innovations on--Handbooks, manuals, etc. | Library technicians--In-service training--Handbooks, manuals, etc.
Classification: LCC Z678.9 .S47 2021 (print) | LCC Z678.9 (ebook) | DDC 025.00285--dc23
LC record available at https://lccn.loc.gov/2021011729
LC ebook record available at https://lccn.loc.gov/2021011730

To AJ, Alyssa, Nora, Danny, and Joanie
The Young Technology Users of Tomorrow

Contents

LIST OF ILLUSTRATIONS	ix
LIST OF TABLES AND TEXTBOXES	xi
PREFACE	xiii
ACKNOWLEDGMENTS	xix
EDITORIAL ADVISORY BOARD	xxi

PART I Fundamentals of Technology

CHAPTER 1. INTRODUCTION TO LIBRARY TECHNOLOGY	3
CHAPTER 2. PLANNING FOR TECHNOLOGY	11
CHAPTER 3. COMPUTERS	19
CHAPTER 4. SOFTWARE APPLICATIONS	29
CHAPTER 5. LIBRARY SYSTEMS	39
CHAPTER 6. OPEN SOURCE	51

PART II Library as Community

CHAPTER 7. CLOUD COMPUTING	63
CHAPTER 8. NETWORK INFRASTRUCTURE	73
CHAPTER 9. ONLINE MEETINGS, PROGRAMMING, AND LEARNING	85
CHAPTER 10. SOCIAL MEDIA	97
CHAPTER 11. MOBILE TECHNOLOGIES	111

PART III Education and the Future

CHAPTER 12. STEM/STEAM AND MAKERSPACES 125

CHAPTER 13. CODING AND ROBOTICS 137

CHAPTER 14. DIGITAL MEDIA TECHNOLOGIES 149

CHAPTER 15. CYBERSECURITY AND APPROPRIATE USE 161

CHAPTER 16. THE FUTURE OF LIBRARY TECHNOLOGIES 171

GLOSSARY 181
INDEX 187
ABOUT THE AUTHOR 191

List of Illustrations

1.1	Typical Library Setting	5
2.1	Gathering Input from Library Users, Staff, and Community	13
2.2	Technology Planning Steps	14
3.1	Assistive Technology	25
4.1	Computer Software Code	31
5.1	Library Patron Barcode	42
7.1	Cloud Computing	64
7.2	Cloud Computing Models	66
8.1	Basic Network Infrastructure	77
8.2	Example of Public Library Network Infrastructure	80
9.1	Online Meeting	87
9.2	Learning by Webinar	92
10.1	Relationship among Platforms, Social Network, and Channels	99
10.2	Library Social Media	101
10.3	Facebook—Groton Public Library, Groton, CT	102
10.4	Twitter—Ledyard Public Library, Ledyard, CT	103
10.5	Instagram—Groton Public Library, Groton, CT	105
11.1	Working with Smart Devices	114
11.2	Using Library App Remotely	117
12.1	Makerspace	128
12.2	3-D Printer	132
13.1	Building a Robot	141
13.2	Learning to Code	144

14.1	Digital Audio Workstation	152
14.2	Creating a Library Announcement	156
15.1	Secure Library Computers	164
16.1	Future Library Innovation	174
16.2	Learning with Virtual Reality	175

List of Tables and Textboxes

TABLES

1.1	Library Services Use Technology	6
4.1	Example of File Extensions	32
5.1	Current Models of Discovery	47
6.1	Common Needs Fulfilled by Open Source	54
8.1	Libraries Use Five Types of Broadband	76
8.2	Network Infrastructure Components	77
9.1	Best Practices for Online Meetings	89
12.1	Types of Makerspace Equipment	131
14.1	Examples of Podcasts Sources	150
14.2	Sources of DAWs Tutorials	153
14.3	Digital Media Lab Software Considerations	157
14.4	Digital Media Lab Equipment Considerations	157
15.1	Use of Library Computers	163

TEXTBOXES

2.1	Elements of a Technology Plan	14
2.2	LSS Support Needs Assessment	15
3.1	Common Operating Systems	21
4.1	Examples of Software for Patron Academic Computers	35
5.1	Key Benefits of an Integrated Library System	41
14.1	Audio File Formats	150

Preface

Aligned with the revised national American Library Association Library Support Staff Certification (ALA-LSSC) competency standards, *Using Technology in the Library Workplace: An Introduction for Support Staff* provides clear explanations on key principles and concepts of library technology and how Library Support Staff (LSS) can support or perform its functions. In today's libraries LSS use a variety of technology to perform their work. They also are expected to be able to instruct, support, and problem solve many of the technology issues around patrons' technology needs.

This book is aimed to add to the knowledge and skills LSS need to use technology to support how patrons find, read, and view information. Divided into three parts, part I provides readers an introduction to the "Fundamentals of Technology." In the first six chapters readers learn how library staff plan for, acquire, and use hardware, software, and Integrated Library Systems. Examples of how libraries provide assistive and adaptive technologies to improve services for all patrons are found in this section.

The second section of the book, part II, discusses "Library as Community." Cloud computing, networks, social media, and mobile technologies provide remote connectivity that improves patron services. LSS learn in chapters 7 through 11 best practices to use external sources to enhance information opportunities and to connect library services to communities through online meetings, programming, and social media.

The final section of this book, part III, provides topics around libraries using technology to enhance "Education and the Future." Libraries support lifelong learning with STEM/STEAM programs that integrate science, mathematics, engineering, technology, and the arts. Many libraries also offer programs on coding with a focus of twenty-first-century career opportunities. Digital media, artificial intelligence, virtual reality, simulations, and many other technologies that once were thought to be science fiction at best are growing more common in our libraries. At the same time LSS often have the most contact with library technology and the people who use it. They need to be able to recognize and know steps to take when they suspect cyber threats and inappropriate use. This book concludes with a chapter on trends and technological directions LSS may encounter in the not too far future.

This book is essential for those who work in libraries who need to know and apply the fundamental technologies that are critical to library services and programs. It is also essential for those LSS who have or will be undertaking technical or leadership roles and responsibilities for ensuring the functioning of library hardware, software, and how they are used. Imbedded throughout the book are tables and textboxes that provide examples or give easy to understand information about a concept or related topic. At the end of each chapter is an extensive list of online references and suggested readings for further exploration of library technologies. This important handbook is geared to improve the reader's knowledge and skills so that the library can provide equity and reliable access to its technology and systems.

Each chapter is broken down with short subheadings to make complex topics easy to find, read, and understand. Tables and illustrations are abundantly used throughout the text to present key ideas simply and clearly.

The text is written for three intended audiences: working library staff, college instructors, and students in college library certificate or degree programs. No matter the type of library, there is even greater need today for LSS to understand how technology supports the work of staff, the needs of its customers, library functions, services, and programs.

There is a shortage of practical texts written for LSS on technology. Other books on this topic are written at a level that is aimed for professional librarians or are highly technical in other areas of business that do not address the library workplace. Written in clear language the author can help LSS understand the context behind the functions and uses of library technology with many examples and practical suggestions. Students who are training to work in libraries and those who currently are employed as LSS will want this book because it provides understandable explanations about today's challenges and updated accepted practices of library technology. At the end of each chapter there are discussion questions and guided practice exercises for current issues LSS may encounter.

Professors in library technology certificate or associate degree programs will want this book as a primary instructional resource. With extensive chapter bibliographies, this book supports the curriculum and instruction in teaching current issues and practices in technology in LSS academic programs.

Students will find this a useful text for the way the information is presented in clear, nontechnical language. There is an abundance of tables, textboxes, and figures that make concepts easier to understand. Suggested websites and readings at the end of each chapter can further students' knowledge of topics that are introduced in the book. Many references are from academic journals that are cited for further reading.

The structure of each chapter begins with the specific ALA-LSSC technology competency standard it will address. Following subchapter headings are definitions of key terms that explain how the term applies in library administration. The key terms are defined in the context of both their importance to administration but also how that effective library technology relates to library customer services and enhanced library functions. Each chapter has an introduction where the upcoming topics and content are foreshadowed. Background knowledge, practical examples, and many step-by-step instructions abound in every chapter. The aim of this book is to describe library technology in clear and direct ways so that the reader has both a basic understanding and the immediate knowledge of how to apply principles and processes to their work. This book has broad appeal because of its topic coverage and practical suggestions. The reader can immediately put into practice many of the ideas and skills gleaned from each chapter.

The scope of the book addresses many different aspects of technology staff should know about and be able to perform in their working with others and with patrons. Sequenced in sixteen chapters, this book is laid out as follows:

Part I: Fundamentals of Technology

Introduction to Library Technology—LSS are introduced to key types of library technology and how they are used in practice. How LSS obtain technology proficiency through working with peers, attending webinars, reading current journals, subscribing to listservs, volunteering, and other opportunities is discussed.

Planning for Technology—The importance of technology planning is presented as well as the essential roles LSS have in the process. By being involved with a needs assessment, LSS greatly contribute to the success of the library having the right technology for its work and user services.

Computers—LSS are expected to be proficient computer users, but do we understand how they work? Fundamental components are explained as well as basic trouble-shooting solutions. Assistive technologies that provide access and equity and how they are used are discussed.

Software Applications—Presented are basics such as the differences between computer languages, file types, and how they are applied. Software as a Service (SaaS), library ownership versus leasing, problems with malware, devices and drivers are all topics LSS work with and should be familiar with. Readers learn about copyright and how libraries support users with educational software.

Library Systems—The Integrated Library System (ILS) is the backbone and workhorse of library technology. Using its modules of circulation, acquisitions, cataloging, and others, LSS perform a high level of services to customers. Fixes, releases, and other terminology and functions of the ILS are explained. ILS and Discovery Systems are compared.

Open Source—Closed source software is licensed and has proprietary ownership subject to copyright and other regulations. Open source software is without these restrictions. While libraries obtain significant savings with open source, there are compromises of other benefits of closed source ILS. Major open source ILS are presented in this chapter.

Part II: Library as Community

Cloud Computing—Libraries and their users use cloud computing for all types of data storage and retrieval. A significant shift to cloud or outsources storage occurred when computing devices and smartphones became smaller and more powerful but could only function if the data they needed was stored offsite of the device. Fundamentals and service models library use are discussed along with practices and recommendations for both LSS and patrons.

Network Infrastructure—Technology as we know it today would not exist without robust networks that transmit data to and from our devices from servers around the world. This chapter discusses the essential elements of networks that provide the internet as well as comparative differences among browsers, Internet Service Providers (ISP), and broadband options. Network equipment is described and how LSS can troubleshoot basic network problems are suggested.

Online Meetings, Programming, and Learning—In just a few months the COVID-19 pandemic changed how library staff attended meetings, created and shared programs, and were able to enhance other learning opportunities online. Here, best practices for hosting and participating in online meetings as well as how LSS can be involved with online programs and partake in webinars and other forms of educational advancements are explored.

Social Media—Libraries no longer rely on traditional paper and print methods to market their programs. Rather social media has proven to be much more effective. Libraries reach different audiences with multiple social media platforms. In this chapter readers will find social media terminology, examples of what social media policies include, and expectations of users' and staff behaviors.

Mobile Technologies—What is that small thing in your pocket? On your wrist? In your ear? Most likely it is a powerful mobile technology that allows information seekers access to almost anything that can be had on a larger computer, including the online catalog. LSS learn the importance of library users being able to access the library with their new personal devices and how they can help them.

Part III Education and the Future

STEM/STEAM and Makerspaces—Libraries are places of life-long learning. Many K–12 schools and academic and public libraries found that people both young and old are drawn to a dedicated, collaborative space where they can learn through making. Libraries support career development and other purposeful learning by providing lab space that has the equipment and supplies that support an integration of science, technology, engineering, the arts, and mathematics. Readers learn how LSS are essential to the success of makerspaces.

Coding and Robotics—Librarians code? Yes, we are coders with years of experience creating MARC cataloging records. Today, teaching coding and robotics, often related to makerspaces, are successful endeavors in many school and public libraries. Here, basics of coding and robotics and how LSS can become involved in these efforts are explored as well as where libraries can obtain robotic resources for basic through advanced levels.

Digital Media Technologies—Digital technology significantly changed how music is made and how films are created and rendered. Libraries had a long tradition of circulating media and supporting its use. LSS who have the interest and develop the skills of using computers, software, cameras, and other peripheral equipment can instruct and support a library's popular digital workplace that offers patrons the ability to be creative and express themselves audibly and visually.

Cybersecurity and Appropriate Use—Cybersecurity is the combination of people, policies, processes, and technologies employed by libraries and businesses to protect their technology. LSS work directly with technology and are in the position to observe how patrons may also be using it. This chapter informs readers what to be aware of in terms of potential threats and steps to take if their technology is jeopardized. It also discusses appropriate use and why libraries should have stated and approved policies to this end.

The Future of Library Technologies—It is not trite to say the future is now. Look around and see robotics, artificial intelligence, virtual reality, and many more technologies folded into our daily lives. With the next generation network, the internet as we know it will expand to be an Internet of Things (IoT) that will seamlessly and automatically run from computers getting instructions from the cloud and other networked sources. Today, libraries are experimenting with some of these technologies that, in the not too far future, will change how they function and provide user services.

Using Technology in the Library Workplace: An Introduction for Support Staff covers new ground as its content aligns with technology competencies established by the American Library Association Library Support Staff Certification Program (ALA-LSSC). Each chapter addresses one or more of the competencies in ways that the reader can understand each requirement in real and practical applications and examples. In this book technology competencies are turned into examples of library practice that LSS can absorb and practice daily at work.

This text provides a different perspective than most books or materials written for library professionals. Simply put, the majority of library literature is aimed for professional librarians. Works are often highly theoretical and not practical. Other books on this topic of technology are written at a level that is aimed for professional librarians and not support staff. However, 85 percent of library support staff do not hold professional degrees yet will assume many of the functions and responsibilities of working with library technologies.

The many examples within this book can help the reader become more proficient and confident using the functions of library technology. At the end of each chapter are discussion questions that are written to refocus the reader to the more important or salient parts of the chapter. There is a learning activity at the end of each chapter that either an instructor can use with a class or the reader can work through independently or with other staff to gain experience or additional practice with ideas or process described in the text. Using this handbook as a guide, LSS will be able to apply the ALA-LSSC standards of technology and demonstrate their understanding of these important competencies in their daily practice and work performance.

Acknowledgments

I acknowledge all the librarians, library support staff, library boards, users, and community members who guided and supported my own learning, experimentation, and practice in library technology.

I also acknowledge my father, Harry J. Keen, who was an early experimenter and engineer of technology. He provided many opportunities for his curious eight children to have hands-on experiences with his gadgets and inventions.

With special appreciation I acknowledge my editorial advisory board who provided me with important feedback during the stages of writing this book.

I thank my executive editor, Charles Harmon, for his confidence in me and for his supportive advice throughout my writing process.

Editorial Advisory Board

Sandra Smith Rosado, MLS
Eastern Connecticut State University
83 Windham Street
Willimantic, CT 06226

Austin Stroud, MILS, MSEd
Ivy Tech Community College
50 Walnut Street
Lawrenceburg, IN 47025

Anastasia Weigle, MSLIS, PhD
University of Maine—Augusta
46 University Drive
Augusta, ME 04330

PART I

Fundamentals of Technology

CHAPTER 1

Introduction to Library Technology

Library Support Staff (LSS) know the general trends and developments in technology applications for library functions and services.

Topics Covered in This Chapter
Library Technologies
Technology Proficiency
   Workshops and Training
   Journals and Listservs

Key Terms
Analog: Libraries circulated these sound and film tapes for many years. Recorded in a continuous line with a beginning and end, one had to play or fast forward from the beginning of the tape to find a certain frame or location.
Digital: This standard of today's technology uses binary code to create, store, and process data. Computers read data that is either expressed as "on" (1) or "off" (0). Letters and numbers are converted into binary code. Search and other functions are much more efficient with digital than analog.
Library Support Staff (LSS): Term used by the American Library Association for people who work in libraries who do not have graduate library degrees. LSS are approximately 85 percent of library workers performing a wide variety of duties and services.
Listservs: Used by library staff, these are applications that deliver email messages on a topic or theme automatically to subscribers on the electronic list.
Webinar: Online event for sharing ideas or delivering instruction to improve knowledge and skills on topics related to libraries.

Every aspect of library service relies on technology, and **Library Support Staff (LSS)** need to be able to use it in order to perform their work. We live in a dynamic, changing technology environment that is influenced by consumer trends, economics, and rapid invention. These and many other factors push technology innovation that, in turn, changes how libraries serve their patrons.

Technological changes in the 1990s brought dramatic new options to Americans.[1] With the rapid development of institutional and personal computing, the internet, and electronic communications, the methods, tools, services, and systems librarians had traditionally used were transformed. No longer was the bibliographic data of a book typed on stock cards that were then filed manually into a large piece of furniture called a card catalog. Computers replaced the card catalog with the online catalog in a matter of a few short years.

School, academic, and public libraries once offered educational, recreational, and documentaries in 16 mm or other film formats for classroom or large group showings. Prior to the 1980s, libraries owned or circulated film projectors that had a take-up reel to catch the film after it was unwound and passed in front of an intense light. Sound was tracked on the film and amplified through speakers. Film would wear or break in the most inopportune places and times.

For most of the twentieth century libraries used and circulated **analog** media and specialized equipment for each format. How people viewed movies rapidly changed in the last quarter of the twentieth century as new formats developed and the price of equipment became affordable for the home. Film was quickly replaced with video home systems in the early 1980s.[2] Two new competing formats were developed almost simultaneously: Betamax by Sony and Video Home Systems, or VHS, by Victor Company of Japan. Homeowners did not need two different recording tapes, and ultimately VHS won the race because of its two hour length and ease of recording with portable cameras. Families quickly converted from the old 8 mm home films that required expensive development to VHS that could be immediately played back. Many library programs began to record on VHS and circulate to patrons or were archived. Libraries could reliably circulate these magnetic tapes protected in sealed plastic containers that inserted into a VHS player. VHS tapes were easy to use and had little breakage. VHS transformed circulation of educational and recreational visual content in libraries because now patrons could view movies and films in their homes. Patrons purchased the home equipment, but they relied on their libraries for their VHS collections on numerous topics and for all ages.

But for all the benefits of VHS, it was short-lived. The breakthrough of personal computing in the mid-1990s resulted in an almost overnight switch of analog content to **digital** format. Analog content, such as film and VHS, are transmitted in electronic signals or pulses that are continuous, with a start and a finish. In contrast, digital content such as CD-ROM and DVD, are electrical signals encoded into binary numbers of 0 or 1 for rapid and more efficient transmission.[3] While patrons purchased home digital equipment in record numbers, librarians were quickly shifting funds to acquire the new music and movie formats in CD and DVD. At the same time, the way library data was being managed and stored was quickly shifting from file cabinets, circulation drawers, and card catalogs to computers and databases, changing how librarians worked. The technology revolution of the late twentieth century created the fastest and most significant changes to the operation, collections, and services libraries offered their patrons than any time in the prior two centuries. LSS, who once circulated primarily printed books, were now handling an assortment of digital media.

LIBRARY TECHNOLOGIES

Walk into any library and be greeted with banks of computers, digital announcements, databases, and educational technology. Today, wireless connectivity is the norm to support the significant numbers of patrons' personal technology, such as cell phones, tablets, and laptops. The majority of library users today conduct their searches on their mobile phones and devices using the library's Wi-Fi.

What is the current state of technology and how do LSS support it? In a typical day, LSS help manage collections and circulate items using an Integrated Library System where acquisition, cataloging, and circulation data efficiently supports library services. LSS show patrons how to use online catalogs, self-checkout, and features of the library website. LSS may be expected to help users download an e-book or stream video content on a wide variety of personal computing equipment. LSS introduce patrons to databases to search information and support users with educational programs. Some LSS also work with media creating video, audio, and other programs that support a variety of library initiatives. LSS may input announcements on electronic boards, use graphic software programs to prepare library newsletters, post shared calendars, and use social media to promote the myriad services and programs the library sponsors each month.

Figure 1.1. Typical Library Setting. *monekyBusinessimages/iStock/Getty Images Plus via Getty Images*

Table 1.1. Library Services Use Technology

Circulation Services	Online catalog
	ILS
	Self-checkout
Technical Services	Cataloging and acquisitions
	Statistics reports
	Inventory
Hardware	Computing devices
	Multimedia
	Peripherals—printers, scanners, copiers, etc.
Mobile Devices	Smartphones
	Tablets
	E-readers
Digital Information Services	E-books
	Subscription databases
	Internet
Infrastructure	Wi-Fi
	Network equipment (routers, switches, etc.)
	Cable network
Security/Theft	Radio frequency identification (RFID) tags
	Security systems
Media	Streaming video
	Video and audio files (MP4, MP3)
Makerspaces	3D printers, scanners
	Laser, CNC, sewing machines
	Electronics
	Video, sound, and photography equipment
Marketing	Graphic, editing software
	Publications software (newsletters, fliers, etc.)
Projection	LCD or DLP projectors
	SmartBoards
	Microphones, mixers, etc.

In this book we will learn how LSS can most effectively use these and other technologies in their daily work. While technology was once primarily machines, today the term "technology" implies the art and science of applying our knowledge in all sorts of human endeavors such as engineering, medicine, culture, music, and so forth. It is no surprise that libraries, institutions dedicated to helping people find information to enhance their acquisition of knowledge, would use current technologies to enhance users' experiences and services. Table 1.1 provides just a few examples of the technologies[4] that LSS may use in their daily work.

LSS who are proficient users and are adept at solving problems with technology are highly desired by library directors. Below are some of the technology qualifications and competencies required of LSS on the job today.

TECHNOLOGY PROFICIENCY

Library directors seek LSS who are able to use, problem solve, and demonstrate an aptitude for working with a wide variety of hardware, software, and integrated technologies. Not only should LSS be proficient with current technology, they should also know about and keep up-to-date with emerging technologies that have the potential to improve library services. The following are examples of technology qualifications sought by libraries:

- Experience with social media and online marketing platforms, knowledge of/interest in new and emerging technologies
- Knowledge of computers and technology; daily tasks include circulation, processing library materials, marketing, and creating displays
- Assist with the implementation and use of various technologies; responsible for troubleshooting technological difficulties and the setup for events
- Respond to help requests from end users via telephone and email in a courteous manner
- Maintain, monitor, and troubleshoot end user workstations and related hardware.
- Work with other IT staff to complete administrative tasks

It is important to stay up-to-date with new technology because it is constantly changing. LSS have many options to enhance their skills and stay current by attending workshops and trainings, reading technology reports and journals and subscribing to **listservs** and other resources from professional organizations. When the library is considering using a new technology, LSS can volunteer to be a member of the trial.

Workshops and Training

Each state has its own library, and the majority offer online training. Some offer locally produced workshops and **webinars** that library staff can attend in "real time." The majority of state libraries support WebJunction, a branch of the Online Computer Library Center that provides a wide variety of timely online training in technology and other topics. Training sessions are often archived and may be accessed at a later date. For example, the Indiana State Library[5] utilizes WebJunction. It offered webinars for library staff on available free tools for working with social media, e-books, data analytics, and digital collections, among many other topics.

The Colorado State Library[6] offers a wide variety of technology opportunities through its online Library Learning & Creation Center. Featured recently are makerspaces with links to learning about such things as 3-D printers, successful strategies for setting up a makerspace, free tools, more than one hundred makerspace products and materials, and many more helpful links. If your state library does not offer technology training or webinars, look to other states to discover opportunities to enhance technology knowledge and skills.

Journals and Listservs

There are excellent articles written about library technology. Searching academic or professional databases will result in a plethora of timely literature. Reading articles cited at the end of each chapter in this book is an effective way to accelerate knowledge of library technology. For example, Marshall Breeding,[7] an independent consultant for library technology, writes practical advice for library staff and provides comprehensive and objective information about the many different types of technology products that enhance library services.

Another suggestion is to read the technology sections or reports of major newspapers and media outlets. *The New York Times, The Wall Street Journal,* and *USA Today* provide information about future technology and trends. Websites CNET, ZDNet, and TechCrunch provide breaking news about technology in easy sound and video bites that are comprehendible and thought provoking.

Many professional organizations provide resources for their members to communicate and share ideas about technology and other topics. An example of a listserv for LSS is LIBSUP-L,[8] which discusses current issues, training opportunities, and a wide variety of public and technical services topics.

The American Libraries Association publication *American Libraries* has a website called American Libraries Live[9] that provides access to archived episodes of web and video conferences on timely topics, including technology. You may have to upload video conferencing software to view a session. American Libraries Live is a fine way to gain new learning about how technology is and will be used in libraries.

Library directors and technology specialists seek staff who are willing to support their new initiatives and projects. If you work at the circulation desk and your director would like to trial self-checkout, rather than resist, be open-minded and offer to work with them in beta testing. Be the person who is curious about how technology can free up staff so they will be able to perform other exciting and more meaningful work. Your manager and peers will soon see you as a technology leader.

CHAPTER SUMMARY

It is critical that LSS know the general trends and developments in technology applications for library functions and services. Today, LSS cannot perform their work without a high level of technology knowledge and aptitude. Not only do LSS need to be able to work with technology on the job, but they also are called upon by patrons to help and support their use of technology on their own mobile devices. Library content and services are and will continue to be heavily reliant on digital equipment and content now and in the future.

DISCUSSION QUESTIONS

1. Why are technology skills valued by library employers?
2. Describe ways LSS can keep current with learning new technology applications.
3. How do you personally learn about technology? How may you improve your learning?

ACTIVITY

Visit two types of libraries and observe their technology. For example, you may visit a public and a school library, or an academic and a special library. Talk with two LSS at these libraries about how they use technology on the job. Have expectations for technology skills changed since they began their work? How do they obtain their training? What are some of their most serious challenges with technology? What are their successes? Write a two-page paper on the results of your interviews, comparing the two different sets of interview data. What conclusions can you draw about technology expectations for LSS?

NOTES

1. Independence Hall Association, "Toward the New Millennium: Living in the Information Age," U.S. History: Pre-Columbian to the New Millennium, last modified 2019, accessed December 27, 2019, https://www.ushistory.org/us/60d.asp.

2. Museum of Obsolete Media, "Video Format Timeline." Museum of Obsolete Media, last modified 2020, accessed February 2, 2020, https://obsoletemedia.org/video/.

3. Diffen, Analog vs. Digital, last modified 2020, accessed February 2, 2020, https://www.diffen.com/difference/Analog_vs_Digital.

4. Vanderbilt University, "Hardware and Software in the Libraries," Jean and Alexander Heard Libraries, last modified October 15, 2019, accessed February 8, 2020, https://www.library.vanderbilt.edu/technology/hardwaresoftware/.

5. Indiana State Library, "Continuing Education Toolkit for Library Professionals," Current Training Opportunities, last modified 2020, accessed February 8, 2020, https://continuinged.isl.in.gov/find-training/2019-free-trainings/.

6. Colorado State Library, "Create Your Own Path to Learning," Library Learning & Creation Center, last modified 2020, accessed February 8, 2020, https://create.coloradovirtuallibrary.org/.

7. Marshall Breeding, "Library Systems Report 2018," American Libraries, last modified May 1, 2018, accessed February 2, 2020, https://americanlibrariesmagazine.org/2018/05/01/library-systems-report-2018/.

8. Infoworks Technology Company, "Library E-Mail Lists and Newsgroups: Support Staff," Internet Library for Librarians, last modified 2017, accessed February 9, 2020, http://www.itcompany.com/inforetriever/emailstf.htm.

9. American Library Association, "American Libraries Live," American Libraries, last modified 2020, accessed February 9, 2020, https://americanlibrariesmagazine.org/al-live/.

REFERENCES, SUGGESTED READINGS, AND WEBSITES

American Library Association. "American Libraries Live." American Libraries. Last modified 2020. Accessed February 9, 2020. https://americanlibrariesmagazine.org/al-live/.

Breeding, Marshall. "Library Systems Report 2018." American Libraries. Last modified May 1, 2018. Accessed February 2, 2020. https://americanlibrariesmagazine.org/2018/05/01/library-systems-report-2018/.

Colorado State Library. "Create Your Own Path to Learning." Library Learning & Creation Center. Last modified 2020. Accessed February 8, 2020. https://create.coloradovirtuallibrary.org/.

Diffen. Analog vs. Digital. Last modified 2020. Accessed February 2, 2020. https://www.diffen.com/difference/Analog_vs_Digital.

Independence Hall Association. "Toward the New Millennium: Living in the Information Age." U.S. History: Pre-Columbian to the New Millennium. Last modified 2019. Accessed December 27, 2019. https://www.ushistory.org/us/60d.asp.

Indiana State Library. "Continuing Education Toolkit for Library Professionals." Current Training Opportunities. Last modified 2020. Accessed February 8, 2020. https://continuinged.isl.in.gov/find-training/2019-free-trainings/.

Infoworks Technology Company. "Library E-Mail Lists and Newsgroups: Support Staff." Internet Library for Librarians. Last modified 2017. Accessed February 9, 2020. http://www.itcompany.com/inforetriever/emailstf.htm.

Museum of Obsolete Media. "Video Format Timeline." Museum of Obsolete Media. Last modified 2020. Accessed February 2, 2020. https://obsoletemedia.org/video/.

Vanderbilt University. "Hardware and Software in the Libraries." Jean and Alexander Heard Libraries. Last modified October 15, 2019. Accessed February 8, 2020. https://www.library.vanderbilt.edu/technology/hardwaresoftware/.

CHAPTER 2

Planning for Technology

Library Support Staff (LSS) know the general trends and developments in technology applications for library functions and services.

Topics Covered in This Chapter
Technology Plans
Needs Assessment

Key Terms
Needs assessment: Staff, patrons, and community thoughtfully and systematically analyze and determine what they currently have and what would be required to improve technology services.
Strategic plan: Fundamental to the existence of the library, this type of plan states its mission, vision, values, and long-term goals.
Technology plan: This is the result of a process of determining how the library can best use technology to further its mission.

The word "plan" is simple, but what it represents is not. As a verb, to plan requires critical thinking, meaningful intent, actions, and often hard work. As a noun, a plan is the written description, prototype, or blueprint on how to accomplish goals or objectives in a timely, cost-effective, and efficient manner. Planning may be done in work groups that recommend new ideas or directions to a department or institution. There are many types of plans available to guide institutional success. Plans can focus on finance, marketing, technology, or daily operations. Plans could lay out long-range stability efforts and growth of the library. All organizations need to have plans that are well written and shared with their members for a common direction to follow.

Depending upon the size of the organization, planning may be formal or informal. Informal planning often lies within the conversations of individuals or a small group of leaders and is not communicated to the entire staff in a straightforward way. Formal planning is based on discussion and agreement among stakeholders. It is documented and disseminated so that the actions needed to reach the objectives are clear to all. Whether formal or informal, plans tend to fall into one of these four categories:[1]

1. Strategic plans set the long-term direction about the mission, goals, and actions of the organization.
2. Operational plans support the day-to-day running of the organization.
3. Tactical plans ask specific questions about what needs to happen to accomplish a strategic goal.
4. Contingency plans guide decisions during a time of unexpected change or crisis.

Libraries are most successful when all four types of plans are in place and understood by staff.

The word "strategic" is synonymous with the words "critical," "vital," "important," and "key." A **strategic plan** is fundamental to the existence of the library. It should state the library's mission, vision, values, and long-term goals. The strategic plan provides a high-level overview of the entire library's services, programs, facility and equipment, staffing, and other supports. It is meant to provide direction for long-term decisions, often for a defined period of five or more years. Strategic plans require agreement among library stakeholders that include a balanced representation of staff, administration, users, and the outside or external community. If your library is undergoing the strategic planning process, consider becoming involved either in your role as LSS or a community member.

Once the strategic plan is in place, other plans such as operational, tactical, and contingency have a much better chance of being successful because they are all aligned with the common mission, vision, and values of the library. The library technology plan should be aligned with its strategic plan. For example, if a goal of the strategic plan is to increase and support access of online digital information services, in the technology plan there could be specific action steps to acquire enhanced Wi-Fi capacity.

TECHNOLOGY PLANS

The library **technology plan** is part operational (such as budget), part tactical (such as what technology to acquire), and part contingency (such as what to do if there are flood, fire, or security issues).

Libraries have limited budgets, and they cannot make expensive mistakes when purchasing technology. Mistakes may range from paying too much, selecting technology patrons will not use, or acquiring technology that has too short a shelf life. An example of these mistakes would be a library that purchased a large number of black-and-white Kindles at full price just prior to the onset of color tablets and smartphones. Once lightweight color tablets and smartphones became ubiquitous, patrons wanted to view e-books in color on their own devices. With a current and approved technology plan, libraries can improve how they acquire technology for their work and for their users. This chapter explores the mechanics of library technology planning and how LSS can be active participants in the process.

A technology plan should be an evolving document that can be amended as needed. It should reflect the library's goals and needs. It is also a road map to success and a necessary ingredient in acquiring additional funding.[2]

LSS who use library systems and technology to accomplish work-related tasks as well as support customers' use of technology can be important members of the technology planning process. Because they have firsthand knowledge of how library technology performs and they can discuss with customers their library technology experiences, LSS can provide an accurate picture about what functions well and what does not.

While libraries can put their own individual spin on their technology plans, most plans follow specific processes suggested or required by the residing state library or state department of education. Technology plans are often required as part of applying for outside funding or grants, although they are no longer required for the federal E-rate program. Technology is a large and costly investment, often funded by state and local taxpayers. It is critical that monies that are asked for are well spent in a planned, cost-effective manner. The State Library of Iowa[3] recommends elements of technology plans found in textbox 2.1.

Figure 2.1.   Gathering Input from Library Users, Staff, and Community. *SDI Productions/E+ via Getty Images*

> **TEXTBOX 2.1: ELEMENTS OF A TECHNOLOGY PLAN**
>
> - Mission—State the role of technology in the library's mission. Describe how technology will benefit library customers, staff, and the community.
> - Goals and Strategies—Establish clear goals and realistic strategies for using information technology to improve library services.
> - Assessment of Current Status—Include an assessment of the telecommunications, hardware, software, and other technologies needed to improve library services.
> - Staff Development—Include an assessment of the technology skills staff must be able to perform and how training may be obtained.
> - Evaluation Plan—Include the process that enables the library to monitor progress toward achieving the plan and make mid-course corrections in response to new developments and opportunities as they arise.

Similar to many states, the Missouri State Library[4] offers public libraries support in writing technology plans. It provides a sequential checklist of specific components that they look for in the plan. With each component a state library reviewer will assess whether what they see is "good" or if it needs specific improvement. The first two criteria the reviewer looks for are the library mission and vision. These should come right from the library strategic plan. The vision is then refined to the library's technology vision. In other words, what does the library aim its technology and related services to be? What could it be in both the near and far future?

The next components are about using technology to improve library services. Clear goals, objectives, and realistic strategies should be stated for using telecommunications and information technology. How will the library ensure that its staff knows how to use the new technologies? Now the plan focuses on what the library has in place and what are its needs. A current technology inventory is required as well as an assessment that identifies the technology needs of staff and users. The next two items address how the library will fund the acquisition of new technology and the details of what will be accomplished or implemented during the time span of the plan. Finally, an evaluation process is required that includes project monitoring techniques and how often and by whom the plan is reviewed. Figure 2.2 shows the sequential steps of the checklist.

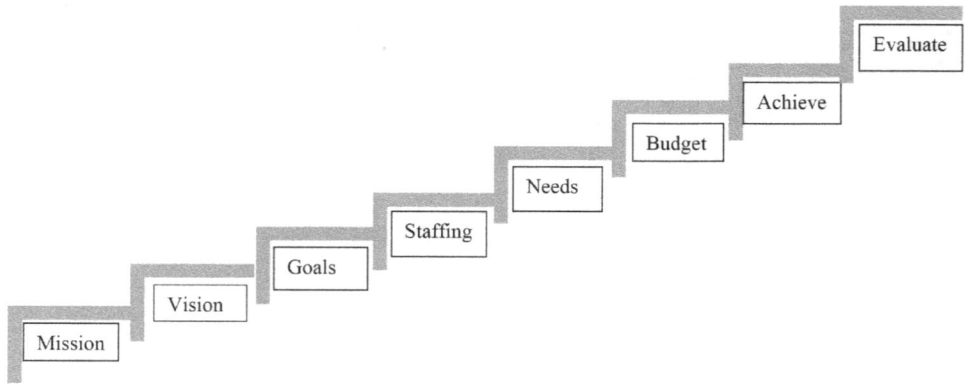

Figure 2.2. Technology Planning Steps.

Planning for Technology

LSS can contribute in many ways to the creation and implementation of the technology plan. By serving on the planning team, LSS can share not only their staff perspective of the need to improve library technology, but they can also communicate their observations and experiences about patrons' needs and usage. The second part of this chapter explores the roles LSS can play in the development and implementation of a successful library technology plan.

NEEDS ASSESSMENT

Every aspect of library operations and services rely on highly functioning and user-friendly technology. Very few libraries, except for perhaps new construction, have been able to acquire technology in a totally planned and fully integrated manner. Most libraries have acquired different technologies in batches or stages around a project, a gift, or other means. Because of this, library technology plans may greatly differ. Where one library has the greatest need to replace an outdated Wi-Fi system, another library that has strong Wi-Fi may be looking to expand its makerspace. While the needs are different, the steps in the planning process remain the same.

About midway in figure 2.2 of the technology plan steps are the actions of taking an assessment of the technologies the library has in its inventory and then making the projection of what it needs. This **needs assessment** step is at the heart of the plan because here are where the decisions are made of what should be kept, what should be discarded, and what new technology should be acquired. It is also critical that the decisions that are made are aligned with the prior strategic planning steps of mission, vision, goals, and staffing. For example, if the goal is to add video services but the library lacks sufficient staff to film, edit, and produce content, even if the equipment is acquired, the goal of offering video services will not be fully achieved. Textbox 2.2 summarizes ways LSS may support a needs assessment.

TEXTBOX 2.2: LSS SUPPORT NEEDS ASSESSMENT

- Survey—LSS work with administration to develop questions around staff and users' technology experiences and future expectations.
- Research—LSS share research about current and future trends in library technologies.
- Data Analysis—LSS compile survey data and help spot themes or recurrent suggestions.
- Communication—LSS work with library administration to communicate to the public and other stakeholders the technology plan and its implementation.
- Staff Development—LSS seek new learning in technology to assist with and be poised to undertake new responsibilities with newly acquired technology.

CHAPTER SUMMARY

LSS are essential to meeting the library's strategic mission and vision for technology implementation and use. A well-written technology plan is developed through input of the stakeholders that include staff, patrons, businesses, and the broader community. There are key elements that are necessary for a library technology plan to be successful and sustaining.

Only after a needs assessment of the current state and the future vision should acquisition and implementation steps be taken. How we evaluate staff and patron use of technology will be ongoing in this text.

DISCUSSION QUESTIONS

1. What are key elements of library technology planning?
2. What is the relationship between library strategic planning and library technology planning?
3. How can LSS support their library technology planning process? Choose one or two steps and be specific.
4. Why is it important for a library to conduct a technology needs assessment? What are the benefits from doing so?

ACTIVITY

Obtain your library's technology plan. If it does not have one, seek one from another library in your area or state. Find the Technology Plan Review for Public Libraries Checklist at the Missouri State Library's website: www.sos.mo.gov/library/certifications/tech_planning.

Step into the role of a reviewer and compare the library technology plan to the checklist. Look for each of the criteria in the plan: Header, Mission, Vision, Demographics, Planning Team, Goals, Objectives, Strategies, Staff Development, Inventory, Needs Assessment, Budget, Implementation, and Evaluation. Rate each criterion as either "Good" or "Needs Improvement." If the criteria need improvement be specific as to what needs to be done for this area to be successful.

NOTES

1. Alvernia University, "Business Management: 4 Types of Planning," Business, last modified 2020, accessed March 2, 2020, https://online.alvernia.edu/articles/types-of-planning/.
2. State of Alaska, "Technology Planning for Libraries: What is a technology plan?" Alaska State Library, last modified December 15, 2018, accessed March 1, 2020, https://lam.alaska.gov/techplans.
3. State Library of Iowa, "Writing a Technology Plan," Tech Plans, last modified 2020, accessed March 3, 2020, https://www.statelibraryofiowa.org/ld/e/e-rate/TechPlans.
4. Missouri Secretary of State, "Technology Planning for Public Libraries," Missouri State Library, last modified 2020, accessed March 4, 2020, https://www.sos.mo.gov/library/certifications/tech_planning.

REFERENCES, SUGGESTED READINGS, WEBSITES

Alvernia University. "Business Management: 4 Types of Planning." Business. Last modified 2020. Accessed March 2, 2020. https://online.alvernia.edu/articles/types-of-planning/.

Missouri Secretary of State. "Technology Planning for Public Libraries." Missouri State Library. Last modified 2020. Accessed March 4, 2020. https://www.sos.mo.gov/library/certifications/tech_planning.

State Library of Iowa. "Writing a Technology Plan." Tech Plans. Last modified 2020. Accessed March 3, 2020. https://www.statelibraryofiowa.org/ld/e/e-rate/TechPlans.

State of Alaska. "Technology Planning for Libraries: What is a technology plan?" Alaska State Library. Last modified December 15, 2018. Accessed March 1, 2020. https://lam.alaska.gov/techplans.

CHAPTER 3

Computers

Library Support Staff (LSS) demonstrate flexibility in adapting to new technology. LSS access and use basic assistive technologies, where appropriate, to ensure that all users have equitable access to technology.

Topics Covered in This Chapter
Hardware
Platforms, Operating Systems, and Central Processing Units
Peripherals
Troubleshooting
Assistive/Adaptive Technology

Key Terms
Assistive technology: These are electronic solutions that enable people with disabilities to live independently. The term "adaptive technology" is sometimes used in a similar way.
Central processing unit (CPU): The CPU executes instructions organized in programs or software that tell the computer what to do.
Mapping: Referring to a network, this is the process of creating a link to another computer, a printer, or shared devices.
Operating system (OS): This is the software that manages the computer's memory and processes, as well as all of its software and hardware.
Peripherals: These are any external devices that provide input and output for the computer.
Platform: A hardware device, such as a desktop or laptop computer, that works with a certain type of operating system and has a central processing unit.
Release: New software or revisions to existing software that is meant to correct and fix a problem or add new features and enhancements to the current version.

HARDWARE

The word "technology" refers to both broad concepts and specific things. Conceptually, technology is the application of science to achieve a practical objective or make a change in how we conduct business,[1] education, healthcare, etc. We use technology to operate libraries. Specifically, technology can be electronic or digital products such as hardware, software, networks, and digital content. Computers are a type of specific technology. The focus of this chapter is on computers, core to technology, and how we use them in libraries.

Look at the numerous lists that rank the impact of inventions, and computers will be near the top. On a list of the greatest inventions of the past one thousand years,[2] computers are ranked seventh for the impact they had on business and the use of the internet. Libraries operate similar to a nonprofit business, and computers are fundamental to almost every aspect of how Library Support Staff (LSS) do their work.

Hardware[3] relates to the physical parts of a computing system, both internally and externally. Internal computer hardware parts, referred to as components, are hidden out of sight within some type of casing and comprise the motherboard, or main circuit or logic board, hard drives, and RAM or random access memory. External computer hardware parts, called **peripherals**, can be the monitor, keyboard, mice, printers, and scanners. Most often decisions about selecting computers are around the components, such as will this computer have the RAM needed to run the functions needed at this workstation or does the motherboard support the speed that will be needed for how the computer will be used? This chapter begins with a discussion on how computers internally work and how LSS render computer support.

PLATFORMS, OPERATING SYSTEMS, AND CENTRAL PROCESSING UNITS

LSS work with a wide variety of computer types or **platforms**. Computers may be stationary, such as desktops or servers or mobile, like laptops, tablets, smartphones, or watches. Computers have platforms, **operating systems (OS)**, and **central processing units**. All three must function in harmony for a computer to work. The computer platform is the basic hardware or device that is designed to work with a specific OS. The platform of a laptop will look and work differently than the platform of a desktop. Examples of platforms are the hardware specific to Dell personal computers, Apple iPads, or Samsung Galaxy smartphones. One of the first things LSS notice when they are supporting a user is to determine the computer platform. What piece of hardware does the user need help with? Depending upon their own personal computing experiences and knowledge base, LSS may be more familiar or comfortable helping a user on a PC platform versus an Apple platform, and vice-versa. It is important that no matter what platform we use in our personal lives, LSS should learn about and familiarize themselves with all the computer platforms offered in the library. Ways to do this is to have others both formally and informally teach how to use the unfamiliar platform. LSS should make opportunities for themselves to use a device meant for customers. For example, LSS should download and read e-books from the library collection on different platforms in order to be familiar with and ready to help new users.

All computers have an OS, the main program of the computer. OS are often referred to as computer platforms. OS manage all the software and hardware functions on the computer.[4] Without the OS, computers do not work. The OS orchestrates the startup of the computer when it is powered on and contains the permission files for users. The OS continues to interface with the user and the software programs. When the user wants to print a page, the OS provides the right connections between the computer and printer. The OS performs the following functions:

- Determines what types of software can be installed
- Coordinates the applications running on the computer
- Makes sure that individual pieces of hardware, such as printers, keyboards, and disk drives, all communicate properly
- Allows applications such as word processors, email clients, and web browsers to perform tasks on the system and use other system resources (e.g., printers, disk drives)
- Reports error messages

OS are extremely valuable commodities because each provide a unique manner in which the platform device functions. OS are not all the same and are proprietary to the inventor or company. Microsoft Windows is the most common OS for personal computers. It has had many updates or new releases over the years. Apple's macOS and iOS-X have had many iterations for its popular devices with regular updates to keep current with innovation. Apple has iOS specific to its many platforms of Macs, iPad, iPhones, and watches. While a library most likely will not be circulating smartphones or watches, users will bring them into the library. Like with the platforms, LSS should familiarize themselves with PC and iOS operating systems so that they are skilled at using the functions of both.

Often, when a small update is made to an OS, it is called a **release**. A release is indicated by a decimal and number, such as the release made to the Apple watch OS6 to OS6.1. LSS encounter different OS depending upon the computer they are using. If they are helping a customer on a library desktop, they most likely will be using Windows 10 (or a higher version). When assisting a child with an educational game on a library iPad, they will be using iOS, and when cataloging a book, the Integrated Library System most likely will have a UNIX-derived OS. Textbox 3.1 offers the most common operating systems.[5]

TEXTBOX 3.1: COMMON OPERATING SYSTEMS

- **Windows**—Microsoft's OS is common for home users and is often included on machines purchased from vendors such as Dell or Gateway. Windows OS uses a GUI, which many users find more appealing than text-based interfaces.
- **Mac OS X** and **iOS**—Apple's Mac OS X is for Macintosh computers. Although a different GUI, it operates similarly to Windows. iOS is used with Apple devices.
- **Linux and other UNIX-derived operating systems**—Frequently used for specialized workstations and servers, such as web and email servers. Advanced knowledge and skills are needed to operate.

LSS should know about releases because they may be involved with installing the updates on work or patrons' computers. LSS may also find the computer may be working slightly differently than it did the day before due to a release that was automatically installed overnight. Sometimes releases can be significant, and the Integrated Library System may have to shut down to users for several hours. These should be announced and planned for, especially if they affect the online catalog or circulation modules. It is important to keep current with releases because often they provide better security against viruses and other threats to the computer.

Lastly, computers have central processing units (CPUs) that are designed to run specific machine language code. The CPU is the component that actually executes instructions organized in programs or software that tell the computer what to do. In order for the computer to run software applications, the applications must be in that CPU's binary code machine language. Today, many libraries offer coding camps or workshops that young people can attend to learn how to write computer programs that, in turn, communicate with a computer's CPU. Historically, application programs written for one platform would not work on a different platform.[6] Today, while some of this has been resolved, do not assume that a program written specifically for an Apple platform will work on a PC. Together, the computer hardware platform, its OS management software, and its CPU must work seamlessly to give the user reliable computing service and experiences. LSS who are interested in learning more about computer processing and coding can volunteer to support presenters in library coding workshops to gain experience and enhance their own knowledge.

Libraries often have circulating and noncirculating computers. School, academic, and special libraries are more apt to circulate computers than public libraries because these libraries serve users who are students or workers of the same institution. Often, the school library circulates carts of laptops, tablets, or Chromebooks for 1-to-1 computing where every student in a school has been provided a laptop, tablet, or other mobile device. Examples of circulating computers are MAC and PC laptops, iPads, Chromebooks, Amazon Fire tablets, and Microsoft Surface laptops. Noncirculating computers are most often desktops that are committed to be at public workstations.

PERIPHERALS

External parts, or peripherals, are the devices that the user interfaces with to support their use of the computing components. More common peripherals found in libraries are monitors, mice, keyboards, printers, and scanners. But peripherals may also be projectors, smartboards, sound speakers, external hard drives, flash drives, and sometimes smartphones and copiers. LSS are often tapped to help customers using peripherals, which can be problematic due to connectivity and incompatibility issues.

Depending upon the type of library, LSS may encounter specialized or unique peripherals. Academic and school libraries often have and/or support subject related technologies that are found in classrooms and computer labs. One university[7] has on its listing of computer peripherals joy sticks, graphic digitizers, light pens, mice, pen pads, trackballs, secure ID access cards, headphones, microphones, and Pro-scope microscopes. Another university[8] allows students and staff to borrow video and **virtual reality** cameras and accessories; presentation peripherals such as projectors, document cameras, webcams, clickers, and remotes; music and art peripherals; audio equipment and accessories; and even a transcription foot pedal and a gaming console. LSS have an important role in the inventory, circulation, and support with customers' use of peripherals. While many of them are just a step above "plug and play," these are sophisticated and often expensive pieces of equipment for LSS to demonstrate and manage. Read and share with other staff the literature that comes with each peripheral. Create shortcut instruction sheets to accompany each device as well as be posted to the library website. Be sure they include handling and care as well as the library expectations for appropriate use and circulation period.

Peripherals
- must communicate with the OS of the computer for it to function;
- may require their own application or other software to be loaded onto the computer;
- augment or change the functionality of the computer into a faster, more efficient, or new machine;
- must have a connection to the computer either wired with USB or another cabling standard, use Bluetooth, or Wi-Fi.

Printers can be a demanding computer peripheral for LSS. Most libraries and user computers on the library Wi-Fi are networked to a central printer. In the print manager software, the library computers are mapped. **Mapping** involves several steps, depending upon the network or OS. Find the place to add a printer. Select network, wireless, or Bluetooth printer and click on the desired printer in the listing of library printers. Choose the correct printer driver. If it is being shared with another computer, the driver may be automatically installed. If the driver is not found, it may have to be manually downloaded from the printer manufacturer's website.

When printing problems occur, LSS have many options to explore. First, is the printer powered on? Next, look at the information window. Is there an error message, such as low ink, a paper jam, or other jobs in the queue waiting to be printed or needing to be cleared? All these messages are actions that LSS can take to resolve the problem. If it is not resolved, look to the individual computer of the user. Is it connected to the network? If so, can other users on other computers networked to this printer successfully print? By asking these questions the LSS is isolating the problem to the specific computer not printing. Finally, check to see if the computer has the printer properly mapped in its OS device or printer manager folder. If it is not found, the driver needs to be reinstalled.

3-D printers are sophisticated pieces of equipment that have some of the same attributes of paper printers, but also have many of their own unique functions. LSS should be trained to use the library 3-D printer. Chapter 12 discusses library makerspaces and the many popular peripherals, including 3-D printers.

TROUBLESHOOTING

To troubleshoot is to investigate and find solutions to technical problems using common sense and taking logical steps to fix the problem. LSS often encounter and resolve connectivity or incompatibility issues.

While it may seem trite, the first thing LSS should look for when there is a connection problem is the wires. Is the wiring snuggly plugged into the wall, the computer, and the peripheral? Is there any fraying or damage in the wires or extension cord? Secondly, check the ports. Ports are the small openings along the sides or edges of the computer where wires are plugged in. Ports are important because they are the hard conduits between the peripheral and the computer components. One port does not fit all! Ports are specific and only accept external hardware compatible with the OS.

The most common ports are USB and PS/2. USB stands for universal serial bus and is used by a wide range of peripheral equipment. PS/2 ports stand for personal system/2 and is found in IBM compatible computers for connecting mice and keyboards. Below are examples of common connectivity issues with PC peripherals.

- *No power*—Check cables and wiring
- *Problems with the port connectors*—Holes clogged with dust or pin damage
- *Error with wireless keyboard or mouse*—Computer may have old operating system
- *PS/2 keyboard and mouse not working*—The keyboard cable should go into the purple-colored port and the mouse into the green-colored port
- *Blocked keys or sensors*—Dirt blocking the keys or sensors prevents PC peripherals from responding to commands
- *Monitor screen or projector screen does not show*—Press the appropriate function key combination to alternate between the monitor and the projector

It is common for printers, scanners, and other peripheral devices to be connected via the home or business wireless network. Both the computer and device have to be recognized on the network. In Windows, the printer would be added to the Devices and Printers folder, indicating if it were a network, wireless, or Bluetooth printer. In the MAC iOS, click on the Apple symbol on the top left-hand corner. Click System Preferences followed by the Printers and Scanners icon. Add the printer. It should automatically be configured and appear in the list of networked printers for the device.

As platforms and OS need to be compatible, so do computers and peripherals. LSS may find that the peripheral is not set up to be compatible with the PC or the PC is not recognizing the peripheral. Common incompatibility issues can be:

- *USB standards don't match*—Newer USB devices may not run on old USB ports
- *Input devices stop working after updates*—Switch USB ports
- *Mouse and keyboard stop working when the printer is turned on*—Check for driver compatibility
- *Printer or scanner not working*—Install the latest printer driver

Some issues such as cleaning ports and uploading drivers also apply to MACs. MAC uses its own specific mini and micro adapters to connect to DVI (digital visual interface) and VGA (video graphic array) ports found on media devices. A brief troubleshooting checklist provides LSS an approach when helping users with technology issues:

- *Keep your cool*—Let the patron know that you are there to help and that you will call in additional supports.

- *Check power supply*—Make sure all connections are snug and that power sources are on.
- *Look around*—Determine if the problem is throughout the library or just one computer.
- *Reboot*—Use the "ten second rule": power down for ten seconds, count to ten, then power up to clear the problem.
- *Compatibility*—Is there incompatibility among platforms and software?
- *RTF and PDF*—Save work in universal formats.
- *Flash drive*—Carry one to save work before trying to resolve problem.

ASSISTIVE/ADAPTIVE TECHNOLOGIES

According to the Association of Specialized Government and Cooperative Library Agencies (ASGCLA), **assistive technology** is a term that describes electronic solutions that enable people with disabilities to live independently. The term "adaptive technology" is sometimes used in a similar way. ASGCLA[9] is a division of the American Library Association and recommends hardware, software, and specific uses of technology for patrons with visual, hearing, or other physical disabilities. As computers and other technology advances, so do the features and functions that are assistive. LSS can support and help challenged patrons with using both PC and Apple computers with built-in accessibility features, such as zoom text or sticky keys that simplify computer commands to one keystroke. Because of advances around e-books and tablets, text on some devices can be enlarged with a simple spread of the fingers. Hyper markup language or html files, common text file types, can be

Figure 3.1. Assistive Technology. *Sladic/E+ via Getty Images*

converted to audio by many applications. Gale Cengage and EBSCO have built-in reader/audio converters in their databases just for this purpose as well as multiple language translators.

Found in Windows settings, Microsoft Ease of Access Center includes programs such as Sound Sentry (which helps hearing-impaired people see audio computer cues), and Sticky Keys (which enables key-combination commands, such as Ctrl-Alt-Delete) to be entered as individual key entries. Sound Sentry can be useful for people who have limited dexterity. Moreover, patrons with visual impairments or learning disabilities may find programs such as the "Magnifier" and "Narrator" helpful. Apple products offer a significant number of tools available that help people with learning, visual, hearing, and physical disabilities access information without any cost to the library.[10] LSS should be aware of and properly trained to be proficient with the available tools. Apple iPads and iPhones facilitate text to speech as part of their operating systems. Simply tap Settings and go to Accessibility. Select Speak Selection. Slide it on and adjust speaking rate to an appropriate setting. Now you can select any text and have it spoken to you.

ASGCLA recommends these text-to-speech programs for patrons with vision loss: JAWS Screen Reader, Open Book Text Reader, Duxbury Braille Translating Software, Braille embosser, and Talking Typer software. For those with hearing loss ASGCLA suggests using text messaging and Sound Sentry, a Windows-based program that also works for Apple computers that converts the warning chimes of Windows into flashes the user would see on the screen. People with other physical disabilities may benefit from devices such as trackballs, joysticks, switches, touch pads, and augmented keyboards. Some people who do not have hand or finger dexterity benefit from using a Madentec tracker, which is a tiny reflective dot on the forehead that allows users to manipulate the computer cursor through head movement.[11] LSS who work with disabled patrons can try and recommend these devices to supervisors for purchase.

CHAPTER SUMMARY

LSS use computers in their daily work and are expected to be flexible, knowledgeable, and competent on multiple platforms and systems. LSS are presented with a wide variety of computing devices belonging to the library as well as the mobile devices owned by patrons. Becoming familiar with features and functions of computer operating systems is a first step in being able to work with multiple platforms. There are many functions embedded in computer operating systems that enhance use for people who are sight or hearing impaired or have other disabilities. LSS can familiarize themselves with these functions and other programs or apps the library offers so that they can support those who require assistance or adaptations to ensure equitable access.

DISCUSSION QUESTIONS

1. In relation to a computer, what are platforms, operating systems, and central processing units? What does each of these do?

2. What are some of the key differences between the operating systems of PCs and Macs?
3. What steps can LSS take to troubleshoot problems?
4. How can libraries provide equal access to computing services to the disabled?

ACTIVITY: INTERVIEW WITH IT DIRECTOR

Arrange a time to interview the library IT director to discuss the library's technology. Are the computers adequate? Do the peripherals support users' needs? Explain. What new computer technology is the IT director planning for and how will it be used? Finally, why does the library have the computer platforms that it does? What would the IT director change?

NOTES

1. Cambridge University Press, "Technology," Cambridge Dictionary, last modified 2020, accessed March 8, 2020, https://dictionary.cambridge.org/us/dictionary/english/technology.

2. Ohio State University, "The Greatest Inventions in the Past 1000 Years," eHistory, last modified 2020, accessed March 8, 2020, https://ehistory.osu.edu/articles/greatest-inventions-past-1000-years.

3. Sharpened Productions, "Hardware Definition," TechTerms, last modified 2020, accessed March 10, 2020, https://techterms.com/definition/hardware.

4. Western Governors University, "5 Most Popular Operating Systems," Information Technology, last modified October 2, 2019, accessed March 9, 2020, https://www.wgu.edu/blog/5-most-popular-operating-systems1910.html.

5. Department of Homeland Security, "Understanding Your Computer: Operating Systems," CISA - Cyber Infrastructure, last modified September 27, 2019, accessed March 9, 2020, https://www.us-cert.gov/ncas/tips/ST04-021.

6. Techopedia, "Definition - What Does Platform Mean?" Techopedia, last modified 2020, accessed March 9, 2020, https://www.techopedia.com/definition/3411/platform.

7. University of Rhode Island, Commodity Codes, last modified 2020, accessed March 13, 2020, http://web.uri.edu › purchasing › files › CommodityCodes-for-website.

8. University of Pennsylvania, "Find Equipment Loans by Category," Penn Libraries, last modified 2020, accessed March 13, 2020, https://www.library.upenn.edu/using-libraries/tech-equipment/equipment.

9. American Library Association, "Assistive Technology," Association of Specialized Government and Cooperative Library Agencies (ASGCLA), last modified 2020, accessed March 13, 2020, https://www.asgcladirect.org/resources/assistive-technology/.

10. Ibid.
11. Ibid.

REFERENCES, SUGGESTED READINGS, AND WEBSITES

American Library Association. "Assistive Technology." Association of Specialized Government and Cooperative Library Agencies (ASGCLA). Last modified 2020. Accessed March 13, 2020. https://www.asgcladirect.org/resources/assistive-technology/.

Cambridge University Press. "Technology." Cambridge Dictionary. Last modified 2020. Accessed March 8, 2020. https://dictionary.cambridge.org/us/dictionary/english/technology.

Department of Homeland Security. "Understanding Your Computer: Operating Systems." CISA - Cyber Infrastructure. Last modified September 27, 2019. Accessed March 9, 2020. https://www.us-cert.gov/ncas/tips/ST04-021.

Ohio State University. "The Greatest Inventions in the Past 1000 Years." eHistory. Last modified 2020. Accessed March 8, 2020. https://ehistory.osu.edu/articles/greatest-inventions-past-1000-years.

Sharpened Productions. "Hardware Definition." TechTerms. Last modified 2020. Accessed March 10, 2020. https://techterms.com/definition/hardware.

Techopedia. "Definition - What Does Platform Mean?" Techopedia. Last modified 2020. Accessed March 9, 2020. https://www.techopedia.com/definition/3411/platform.

University of Pennsylvania. "Find Equipment Loans by Category." Penn Libraries. Last modified 2020. Accessed March 13, 2020. https://www.library.upenn.edu/using-libraries/tech-equipment/equipment.

University of Rhode Island. Commodity Codes. Last modified 2020. Accessed March 13, 2020. http://web.uri.edu › purchasing › files › CommodityCodes-for-website.

Western Governors University. "5 Most Popular Operating Systems." Information Technology. Last modified October 2, 2019. Accessed March 9, 2020. https://www.wgu.edu/blog/5-most-popular-operating-systems1910.html.

CHAPTER 4

Software Applications

Library Support Staff (LSS) know the general trends and developments in technology applications for library functions and services.

Topics Covered in This Chapter
Software Basics
   Computer Languages
   Files
Software Utilities and Supports
   Device Drivers
   Malware
Library Software
   Educational Software
   Copyright
   SaaS—Software-as-a-Service

Key Terms
Apps: An abbreviation for the word "applications," this term is another name for computer programs first coined by Apple.
Computer language: These are unique sets of codes or instructions used for communicating with the computer.
Copyright: This is the right given by the US government to the owner to control the sale and use of the software.
Device driver: A type of utility software application or program, a driver is necessary for printers, scanners, and other device peripherals to interact with computers to perform their functions.
File: This is a set of data created and saved with a program that needs either the program or a compatible one to open, use, or edit the data.

> *File extension:* These are the three or four letters at the end of the file name that identify the type of program that was used to create the file.
> *Instruction sets:* A main category of software, these are commands that are built into the central processing unit (CPU) of the computer to command routine tasks.
> *Malware:* This is malicious software that enters a computer without the user's consent to damage files and software, and pose theft or security threats.
> *Program:* One of the main categories of software, this is a set of statements or instructions to be used directly or indirectly in a computer to bring about a certain result.
> *Scripts:* These are the lines of computer language that together make up a program.
> *Software:* This is a set of instructions or programs that instruct computers to do a specific task.
> *Utilities:* These are programs that help and support the performance and functionality of computers for users.

SOFTWARE BASICS

A computer is an instrument that needs **software** to instruct it so that users can perform tasks. Computer hardware is built to process information; however, computers need programs, applications, scripts, and instruction sets called software[1] to perform specific functions such as word processing, calibrations, gaming, streaming video, making predictions, solving problems, and so forth. The aim of this chapter is to help Library Support Staff (LSS) understand the basics of software so that they can better use it for their own work and to support the information needs of users. Related to software are the Integrated Library System (ILS) that is explained in chapter 5 and the topic of open source software, which is taken up in chapter 6.

As computers need software to perform functions, software needs specific computer hardware components. Examples of these hardware components are the CPU or computer processing unit, RAM or random access memory, hard drives, video and sound cards, speakers, monitor, and mouse. Each piece of software is particular with its own characteristics and purpose. Software is code written in a specific **script** of **computer language** that functions when installed on the computer hard drive or uploaded from a server.

The most familiar type of software that LSS use throughout the day are **programs**. Programs direct computers to perform particular tasks for users with or without their interaction. Programs are written in computer languages. The person who writes the program is called a programmer. While most users are not programmers, it is helpful for LSS to understand some of the basics of how software is created.

Another name for programs is **apps**. The term "apps" was once associated with Apple software but now is commonly used for programs that are installed on mobile devices such as smartphones and tablets. LSS may think of apps as being short programs that help do a specific task, such as ordering groceries, locating a ride, or placing a hold on a book from the library online catalog.

Computer Languages

Computer language can be considered low or high level. A low level language such as machine language, turns on or off basic functions of a computer, while a high level language, such as JavaScript, is used for writing much of the software we use on our devices today.

With hundreds of computer languages, most programmers specialize in just a few of them in order to write software. Unlike human languages, computer languages do not have vocabularies or alphabets. Rather computer languages are codes, each with unique ways to give the computer commands, arranging text, and writing abbreviations. Some computer languages are written for specific computer platforms, such as Windows or Apple, other computer languages are more universal. Three of the more common computer languages LSS encounter are Visual Basic, C, and JavaScript.[2]

Computer languages are written to work with other parts of the computer, such as its operating system (OS) or sometimes specific hardware. Google, Yahoo, and Chrome are internet **browser** programs that need the OS as a go-between so that users can access websites.[3] These search engines cannot, on their own, open websites. For example, the Netflix streaming program requires certain hardware components, including sound and video cards, to be activated so that the user can view the film on a computer.

In addition to programs, two other categories of software are scripts and **instruction sets**. Scripts are the lines of computer language that, when written in a certain way, are the essence of programs that command the computer to perform the task. The lines of code in figure 4.1 are small parts of scripts. A programmer may adjust or rewrite a few lines of script to fix a bug or a problem, or to make wanted changes to the program.

The third type of software, instruction sets, are commands that the computer will routinely do that are built into the CPU. Instruction sets can also be written into software. Computers function as calculators because of the instruction

Figure 4.1. Computer Software Code. *fotograzia/Moment via Getty Images*

sets found on CPUs and in programs such as Excel, which offer the summation function. Instruction sets also direct the internal workings of the computer for maximum speed and performance. Instruction sets are written in software code and are of most interest to IT and software engineers who support large computer maintenance and functionality.[4]

Files

LSS use files every day on their computers. Are files programs? The answer is no, files are not programs; however, programs format the data contained within files. Think of a **file** as the outside packaging of data. Data is the information being held inside of a file that has been formatted by a particular program. Each package, or file, needs a program to format the data that is created by the user, save the data, and open it at another time so the data can be edited or used.

Microsoft Word is a program for users to create documents such as reports, stories, assignments, and so forth. The data in these formatted documents is tucked inside the special packaging of a file. There are several options in Word for the "package" such as .doc (Word document), .rtf (rich text format), .txt (plain text), .pdf (portable document file), and wps (Works). These three or four letters that follow the name the user gives the file are called file extensions. By looking at the **file extension**, LSS can determine what program may open the file. Other examples of programs and format types with extensions can be found in table 4.1.

As technology advanced and became universal, file converters were developed for some file types. Especially for media, converters, or programs, are available to change some file types so that they can be used with programs written in other platforms. An example of this is a converter called Real Player,[5] which supports popular and commonly used video formats including MP4, MPEG, MOV, AVI, MPEG, and others and is compatible with Windows, Mac, Linux, Windows Mobile, and Android Mobile. Where once LSS had to tell a patron their film made with iMovie could not play on a PC because of an incompatible file extension, today it can because the library has a file converter installed on each of its patron computers.

LSS are expected to be able to understand, explain, use, and at times, troubleshoot a wide variety of software. In a day's work they may be expected to be proficient with not only the software that supports the operations and services of the library but also with the software that patrons use for their information, research, and productivity needs.

Table 4.1. Examples of File Extensions

Extension	Format	Programs
html	Hypertext markup language	Website software
pptm	PowerPoint macro-enabled presentation	PowerPoint
pages	Pages	Apple or Mac word processing software
mov	Movie	Apple QuickTime movie file
mp4	MPEG 4 video	Windows Media Player and other programs using a file converter
xlsm	Excel workbook after 2007	Microsoft Excel

SOFTWARE UTILITIES AND SUPPORTS

Basic to every computer is its OS. The OS is the software that manages the computer's memory and processes, as well as all of its instruction sets, programs, and hardware. Chapter 3 discusses the vital importance of the OS to computers. Computers as we know them will not work without a functional OS.

Other types of necessary software are referred to as utility programs. **Utilities** help computers perform and function better, and LSS use them in their work. These include antivirus, backup, disk repair, file management, security, and networking programs.[6] Utilities may vary depending on the platform (Windows or Apple) and the OS. The App Store on Apple products are user friendly and easy to find and launch with just a few keystrokes where Windows require a few more steps. The user downloads the utility from Microsoft or other websites (if it is not an automatic update) and then opens and runs the file to install it on the computer. Utilities can do such things as automating tasks and improving the menu bar. For example, the Apple utility clipboard manager boots productivity allowing the user to copy content from one app and paste it into another, eliminating the need to toggle back and forth between different apps. The Keyboard Maestro utility lets the user streamline repetitious sequences, such as opening a certain set of programs and websites that may be part of the user's daily work.[7] LSS may seek utilities such as these to automate tasks and make more efficient use of their time.

If LSS share a computer with others, and often they do, each staff member will have their own account. In a Windows platform, such things as the staff member's desktop and permissions to access some or all of the software installed on the computer is determined by the level of personalization of the account assigned to each LSS. Utilities can also be applications such as screensavers, font and icon tools, and desktop enhancements. Some utility programs help keep your computer free from unwanted software such as viruses or spyware, while others add functionality that allow you to customize your desktop and user interface.[8]

Device Drivers

A **device driver** is a type of utility software application or program that is necessary for printers, scanners, and other device peripherals to interact with computers to perform their functions. Merely connecting a computer to a printer will not allow it to print. Each printer model has a specific device driver needed for the OS to communicate with that printer. A device driver acts as a translator between the hardware device and the programs or OS that use it.[9]

Many common drivers for audio and video equipment are preinstalled on both Windows and Apple OS. However, if your computer does not already have the proper driver installed, it can be manually installed from the device manufacturer's website. For example, if the computer did not already have the driver for a new library HP printer, a simple search of "HP printer drivers" brings one to the HP Customer Support—Software and Drivers Download page where one can either select the correct driver from a large list of links to new HP printers or can submit the product name and printer model to be searched. Installing a driver is a simple process in Windows:

1. Open Control Panel.
2. Click Devices and Printers, and then click add a printer.
3. Select your printer. Click Next and follow the on-screen instructions to install the driver.

Malware

All computers should have installed and run in the background daily, if not more often, utility software that guards against **malware**.[10] Malware is malicious software that enters a computer without the user's consent to damage files and software, and pose theft or security threats. A computer virus where damage is done to the script of a program, thus corrupting it, is a type of malware. If LSS suspect a malware threat to a library computer, that is, something does not look correct or the computer's performance is "off," they should report their suspicions immediately to their supervisor. A scan can be performed to ensure if it is a virus or not. If so, it will be removed. Particularly in libraries where the technology support is limited, LSS should be able to identify the security utility and check to see that the antivirus program is scheduled to run each day, if not multiple times per day. The security utility runs in the background of the computer and should not affect the computer's processing speed or performance. Each file is systematically checked to ensure there is no corruption or suspicious changes to the programs. Utilities are updated regularly through their subscription service to keep current with new and detrimental threats. Having each library computer armed with a functioning security utility is a smart purchase to ensure programs, files, and hardware are not damaged.

In addition to computer viruses, library programs can be damaged by masked threats called Trojans. Trojans pretend to be benign but are purposefully malignant software waiting to be downloaded. In addition to security software that would recognize the Trojan, it is important that libraries have both policy and account security that do not allow for patrons or staff to freely download software on library computers.

LIBRARY SOFTWARE

It is impossible to generalize a LSS work computer as each library sets responsibilities and duties among LSS differently. A staff computer is most often dedicated to a single or small number of people and its function is to primarily support the business operations and services of the library. While there could be dedicated computers for searching the online catalog and other resources, the software that LSS use on a staff computer may be more in line with business software. Programs that may be found on LSS work computers are:

- Microsoft Office or Google Docs: Documents, spreadsheets, presentations, publications, and email
- Purchasing/Financial: Tracking purchasing and budget expenditures with Excel, QuickBooks, FreshBooks, ZarMoney, and Tipalti as examples
- Statistics software: Compile ILS statistics as well as monthly visitors, meeting room use, and website views (Google My Business)

- Management packages: Preparation of reports and meetings using Diligent, Naviant, Municode, or CivicPlus
- Specialized Software: Creation of marketing and library newsletters and materials

Today, more people use their own devices with library Wi-Fi than public access computers. However, libraries are often equipped with banks of computers or dedicated labs for specialized work or for programs that are age appropriate. In addition to Microsoft Office or the expectation to use Google Docs, patron computers should have Adobe Reader, at least two up-to-date browsers (Chrome and Firefox), as well as editing software for film and audio. All staff and patron computers should have the current version of Adobe Acrobat Reader installed so that PDF documents can be readily opened and read. Textbox 4.1 contains a list of software programs that would enhance patron productivity on academic library computers and labs. Some of these programs would also be useful in K–12 school libraries and public library computer labs or centers.

TEXTBOX 4.1: EXAMPLES OF SOFTWARE FOR PATRON ACADEMIC COMPUTERS

Adobe Reader—read PDF	Adobe Acrobat DC—edit PDF	Flash—animation
Illustrator—artwork	InDesign—professional layouts	Photoshop—digital imaging
SPSS—statistical analysis	GIMP—image editing, photo editing/retouching, image	Microsoft Mathematics—solve mathematics problems
Photomath- solve equations and calculations	Audacity—audio recording and editing	Java or JavaScript—view websites that require it

Educational Software

School, public, and academic libraries acquire educational software for their users. There are many different computer learning programs for children that support literacy, numeracy, civics, and culture. Young adults in middle and high school have need for productivity software where they can create assigned projects as well as analytical software where they can compare or contrast events in history, scientific inquiry, and the human condition. Educational software provides opportunities to learn a second language, improve performance on college admission testing, understand computer coding, or enhance skills with STEAM software. School libraries may invest in specific programs that follow the curriculum, such as CAD, or computer assisted drafting, or Noteflight, an online music notation editor for music composition students.

Libraries provide information that reinforces learning for both the young and the old. One way libraries do this is through educational software. Using technology has improved motivation, engagement, and independence in learning. It has also led to increased collaboration, greater engagement and persistence, and better conceptual understanding. With its strong visual elements, such as digital video, multimedia presentations, and drama-orientated software, learners are more effectively engaged.[11]

LSS can be an active part in users' learning by becoming familiar with the educational software offered by their library. An important way to do this is to make a personal goal to use each program. Just as LSS would become familiar with many books to recommend and suggest to patrons, they can as well with educational software once they have personally used the programs. LSS who can talk about the educational benefits and engaging cartoons and games of an early literacy program to a young child, or their parent, will be better able to promote the use (and the skill development) to the family. Likewise, LSS, who have explored the library's educational programs aimed at science or discovery for teens or adults, can authentically promote their value to these patrons. LSS support patrons' use of educational software when they have explored and used each educational software program the library has purchased or subscribed to and are familiar with features, scope of content, and operations so that they can promote benefits of programs and applications to others.

Copyright

Copyright protection for a computer program extends to all copyrightable expressions embodied in the program. Copyright law does not protect the functional aspects of the computer program, such as its algorithms, formatting, functions, logic, or system design.[12] Software that is copyrighted is licensed. A license is an agreement between the owner of the software and the library that is acquiring it by purchase or lease. If LSS suspect a user is unlawfully copying the program, they should report it immediately to their supervisor as this may be a violation of copyright and it is up to the library to uphold the contractual agreement set forth in the license.

Software-as-a-Service

A type of leasing library software is SaaS, or Software-as-a-Service, where libraries and users access software over the internet. Also known as software on demand, SaaS is a model that is becoming more and more prevalent, especially in academic libraries that are moving from ILS to library services platforms (LSPs) (see chapter 5 for more information on LSPs). In SaaS, a service provider hosts the application at its data center and a library or customer accesses it via a standard web browser over the internet.[13] As with other leased or subscription software, updates are automatically applied without customer intervention or extra hardware needed by the library for installation.

CHAPTER SUMMARY

When we think of technology, hardware often comes to mind. However, without software, hardware does not function. LSS can be important members of their library technology support team. LSS who know the basics of software, and are users of their library programs and applications, are better able to keep up with the general trends and developments in technology applications and support patrons who use the technology of library functions and services.

DISCUSSION QUESTIONS

1. What are the differences between the three main categories of software: programs, scripts, and instruction sets?
2. What are the common problems libraries may encounter with malware and what can LSS do to mitigate these problems?

ACTIVITY

Make an appointment to speak with the librarian in charge of library software for public computers. If there is not an updated inventory of the software on each machine, offer to create a spreadsheet that lists all software used. As part of the inventory, include the name and date of the software and vendor. If you can, determine if the software has been revised. Indicate if the software is purchased or leased. Ask the librarian if there is any other information they would like to have on the spreadsheet about the software on the public computers.

Once the inventory is done, analyze it and present your results to the librarian. Look for inconsistences among the computers. Discuss if programs need to be updated. Based on your findings, determine if a software needs assessment would be beneficial to library users.

NOTES

1. Techopedia, "What Is Software?" Techopedia, last modified 2020, accessed April 6, 2020, https://www.techopedia.com/definition/4356/software.

2. Code Conquest, "Common Coding Languages," Code Conquest, last modified 2020, accessed April 8, 2020, https://www.codeconquest.com/what-is-coding/common-programming-languages/.

3. Computer Hope, "What Are the Differences Between Hardware and Software?" Computer Hope, last modified 2020, accessed April 6, 2020, https://www.computerhope.com/issues/ch000039.htm.

4. Computer Hope, "Software," Computer Hope, last modified March 6, 2020, accessed April 2, 2020, https://www.computerhope.com/jargon/s/software.htm.

5. Wondershare, "Top 8 MP4 Players for Windows 10/8/7/Mac," Wondershare, last modified 2020, accessed April 9, 2020, https://videoconverter.wondershare.com/convert-mp4/mp4-players.html.

6. Sharpened Productions, "Utility," Tech Terms, last modified 2020, accessed April 8, 2020, https://techterms.com/definition/utility.

7. Jason Snell, "6 Powerful Utilities that Make the MAC Feel Like Home," *MACworld* 36, no. 7 (July 2019): https://search.ebscohost.com/login.aspx?direct=true&db=aph&AN=136929103&authtype=cookie,cpid&custid=csl&site=ehost-live&scope=site.

8. Sharpened Productions, "Utility," Tech Terms, last modified 2020, accessed April 8, 2020, https://techterms.com/definition/utility.

9. Techopedia, "Device Driver," Techopedia, last modified 2020, accessed April 8, 2020, https://www.techopedia.com/definition/6824/device-driver.

10. Bull Guard, "A Definition of Malware," PC Security, last modified 2020, accessed April 8, 2020, https://www.bullguard.com/bullguard-security-center/pc-security/computer-threats/malware-definition,-history-and-classification.aspx.

11. Kaaya Sadab, "How Technology Improves the Quality of Learning," *Flashes Magazine* 57 (November/December 2019): https://search.ebscohost.com/login.aspx?direct=true&db=aph&AN=139858954&authtype=cookie,cpid&custid=csl&site=ehost-live&scope=site.

12. *Copyright Registration of Computer Programs - Circular 61* (Washington, DC: U S Copyright Office, n.d.), accessed April 9, 2020, http://www.copyright.gov.circs.circ61.

13. Techopedia, "What Is Software as a Service (SaaS)," Techopedia, last modified 2020, accessed April 10, 2020, https://www.techopedia.com/definition/155/software-as-a-service-saas.

REFERENCES, SUGGESTED READINGS, AND WEBSITES

Bull Guard. "A Definition of Malware." PC Security. Last modified 2020. Accessed April 8, 2020. https://www.bullguard.com/bullguard-security-center/pc-security/computer-threats/malware-definition,-history-and-classification.aspx.

Code Conquest. "Common Coding Languages." Code Conquest. Last modified 2020. Accessed April 8, 2020. https://www.codeconquest.com/what-is-coding/common-programming-languages/.

Computer Hope. "Software." Computer Hope. Last modified March 6, 2020. Accessed April 2, 2020. https://www.computerhope.com/jargon/s/software.htm.

———. "What Are the Differences Between Hardware and Software?" Computer Hope. Last modified 2020. Accessed April 6, 2020. https://www.computerhope.com/issues/ch000039.htm.

Copyright Registration of Computer Programs - Circular 61. Washington, DC: U S Copyright Office, n.d. Accessed April 9, 2020. http://www.copyright.gov.circs.circ61.

Sadab, Kaaya. "How Technology Improves the Quality of Learning." *Flashes Magazine* 57 (November/December 2019): 38–41. https://search.ebscohost.com/login.aspx?direct=true&db=aph&AN=139858954&authtype=cookie,cpid&custid=csl&site=ehost-live&scope=site.

Sharpened Productions. "Utility." Tech Terms. Last modified 2020. Accessed April 8, 2020. https://techterms.com/definition/utility.

Snell, Jason. "6 Powerful Utilities that Make the MAC Feel Like Home." *MACworld* 36, no. 7 (July 2019): 77–81. https://search.ebscohost.com/login.aspx?direct=true&db=aph&AN=136929103&authtype=cookie,cpid&custid=csl&site=ehost-live&scope=site.

Techopedia. "Device Driver." Techopedia. Last modified 2020. Accessed April 8, 2020. https://www.techopedia.com/definition/6824/device-driver.

———. "What Is Software?" Techopedia. Last modified 2020. Accessed April 6, 2020. https://www.techopedia.com/definition/4356/software.

———. "What Is Software as a Service (SaaS)?" Techopedia. Last modified 2020. Accessed April 10, 2020. https://www.techopedia.com/definition/155/software-as-a-service-saas.

Wondershare. "Top 8 MP4 Players for Windows 10/8/7/Mac." Wondershare. Last modified 2020. Accessed April 9, 2020. https://videoconverter.wondershare.com/convert-mp4/mp4-players.html.

CHAPTER 5

Library Systems

Library Support Staff (LSS) know the role of technology in creating, identifying, retrieving, and accessing information resources and demonstrate facility with appropriate information discovery tools.

Topics Covered in This Chapter
Integrated Library Systems
    Barcodes
    Modules and Functionality
    Fixes, Releases, and Versions
Library Discovery Systems

Key Terms
Barcode: Often in the form of labels that represent data in a machine-readable form, these are used by libraries to keep track of items and patron information.
Discovery: A name for systems that seamlessly allow users to search multiple databases, catalogs, websites, and other online resources simultaneously.
Federated search: Also known as a metasearch, the user can find results from multiple databases and resources through a single search query.
Functionality: This is a name for the capability of library work the computers and software are able to perform.
Integrated Library System: Known more commonly in libraries as ILS, it is the software and hardware that manage circulation, cataloging, public online catalog, serials, acquisitions, etc.
Library Service Platform: Also referred to as LSP, this is the direction libraries are moving in where the online catalog, databases, software, and many other information services are outsourced and available in a seamless manner.

> *Mainframe computer:* Early computers known for their large size, reliability, high level of processing power, and extensive amount of storage.
> *Modules:* A software package of resources with a distinct service such as circulation or cataloging.
> *Public Access Catalogs (PACs):* Also called PACs, these terminals have access to the library catalog on the main computer or server with limited functionality.
> *Release:* An update to library software, particularly for an update to its ILS.
> *Version:* Library software or ILS modules that are significantly rewritten or revised.

INTEGRATED LIBRARY SYSTEMS

The 1970s saw decisive changes in how librarians performed their work. In the early 1970s, MARC (machine-readable cataloging) became the national and international standard for creating records that could be used by **mainframe computers** and shared among libraries.[1] While personal computers were not yet invented, the following developments for library automation were occurring:

- Lists of titles and other information could be used by many when computerized.
- Financial accounting information was linked to items purchased in the same system.
- MARC records that were developed by the Library of Congress could be purchased at a cost savings to staff labor.
- Online terminals were coming into use in library offices.
- Microfiche cards could be an alternate to the card catalog.

In the 1970s, many library systems believed that technology was too expensive and not cost-effective. However, by the 1980s that opinion changed as technology became significantly affordable and librarians began to focus on new, cooperative ways to harness it.[2]

The introduction of personal computers to the workplace in the mid-1980s changed how libraries circulated and cataloged materials. Library automation enhanced circulation and cataloging. The traditional card catalog was replaced in the 1990s once librarians could store and share MARC records in computer files. Patrons quickly adapted to using "dumb terminals" in the library called PACs or **Public Access Catalogs**. A rather unconventional term, these terminals were peripheral monitors with no computing or processing capability. They only provided the user a look at the catalog records on the central computer. Early PAC terminals had no internet access as they used direct connections or Z39.50 access to the mainframe computer storing the library catalog.

During the next two decades library automation was consolidated and expanded into **Integrated Library Systems** (ILS). In addition to cataloging and circulation, by the late 1990s other services that libraries were learning how to use technology for to automate work and services were in the areas of acquisitions, serials control, reserves, holds, and reference. There would be great efficiencies if multiple functions could be had in one system or product. As personal computers, networks, software, and supporting infrastructure became more advanced, so were enhancements being made to the basic library automation systems of cataloging and circulation.

The Library of Congress (LOC) chose Endeavor Information Systems to create its first ILS. Its plan was to consolidate its five separate and major record systems. The new ILS would integrate its automated databases into a single system containing all relevant bibliographic and access information for **LOC** collections.[3] The library world watched closely as the LOC undertook this important and significant step to move away from separate automated systems to one ILS.

By the early twenty-first century ILS was rapidly being improved upon and many academic and public libraries planned to go this route. Libraries anticipated many benefits from and ILS, as shown in textbox 5.1.

TEXTBOX 5.1: KEY BENEFITS OF AN INTEGRATED LIBRARY SYSTEM

1. Ability to use the MARC record for multiple purposes, including searching the online catalog, acquisitions, inventory, reference sources, holds, serials, reports, and reserves.
2. Patron and items data are in a shared, relational database management system.
3. Quick response time and more independence by users.
4. ILS uses internet tools and services that people were familiar with.
5. Software for each function of the ILS had common features and routines, making learning for LSS and other users easier with transferability of skills.
6. Cost savings in purchasing one system that supports multiple library functions rather than separate systems.
7. Reports and other statistical data is relational and obtainable about all of the ILS functions.

However, with benefits come liabilities. In the early years, a most important consideration was that if the ILS was down or out of operation, all functions of the ILS were also nonfunctional. In other words, all eggs were in one basket. If there was a technological glitch, the library could find itself without access to its circulation, online catalog, and cataloging functions. Security threats, lost data, and file corruption were also a risk. Today however, with modern cloud computing and other safety features, ILS are optimal tools for libraries.

Barcodes

One development that should not be overlooked that made library automation and ILS possible was the invention of the **barcode**. Barcodes represent specific data or information. The representation of patron and item information in barcodes expanded technical possibilities. A library barcode typically is a strip of fourteen unique vertical lines that, when scanned and attached to an item, represent data about that item. Other barcodes have less than fourteen characters. As LSS use bar codes in their daily work, the following list shows how a fourteen-character library barcode[4] is constructed:

- The first character of a patron barcode is typically a "2."
- Item barcodes typically begin with a "3."
- The next four characters represent the specific library or school district.
- Characters 6–13 are specific to either the patron's name or the item title.
- Character 14 is a "check digit" that is established by the automation software and ensures that the data is being scanned and virtually eliminates input errors.

Figure 5.1. Library Item Barcode. *Paul Bruns/Corbis via Getty Images*

Modules and Functionality

Modules are the different applications or services offered by an ILS, several of which have already been mentioned. Traditional modules that typically are standard are: the online catalog, circulation, cataloging, acquisitions, and serials. Libraries may negotiate for other add-on modules or features that enhance services such as reserves, mobile inventory, financial interfaces, reports, language, community profiles, etc.

The ILS is a primary tool for LSS because, like the work they perform, it supports all services of the library. Modules share common item and patron databases so that patrons and materials data can be purposefully accessed or linked for efficient use. Discussed below are the primary functions of key ILS modules with several examples of how LSS may use each one in their work.

Acquisitions module: The purpose of this module is to help libraries use their budgets to select, order, and acquire materials. Through this module patrons are alerted in the online catalog when items are on order. It also facilitates the ordering, invoicing, and payment processes. LSS may use the acquisitions module to:

1. work with the librarian, select and create lists of books and media to be ordered;
2. create records that will appear in the online catalog to alert patrons of items on order;
3. scan or otherwise input item data that items are received;
4. indicate items that are approved for payment;
5. follow ordering status with vendors and make adjustments for items not available;
6. manage accounts for accurate materials budget balances.

Circulation module: This module manages the loaning of library materials to users. Items that are cataloged are "matched," or loaned, to the user at checkout. Circulation module is embedded with parameters of lending policies of the library that govern who can borrow what and for how long. The process of lending library materials is embedded in rules for both patron and item types. In some libraries patrons do their own self-checkout. LSS may use the circulation module to:

1. checkout and manage the process of lending of library materials;
2. check-in materials for shelving and to clear patrons' records;
3. create new patron records and edit or delete existing records to keep the patron database accurate and current;
4. help others know the active status and current location of items;
5. collect and manage the fines when applicable;
6. create and maintain system reports and statistics about how patrons use the library collections;
7. support the other work of technical services, reference, and other library functions;
8. assist in self-checkout;
9. manage the interlibrary loan processes when patrons seek items from other libraries.

Online catalog module: Also referred to as OPAC, or the online public access catalog, this catalog may be its own module in some systems or under either cataloging or circulation in others. LSS may use the online catalog module to:

1. assist others in selecting and locating items in the library;
2. assist users in placing holds on items in their own library or, if it is a shared catalog, in other member libraries' collections;
3. assist others in selecting and locating items in other libraries;
4. verify cataloging information;
5. help and support users' selection of materials using OPAC recommendation lists and services;
6. help and support users' selection of databases if the OPAC offers discovery services.

Cataloging module: This module houses data about the items and materials, both physical and electronic, that patrons can access by being a library user. The cataloging process entails creating a bibliographic MARC 21 record or metadata that describes each item in the library collections. LSS may use the cataloging module to:

1. copy bibliographic information about new items being acquisitioned;
2. create original MARC 21 or metadata records about new items being acquisitioned;
3. edit or make other changes to existing records to update or change elements of data so that the record is current and accurate;
4. create item or holdings records that set the parameters and matrixes for how items can be circulated;
5. delete bibliographic records when items are withdrawn from the collection;
6. update old and incomplete records to provide patrons better descriptions of items;
7. create and maintain system reports and statistics about the collections.

Reserves module: Typically found in academic libraries, the reserves module is used to manage physical and electronic course materials set aside for specific classes for specific periods of time. LSS who work in academic libraries may use the reserves module to:

1. work with others, such as other university branch libraries, OCLC, ILL, or research databases to find, locate, and acquire course readings using citations provided by an instructor;
2. enter or link course readings as directed by a supervisor and/or course instructor;
3. circulate physical copies of course readings through checkout and check-in processes;
4. run reserve reports for an instructor and administration as required.

Serials module: While some libraries are getting away from circulating and maintaining collections of paper periodicals and serials, other libraries, such as academic, school, and special libraries maintain serials collections. A serials module is used for keeping track of journals, newspapers, and other items that come on a regular schedule. Depending upon the ILS provider and the needs of the library, the serials module may be optional. LSS may use a serials module to:

1. catalog individual issues of serials as they arrive in order to keep track of each volume and issue of a serial title;
2. keep serial collections current by providing status, circulation, and location information;
3. help and support users select and locate specific issues either in print or nonprint with bibliographic citations;
4. create and maintain system reports and statistics about the collections.

Electronic databases module: Depending upon the library, many small to medium libraries provide users access to databases via the library web page. Academic libraries have spurred the development of discovery systems and Library Service Platforms as discussed later in this chapter and in chapter 6. Many ILS vendors provide the option of electronic database modules that integrate with the OPAC. LSS may use the electronic databases module to:

1. help and support users view electronic journals and databases via the OPAC;
2. edit or modify electronic journal cataloging records as directed by supervisor to provide local library access and location information;
3. help and support library administration manage electronic records by tracking licensing terms and usage statistics for local and commercial electronic titles.

When library administration seeks a new ILS in addition to modules, **functionality** is one of the most important considerations. Functionality has to do with the expansiveness of services and the quality of the performance of the system. LSS who have an opportunity to serve on a next system search committee for the library ILS have much valuable input and experience to share about ILS functionality, which may improve work performance and services for customers.

Fixes, Releases, and Versions

As with any technology there are both fixes and new developments. When a library purchases an ILS system, it is no longer "new," just as a new automobile loses value as soon as it's driven off the dealer's lot The nature of technology is to be in a continual state of improvement. Vendors hear about problems from their customers, both small and large. Often a small change to the software, sometimes referred to as a patch, will fix the problem. Most of these small fixes can occur during off hours and have to do with one module. If the fix is anticipated to take longer, the library will be notified so that LSS and other users can make alternate plans. There should be minimal occasions when the ILS is down because of a fix. Most vendors, aware of their competition and future sales, are in ongoing product development.

An ILS software **release** is an improvement to the application or module. Releases may be anticipatory of changes to come in another version of the ILS software. A module may have several releases each year, depending upon developments or changes the vendors make for ongoing improvements. LSS may be affected by releases that change the sequence of steps or the order of processing specific tasks.

Related to releases are **versions**. The first version is a new application or software and is most often numbered 1.0. A second major overhaul, or new version of this application, may be version 2.0 and so forth. Release numbers extend beyond the decimal of the version. The first release or improvement to version 1.0 could be numbered 1.1. The second release that would build upon version 1.1 would result in the application now being called version 1.2. When a new version is ready, LSS should be prepared for some amount of downtime because a new version may affect more than just that one module in an integrated system. Libraries always want to keep current with the ILS vendor fixes, releases, and new versions.

Because ILS are designed for accessing and sharing resources in cost-effective ways, consortia of libraries have developed around the ILS. The consortium may be large or small, but what is common is the shared ILS where all patrons have borrowing privileges to members' collections and resources, such as cataloging records, mutually purchased or created. LSS who work in consortium libraries learn the common practices and policies developed around the use of the ILS. They are in communication with other libraries' LSS to ensure each library's customers are well serviced.

Academic consortia have specific needs that have led to the next phase of ILS development called discovery or just library systems. This development is in a state of flux, but what is certain is that the public, school, and special libraries will be brought along with these changes.

LIBRARY DISCOVERY SYSTEMS

The vision and needs of academic libraries are leading the industry from ILS to discovery systems. **Discovery** is the activity of locating library resources by its users by browsing or searching. Searching can take place by tools or services offered by the library or outside vendors.[5] Because there are many options and no two libraries have the exact same resources or needs, the terminology and concepts can be confusing. LSS use and support discovery with patrons, that is, they help users locate information and other resources. The end goal of discovery systems is to maximize the number and best results from multiple database and resources in one **federated** or a single search query. Table 5.1 describes the various levels of discovery.[6]

Librarians are trained to select the best resources for their library users. Rather than do bulk purchasing of preselected titles, many want to pick and choose book titles and other items for their collections based on users' needs and interests. Discovery services often come prebundled in journals, books, and other resources. Library services platforms offer the functions of the ILS with more coordinated and thorough management of the library's resources. The trend is for library services platform vendors to either partner with or provide themselves the bundled discovery services, making it cost-effective for libraries to purchase a fully integrated system from the same vendor. The downside is that librarians have less choice to mix and match when it comes to the selection of the library resources.[7]

Libraries that use discovery systems and library services platforms (LSPs) are using the Software-as-a-Service (SaaS) model to access resources whereby the majority of the programs and services are physically located and managed on remote servers and not on local library systems. The local library is being "served the use of soft-

Table 5.1. Current Models of Discovery

Model	Description
Online catalog with no indexed-based discovery	Model for most public libraries. Users search the online catalog only to locate local or consortium materials. The library website offers its patrons separate and independent searchable databases.
Index-based discovery service with separate online catalog	Public libraries in states that offer digital library services, K-12 schools, and small academic libraries. Discovery service is separate from the online catalog and offers a wide variety of databases.
Online catalog with integrated index-based discovery	The discovery service is integrated with the online catalog. When the user queries a keyword or term, both items from the library's collections and the resources of the discovery service will be listed in the search results.
Discovery service with ILS integration	Includes above features and ability for patrons to use other functions or modules of the ILS, such as placing holds, creating personal lists, etc.
Bundled discovery service with **Library Service Platforms (LSP)**	For academic libraries that rely on OCLC or Ex Libris management systems for their online catalog in lieu of an ILS, this model pairs the discovery system with management system purchased from the same vendor.
Fully integrated discovery service with Library Service Platform	This is a highly managed outsourced system that full integrates the library resources, OCLC or ExLibris catalogs, websites, databases, and all searchable products into one federated search

ware" via a network. For example, a library using an LSP for online searching of its books has its holdings identified and viewed from a global catalog such as OCLC WorldCat. See chapters 4 and 7 for more information about SaaS.

Challenges for academic libraries as well as all libraries that move to discovery services is that they now will rely on massive indexes with volumes of bibliographic citations that will not all be accompanied by full text. Another challenge for libraries investing in discovery services are patrons' preference to first use Google and Google Scholar, which they may be more familiar with.[8]

CHAPTER SUMMARY

Technology has changed how LSS work in a short span of fifty years from initial computerization of lists to fully integrated discovery and library platforms systems. Undoubtedly, searching and management tools will evolve with new releases to software occurring regularly. LSS who are knowledgeable users of modules of the library ILS and keep current with its software releases, inform and support users of the changing systems. Such LSS become valuable members of technology teams who evaluate and select new products and platforms because of their interest and experiences.

DISCUSSION QUESTIONS

1. What are some of the key benefits of libraries using an ILS for their work and services?
2. How does the ILS benefit patrons?
3. What are the differences among fixes, releases, and ILS software versions?

4. Compare and contrast ILS and discovery systems. Why are discovery systems replacing ILS?

ACTIVITY

Compare the library systems of two libraries of the same type that use different ILS or discovery systems. Arrange to interview the two people who manage the ILS or discovery systems. Before your visit, become familiar with each library's online catalog, finding the name of each vendor. Research the vendor and system before your appointment so that you have background knowledge of the product and its features.

Interview each librarian. What do LSS say about the system? Is it user friendly? What tasks do LSS perform on the system? Do patrons like the public catalog? What improvements could be made? What support is contracted from the vendor and what is expected of the library staff? Write a report about your findings from the interviews and your research. Which system would you recommend and why?

NOTES

1. Library of Congress, "A Half Century of Library Computing," Library of Congress Blog, last modified 2020, accessed March 28, 2020, https://blogs.loc.gov/loc/2014/01/a-half-century-of-library-computing/.

2. Sandra Shores, "Information Technology and Libraries at 50: The 1970s in Review," *Information Technologies & Libraries* 37, no. 2 (June 2018): https://search.ebscohost.com/login.aspx?direct=true&db=aph&AN=130397503&authtype=cookie,cpid&custid=csl&site=ehost-live&scope=site.

3. "LC Plans New ILS to Serve Nation's Libraries," *American Libraries* 29, no. 10 (November 1998): https://search.ebscohost.com/login.aspx?direct=true&db=aph&AN=1277496&authtype=cookie,cpid&custid=csl&site=ehost-live&scope=site.

4. The Library Store, "Library Barcode Basics," The Library Store, accessed March 29, 2020, https://www.thelibrarystore.com/barcode-basics.

5. Marshall Breeding, comp., *Index Based Discovery Services: Current Market and Trends*, report no. 54 (n.p.: Library Technology Reports, 2018), https://search.ebscohost.com/login.aspx?direct=true&db=aph&AN=133042987&auth.

6. Ibid.

7. Marshall Breeding, "Discovery Services: Bundled or Separate?," *American Libraries* 50, no. 1/2 (January/February 2019): https://search.ebscohost.com/login.aspx?direct=true&db=aph&AN=133975635&authtype=cookie,cpid&custid=csl&site=ehost-live&scope=site.

8. Marshall Breeding, "The Ongoing Challenges of Academic Library Discovery Services," *Computers in Libraries* 40, no. 1 (January/February 2020): https://search.ebscohost.com/login.aspx?direct=true&db=aph&AN=141250481&authtype=cookie,cpid&custid=csl&site=ehost-live&scope=site.

REFERENCES, SUGGESTED READINGS, AND WEBSITES

Authormaps. "How Librarians Use ISBNs and Barcodes." Authormaps. Accessed March 29, 2020. http://authormaps.com/how-librarians-use-isbns-and-barcodes/.

Breeding, Marshall. "Discovery Services: Bundled or Separate?" *American Libraries* 50, no. 1/2 (January/February 2019): 71. https://search.ebscohost.com/login.aspx?direct=true&db=aph&AN=133975635&authtype=cookie,cpid&custid=csl&site=ehost-live&scope=site.

———, comp. *Index Based Discovery Services: Current Market and Trends*. Report no. 54. N.P.: Library Technology Reports, 2018. https://search.ebscohost.com/login.aspx?direct=true&db=aph&AN=133042987&auth.

———. "Library Systems Report." *American Libraries* 50, no. 5 (May 2019): 22–35. https://search.ebscohost.com/login.aspx?direct=true&db=aph&AN=136428975&authtype=cookie,cpid&custid=csl&site=ehost-live&scope=site.

———. "The Ongoing Challenges of Academic Library Discovery Services." *Computers in Libraries* 40, no. 1 (January/February 2020): 9–11. https://search.ebscohost.com/login.aspx?direct=true&db=aph&AN=141250481&authtype=cookie,cpid&custid=csl&site=ehost-live&scope=site.

"LC Plans New ILS to Serve Nation's Libraries." *American Libraries* 29, no. 10 (November 1998). https://search.ebscohost.com/login.aspx?direct=true&db=aph&AN=1277496&authtype=cookie,cpid&custid=csl&site=ehost-live&scope=site.

Library of Congress. "A Half Century of Library Computing." Library of Congress Blog. Last modified 2020. Accessed March 28, 2020. https://blogs.loc.gov/loc/2014/01/a-half-century-of-library-computing/.

The Library Store. "Library Barcode Basics." The Library Store. Accessed March 29, 2020. https://www.thelibrarystore.com/barcode-basics.

Shores, Sandra. "Information Technology and Libraries at 50: The 1970s in Review." *Information Technologies & Libraries* 37, no. 2 (June 2018): 7–8. https://search.ebscohost.com/login.aspx?direct=true&db=aph&AN=130397503&authtype=cookie,cpid&custid=csl&site=ehost-live&scope=site.

CHAPTER 6

Open Source

Library Support Staff (LSS) are able to assist and train users to operate public equipment, connect to the internet, use library software applications, and access library services from remote locations.

Topics Covered in This Chapter
Source Code
    Closed Source
    Open Source
Cost-Benefit
    Licensing
Open Source ILS
    Koha
    Evergreen
    Other Systems
Technology Support
Customization

Key Terms
Closed source: This is software that is proprietary and has significant restrictions in the license that limits the ways the library can use it.
Cost-benefit: This is an analytical process used to compare price and value.
License: In terms of software, it is a legally binding agreement that specifies how the software can be used by the library.
Machine language: Also known as object code, this is the binary code made up of strings of 0s and 1s used to command computers to execute program software.
Object code: Also known as machine or binary code, source code is translated into this machine language so that computers can execute software.

> *Open source:* This is software that is freely shared at a very low cost with libraries to manage circulation, cataloging, and other modules and functions of service.
> *Programming language:* This is the source code written in human-readable instructions according to a particular format or configuration.
> *Proprietary:* Closed sourced software that libraries purchase that is copyrighted and licensed.
> *Public domain:* The term given when everyone has equal rights to an item or property.
> *Source code:* These lists of human-readable instructions are written by a programmer when developing a computer program or software.

SOURCE CODE

People have talked in code for centuries in order to communicate. Codes can be straightforward, or they can be used to cloak or disguise conversation. Codes may use words, letters, numbers, and symbols in a nonconventional way to communicate ideas. Coding is what programmers do when they write software. Computer software and programs are written and executed in **source code** and **object code**. Each of these codes are also referred to as a language. Source code is written in programming language. Object code is compiled into machine language.

Source code is human-readable instructions. Coders are programmers, and source code is **programming language**. People learn how to develop and write source code or programs for specific tasks, processes, communications, and millions of other applications for computers to execute. Library Support Staff (LSS) use the programs of Adobe, Google, and Microsoft in their work to enhance or expand information services for users. The programmers of these three popular products write software source code in the programming language C++. Source code or programming language must be written before the second language.

The second language is the object or binary code also known as **machine language**. Programming languages are translated into machine language. The source code is run through a compiler to turn it into object or binary code that a computer can understand and execute. A compiler is a software program that converts source code written by a human programmer into binary code primarily of 1s and 0s that is understood by the central processing unit of the computer. The two languages communicate between each other in order for a computer to execute a command. The word "source" in computer vocabulary refers to the origin of the code or script of the software. In other words, what is the source of the code?

Closed Source

Source code may be closed or open. The software discussed in chapters 4 and 5 is **proprietary** licensed or **closed sourced**. The rights to such software to use and control it are "closed" because they are owned by an individual or company. Microsoft Word is a licensed, closed source proprietary software. If the software is proprietary or closed source, there will usually be significant restrictions in the **license** that limits the ways LSS and others can use it. Many companies carefully guard their source code so that users cannot see or modify it. Microsoft Office has strict licenses that control and regulate the number of users and computer installations. A closed sourced Integrated Library System (ILS) is a substantial investment for the library. In addition, for the annual license and fees to use the software in an agreed upon manner, the library agrees to pay for new software development, system installation, new releases or revisions, fixes to software bugs, customization, and ongoing customer and technical support.

Open source

Open source software is not patented or copyrighted by developers or companies. Many libraries choose open source as an alternative to purchasing or signing contractual agreements for proprietary, closed source ILS. Open source software is significantly less expensive than closed sourced and there is no large initial purchase to download, install, and use it. Most open source software is free of licensing restrictions.

Open source programs are in the **public domain** and free of licensing. The term public domain means that it belongs to the public for anyone's use and cannot be copyrighted. Any modifications or extended versions of the software must also be free. The following are the four essential freedoms[1] for users of open source software:

1. Autonomy: The freedom to run the program as you wish, for any purpose.
2. Creativity: The freedom to access and change source code to enhance or improve the program.
3. Sharing: The freedom to redistribute copies of the program without permission.
4. Collaborative innovation: The freedom to share copies of your modified versions with others, including the open source community.

In order to be considered free of copyright and declared open source, the developer must ensure users have these four freedoms. If the programming language source code is open, it may be copied, modified, shared, and used without restrictions.[2]

COST-BENEFIT

Cost-benefit is a comparative process between price and value. As consumers, LSS run cost-benefit analysis often, if not daily, in their lives, asking if the price of an item is worth the benefit that can come from it. Each year libraries look for ways to maximize their budgets. Decisions are made whether the cost of items and services will provide sufficient value to their users.

The online catalog is fundamental to the existence of the library. Not only does the catalog display in real time the status of all the library items, but for many libraries it is linked to discovery services of databases and other digital content. The online catalog and the services that support it are one of the most expensive investments libraries make in technology.

The dilemma many libraries face is that while proprietary online catalog systems enhance locating and using information, many libraries cannot afford the cost, creating the potential for troublesome inequity among libraries and user services.

Table 6.1. Common Needs Fulfilled by Open Source

Library ➡	Common Need	⬅ University
Every library has unique circulation parameters.	Software is distributed with its source code so that end user organizations and vendors can modify it for their own purposes.	Information and research needs greatly vary even between departments.
Licensing fees are an additional annual expense in the library operating budget that compete with salaries, books, maintenance, etc.	The single major advantage is no licensing fees.	The need to license software can vary from year to year depending upon the research focus.
Libraries have to respond to their communities, including disruptions to budgets.	Open source provides users flexibility to change to another software because they are not locked into steep or long term contracts with a vendor.	Researchers need to be responsive to change, including their commitment to a particular software.
Legacy (meaning there is no further software development) systems can be a crisis for libraries who then must find another ILS to contract with and migrate data.	The software will continue to be enhanced by users and programmers because it is not restricted by copyright or patent laws.	Faculty and students may invest in software that is specific to their needs only to find that the proprietary developer no longer is gaining financial advantage from it and has it discontinued.

The free software movement stemmed from a similar situation that universities faced with the expense of software that was making academic research and the information faculty and students needed unaffordable. Open source fulfills many common needs of both universities and libraries as shown in table 6.1.

Licensing

Software developers and commercial owners protect their property through a license. A software license is an agreement between the library and the owners that allows the library to use the software in particular ways so not to infringe on their copyright. The license controls how the software is used. Can it be copied, shared, or modified? Can the source code be seen or is it encrypted or otherwise hidden?

Free or open source software usually does not need permission to use it. If licensed under a free software or open source license, such as the free software movement, users are allowed to make unlimited copies, modifications, and distributions of the software. Unlike proprietary or closed software, there is no license key or product key for authorization for open source that can be transferred between and among computers without penalty.

In order for software to be considered open source, it has to meet the following criteria:[3]

1. Free distribution: If there is a license it cannot restrict anyone from selling or giving away the software.

2. Source code: The program must include source code in the preferred form in which a programmer would modify it. No one can deliberately conceal or obstruct source code.
3. Derived works: Modifications and derived works from the original open source program is allowed to be distributed under the same terms of the original software.
4. Integrity of author's source code: Any restriction in the original software license must be respected.
5. Antidiscrimination: The license cannot discriminate against any person, groups, or fields of endeavor.
6. Licensing: Adhere to requirements discussed.

In addition to advantages already stated about cost and flexibility, open source has practical and professional benefits around collaboration and community.[4] A community of users provides many practical and professional benefits. Open source programs are reviewed and modified by collaborators who may find problem "bugs" and create "fixes" to the software more readily. Unlike proprietary software, open source can be continually modified, refined, and enhanced and shared to meet the needs of its users.

OPEN SOURCE ILS

In its infancy many librarians considered open source nonconventional and even radical. Were the cost savings worth the risk to take the chance on nonproprietary software for delivering the core services of the library? Without a standard license and purchase agreement with a vendor, were there any performance warranties if and when things went wrong? ILS dependability and reliability were critical. Today, much of the uncertainty about ILS open source has changed. With well over a thousand libraries now being open source, there are many positive experiences and proven products. Below is the most commonly used ILS open source that LSS will encounter.

Koha

Koha, a successful open source ILS, has its roots in the fears that were associated with the turn of the twenty-first century. Called Y2K, short for "the year two thousand," was a real concern that the central processors of millions of computers around the world would not work come January 1, 2000. In 1999, a group of three New Zealand libraries called the Horowhenna libraries were afraid their aging ILS would not withstand the potential date problems of Y2K. When they failed to find a commercial vendor to purchase an alternative to their failing system, they hired a small software firm, Katipo, to create an ILS that would withstand Y2K. What resulted was the initial version of the open source ILS software Koha. The name Koha means "gift" in the Maori language. Today, Koha is one of the two largest and most widely used open source ILS in the world.

Because open source ILS for libraries was so unusual and rare, Katipo decided to forgo copyright or patent rights to Koha and release the software to an open source general public license. They thought it made better business sense to have Koha open source so that it could be more readily customized for libraries based on their unique needs. If the software were closed, they would lose this ability. The hunch paid off for Katipo, and in 2002 a group of libraries in Nelsonville, Ohio, became the first Koha libraries in the United States.[5] Key to Koha's success was not only its quick customization, but also its network of service providers.

Evergreen

Equally successful is the open source ILS software Evergreen. Evergreen was a response to the needs of the Georgia Library System's than 275 libraries in 2006 for an expandable, shared catalog. Today, with more than two thousand worldwide library users, Evergreen is known for being a reliable, open source, full ILS. Evergreen also has the functionality of a metadata search engine, a robust message-passing system, a transaction processing engine, and web applications.[6] Like Koha, libraries that chose Evergreen can enter agreements with outside technical and service support.

Evergreen was first developed as a shared ILS for a large group of libraries, and it continues to be an attractive choice for state and regional consortia. It offers much choice on how information is expressed, and permissions are given in a tree-like hierarchy for library branches, departments, and other group units. This flexibility is attractive, if not necessary, among consortia of differing library types, sizes, and purposes.

The Central/Western Massachusetts Automated Resources Sharing (C/W Mars), a group of approximately 150 academic, public, and special libraries, found Evergreen to be the right solution when changing ILS. Because Evergreen was successfully designed to serve large consortia, C/W Mars found its functionality and speed robust. Librarians appreciate the individual control they have as well as feeling empowered because their input is heard by Evergreen open source developers.

Common to both Koha and Evergreen is the sense of collaboration and community among the users. Unlike in a competitive marketplace abundant with secretive practices to discourage collaboration, open source encourages communities of software developers to work together and share for a better product. In turn, library users also communicate and participate in focused groups and other forms of learning for each other and for the advancement of the software.

Other Systems

There are many other open source developers of ILS for libraries. The Library of Congress maintains a list of all ILS that are compatible with the MARC 21 standard. Of the fifty MARC systems on the list, five are designated as open source. Three examples of other open source ILS are:

1. Catalis: A web application that allows creating, importing, and editing MARC 21 bibliographic records. Catalis is distributed free under the MIT license. Catalis website, documentation, and user interface are in Spanish.
2. ISISMarc: This software was developed in cooperation with the Library of Congress and the Ministry of Education of Argentina. ISISMarc is particularly adapted for handling MARC 21 and UNIMARC records.

3. LibLime: Its mission is to make open source software accessible to libraries. To that end, LibLime develops and markets affordable and customizable open source library technology solutions and provides full vendor services including migration assistance, training, and software maintenance, support, and development.

TECHNOLOGY SUPPORT

Key to the success of open source software and systems for libraries is the ever-growing availability of service and technical support. While it may feel like the library may be going it alone with open source, in reality this is not the case. Libraries have a wide choice of open source expertise through commercial vendors specializing in software customization, installation, hardware, and infrastructure support. These companies offer source programmers who will correct problems and make enhancements to ILS and other open source programs.

A few years after the first installation of Koha, a systems administrator of the Nelsonville Public Library, the first Koha installation in the United States, founded LibLime, which provided customer support and expanded the use of Koha. Librarians had more confidence in changing to open source knowing they could contract for support. Today, there are several companies in addition to LibLime: PTFS Europe, Tind, and ByWater Solutions offer Koha support with ByWater Solutions dominating the field servicing the majority of Koha libraries.[7] Another well-established open source ILS, Evergreen, is primarily supported by the company Equinox. There are four main areas of service ByWater Solutions provides:[8]

1. Data migration: Data migration is moving patron and item information from one ILS system to a new one. Data must be analyzed and tested for both its quality and quantity before going live on the new ILS.
2. Support Hosting: Library data is saved, stored, and retrieved in a real time, interactive manner on off-site servers. The company is responsible for backups and other means to secure and protect data on the outsourced servers.
3. Training and Education: Library staff need new and ongoing training. In addition to supplying manuals, tutorials, webinars, and videos, there should be accessible training staff available from the company.
4. Custom Development: Libraries benefit from custom programming not only for their own unique needs but also because these improvements will be shared in the open community that, in turn, spurs the development of better software.

In addition to outside technical support, for each open source software there is a community of developers, designers, and users. LSS who work with open source can seek participation in the professional learning community with staff in the many other libraries that also use the same software. Communication may take place on blogs, email, or social media dedicated to discussions about the product. In these discussions, ideas are often shared regarding innovation and improvement. Software developers and technical support participate in the community so that they can glean ways to improve service and software to libraries. These communities are think tanks for the future development of customized library software and systems.

CUSTOMIZATION

Because of the free software movement and the creative thinking of those who pioneered open source, ILS library technology and software have continuously improved for the integration of other library applications. This final section provides examples of how customized open source applications are being utilized for web searching, digital collection management, and using data to support decision-making.

Libraries need to have professional and functional websites. Drupal, an open source content management software, builds customized, versatile, structured content on the web. Users can integrate Drupal with external services, such as databases, resources, and other applications. Examples of how a website created with Drupal would meet library users' needs are:

- Site themes can easily be changed with thousands of prebuilt templates.
- Audio and video are supported so that media can be played directly from the library website.
- The library website does not need separate software to be viewed on mobile devices.
- Every version of each web page is saved so that editors can go back to earlier versions.
- Permissions can be given to multiple staff to edit a page.

Libraries use open source to manage local digital collections. Two options are DSpace and Greenstone. DSpace preserves and provides customizable access to repositories of digital content and improves the searching of digital collections.

Greenstone is a multilingual open source tool developed and distributed in cooperation with UNESCO and the Human Info NGO in Belgium with the purpose of building and distributing digital library collections. LSS who work in a small library may suggest Greenstone as it operates from even removable media such as a USB flash drive and DVD.

Libraries collect and keep track of all types of data to help make decisions. Measure the Future can be used to record how many visitors pass by library exhibits and to collect data on what parts of the exhibits were most popular.

ShelfReader, is a practical data tracking software that accurately sorts LC call numbers to verify shelf ordering. It can identify items that are still checked out to patrons, have been marked missing or lost, or are in transit between locations. With the support of this program, LSS can make decisions about true item status and shelf order.

These examples are just a few of the ways the communities of developers, designers, and users are rapidly developing and improving upon customized open source programs that enhance library services.

CHAPTER SUMMARY

Open source has changed from once being thought of as experimental and high risk to being widely accepted as a viable option for libraries. LSS may have witnessed their library migrating from a commercial ILS to an open source system. In addition to being cost-effective, major considerations for libraries to move to open source are the free licensing, the reliable outsource support, and to commit to products that will only get better because of the large communities of users who share ideas for improvement and new developments.

DISCUSSION QUESTIONS

1. What is source code and how does it differ from machine or object code?
2. What are the main differences between open source and closed source?
3. Why should libraries consider open source? What advantages would it have? What disadvantages?
4. What is the meaning of "free" when used in describing open source?
5. What role do open source communities have for the future of libraries?

ACTIVITY

Speak with two system librarians who work in libraries that use two different open source ILS. For example, one library may use Koha while the other uses Evergreen.

Interview the librarians about their experiences with their ILS. Were they involved with data migration from a closed sourced ILS to the open source ILS? What technical support vendor do they use and are they responsive to the library needs? What customization of the ILS has been made for their particular library? Overall, are they satisfied with the ILS? Ask them to explain the advantages and disadvantages of having an open source ILS. Compare the two sets of interview data. What conclusions can be reached about open source ILS?

NOTES

1. Free Software Foundation, "What Is Free Software?," GNU Operating System, last modified 2019, accessed May 6, 2020, https://www.gnu.org/philosophy/free-sw.html.

2. Ariel Gilbert-Knight, "Making Sense of Software Licensing," Making Sense of Software Licensing, last modified March 9, 2012, accessed May 2, 2020, https://www.techsoup.org/support/articles-and-how-tos/making-sense-of-software-licensing.

3. Opensource.org, "The Open Source Definition," Open Source Initiative, accessed May 6, 2020, https://opensource.org/docs/osd.

4. "Open Source," in *Computer Desktop Encyclopedia* (n.p.: The Computer Language Company, 2019), https://search.ebscohost.com/login.aspx?direct=true&db=sch&AN=136047492&authtype=cookie,cpid&custid=csl&site=ehost-live&scope=site.

5. Marshall Breeding, "Koha: The Original Open Source ILS," *Library Technical Reports* 53, no. 6 (August/September 2017): 9–10, https://search.ebscohost.com/login.aspx?direct=true&db=aph&AN=129347417&authtype=cookie,cpid&custid=csl&site=ehost-live&scope=site.

6. Evergreen Project, "Evergreen—Open Source Library Software," Evergreen, last modified 2020, accessed May 7, 2020, http://evergreen-ils.org/.

7. Marshall Breeding, "Koha: The Original Open Source ILS," *Library Technical Reports* 53, no. 6 (August/September 2017): 10–11, https://search.ebscohost.com/login.aspx?direct=true&db=aph&AN=129347417&authtype=cookie,cpid&custid=csl&site=ehost-live&scope=site.

8. ByWater Solutions, "Support for Libraries," ByWater Solutions, last modified 2020, accessed May 7, 2020, https://bywatersolutions.com/.

REFERENCES, SUGGESTED READINGS, AND WEBSITES

Breeding, Marshall. "Koha: The Original Open Source ILS." *Library Technical Reports* 53, no. 6 (August/September 2017): 9–17. https://search.ebscohost.com/login.aspx?direct=true&db=aph&AN=129347417&authtype=cookie,cpid&custid=csl&site=ehost-live&scope=site.

———. "Library Systems Report." *American Libraries* 50, no. 5 (May 2019): 22–35. https://search.ebscohost.com/login.aspx?direct=true&db=aph&AN=136428975&authtype=cookie,cpid&custid=csl&site=ehost-live&scope=site.

ByWater Solutions. "Support for Libraries." ByWater Solutions. Last modified 2020. Accessed May 7, 2020. https://bywatersolutions.com/.

Drupal- Open Source. "Drupal." Drupal. Last modified 2020. Accessed May 8, 2020. https://www.drupal.org/.

DSpace. "About DSpace." DSpace. Last modified 2020. Accessed May 8, 2020. https://duraspace.org/dspace/about/.

Evergreen Project. "Evergreen—Open Source Library Software." Evergreen. Last modified 2020. Accessed May 7, 2020. http://evergreen-ils.org/.

Free Software Foundation. "What Is Free Software?" GNU Operating System. Last modified 2019. Accessed May 6, 2020. https://www.gnu.org/philosophy/free-sw.html.

Gilbert-Knight, Ariel. "Making Sense of Software Licensing." Making Sense of Software Licensing. Last modified March 9, 2012. Accessed May 2, 2020. https://www.techsoup.org/support/articles-and-how-tos/making-sense-of-software-licensing.

Greenstone. "Factsheet." Greenstone Digital Library Software. Last modified 2020. Accessed May 8, 2020. http://www.greenstone.org/factsheet.

Library of Congress. "MARC Systems." MARC Standards. Last modified May 1, 2020. Accessed May 7, 2020. https://www.loc.gov/marc/marcsysvend.html.

Matthews, Billy, and Elizabeth Zoby. "Open Source Tools: Sharpen Your Websites With Drupal." *Computers in Libraries* 37, no. 9 (November 2017): 10–14. https://search.ebscohost.com/login.aspx?direct=true&db=aph&AN=126280995&authtype=cookie,cpid&custid=csl&site=ehost-live&scope=site.

"Open Source." In Computer Desktop Encyclopedia. N.p.: The Computer Language Company, 2019. https://search.ebscohost.com/login.aspx?direct=true&db=sch&AN=136047492&authtype=cookie,cpid&custid=csl&site=ehost-live&scope=site.

Opensource.org. "The Open Source Definition." Open Source Initiative. Accessed May 6, 2020. https://opensource.org/docs/osd.

Stanford University. "Software: Machine Code and Programming Languages." CS101. Accessed May 2, 2020. https://web.stanford.edu/class/cs101/software-2.html.

Smith, Tim. "The Closer." *Library Journal* 145, no. 5 (May 2020): 37. https://search.ebscohost.com/login.aspx?direct=true&AuthType=cookie,ip,cpid&custid=csl&db=f5h&AN=142941965&site=eds-live.

PART II

Library as Community

CHAPTER 7

Cloud Computing

Library Support Staff (LSS) are able to assist and train users to operate public equipment, connect to the internet, use library software applications, and access library services from remote locations.

Topics Covered in This Chapter
Fundamentals of Cloud Computing
Service Models
    SaaS
LSS Use Cloud Computing
Informed Practices
Advice for Users
    Recommendations for Patrons
    Recommendations for LSS

Key Terms

The Cloud: Resources such as servers and other infrastructure provided mostly offsite for users to retrieve programs and applications as well as to share and store files and data.

Gateway: Z39.50 is a protocol developed for libraries to directly connect to other online catalogs as well as to vendor cloud resources.

Vendor Host: In cloud computing this is a company or individual who contracts cloud services with libraries who access their software and content remotely.

Virtualization: This is the process that allows the sharing of applications to multiple customers and companies.

FUNDAMENTALS OF CLOUD COMPUTING

Clouds are what we see when we look at the sky. As expansive storage receptacles, they hold droplets of moisture that may be released as rain or snow. Clouds are also ethereal and untouchable. They spur our imagination of far-off lands as they float above us. Easier to draw than to technically describe, early computer networks were depicted as clouds that held a lot of connections elsewhere that supported, or hovered over, computers. These cloud-like connections enabled people to use the internet for more purposeful work and communications.

Networks are the cloud connection of computing devices that support specific operations and services. Library Support Staff (LSS) have personal home networks that may be made up of their phone, TV, computer, printer, game, and streaming devices. Common to all is the internet connection through the home Wi-Fi. While the term "cloud" comes from early network diagrams, today it is ubiquitous with computing services available over the internet.

The Cloud is offsite resources that enable users to access programs and applications as well as to share and store files and data. Using the internet to engage with these myriad services is called cloud computing.[1] Libraries, like almost all institutions, use the cloud to access, store, retrieve, share, and use data.

There are many companies that host cloud computing for all kinds of government, educational, nonprofit, and commercial institutions. LSS perform many tasks in the cloud, such as working with budgets and other documents, backing up circulation data in an Integrated Library System (ILS) vendor cloud, or assisting patrons with research, obtaining information from cloud-hosted databases.

Cloud location, power, cooling, network, and security are in place so that applications and data can be stored, accessed, shared, retrieved, and used reliably and efficiently. The Cloud is usually managed by an external company. Only large aca-

Figure 7.1. Cloud Computing. *mathisworks/DigitalVision Vectors via Getty Images*

demic or other library institutions would have the staff to manage their own private cloud. While there are countless cloud computing platforms, they all fall into one of four categories:[2]

1. Private Cloud: Highly restricted, it is used in banking, medicine, and government. LSS who work in government or special libraries may use a private cloud for their work.
2. Public Cloud: Providing infrastructure and services to the public that are shared among multiple organizations, data remains private to the organization unless explicitly released. LSS use the public cloud for email, social media, sharing files, and other work related to their job.
3. Hybrid Cloud: Cloud resources are a blend of public and private cloud computing platforms such as the Library of Congress. LSS would have designated access to specific cloud computing to perform duties.
4. On Premises: LSS who work at some special or academic libraries may use the cloud that are local only to the institution.

SERVICE MODELS

Each of the four cloud categories use one of three service models that engage with software, programs, and infrastructure. Successful library operations and services rely on an effective coordination of hardware and skilled programmers who write, manage, and maintain cloud resources. The end goal of infrastructure and programming is to provide software as a service to users.[3] These three service models[4] work in harmony with each other for successful performance that meet or exceed librarian and patrons' expectations. The service models are:

Software-as-a-Service (SaaS): While the storage is normally shared, the data between organizations is strictly partitioned. Per agreement, software in the cloud is accessible to all or designated groups of users via the internet on a variety of devices from in-house library computers and workstations to remote access via patron smartphones. The library is not responsible for either the infrastructure or programming services that support SaaS.

Platform-as-a-Service (PaaS): Library operations are enhanced by application developers who work with librarians in this second model to create or customize applications and manage data pertinent to the functions and services of the library. Application developers are the go-between and work directly with both the end user library and the network architect.

Infrastructure-as-a-Service (IaaS): Network architects manage infrastructure that include virtualization, networks, storage, and servers. **Virtualization** is the process that allows the sharing of applications to multiple customers and companies. For reasons such as cost savings or efficiency, depending upon the vendor host agreement, the library may have some control over applications, operating systems, storage, and networking components.

Software-as-a-Service

Ongoing software improvements enhance library operations and services. Figure 7.2 shows two forms of the service models for libraries. The triangle on the left is more traditional in that robust infrastructure, supported by creative programming, work together to create users' software. The triangle on the right tells the story from a library perspective. Librarians have a long history of being innovators of technology. In this second inverted triangle SaaS is broadly represented at the top, showing how the focus of software development is built upon the needs of the library community who communicate their ideas with the programmers and infrastructure innovators. SaaS are represented in both triangular models but in the second model, librarians and staff drive software development that is unique and specific to library services and operations.

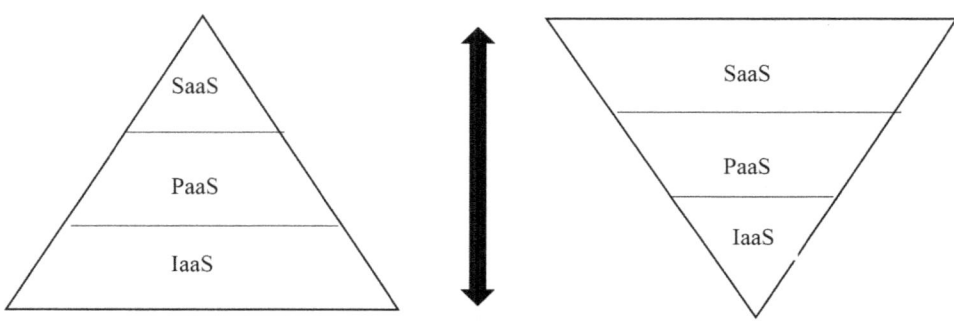

Figure 7.2. Cloud Computing Models.

The benefit of the cloud is the ability for more than one person to have shared access to a file. This action is called file sharing. While it is possible to allow outsiders to have access to a local desktop hard drive, it is much safer and easier to upload the file to a "neutral" third-party cloud. The creator of a file or folder gives varying degrees of permission to others to access and use the file. At a most restrictive level, the file, or parts of it, can only be read but not changed. On the other extreme, the file owner may give full editing rights to others to collaborate and make global changes to the work.

LSS use file sharing to gain information, to review others' work, or to create group slide presentations, documents, or media. LSS may also edit data such as in cataloging to complete MARC records or to support library programming with marketing or products for upcoming events. Successful libraries are the sum of the work of many, and file sharing is an ideal way for staff, particularly those who may not be on the same schedule, to collaborate together.

There are several ways to share files.[5] Three common ways that LSS may share files are:

1. Centralized file hosting server installations on networks such as with the library ILS. Library item and patron information is stored on a vendor host server. LSS use the data from the vendor host server for different applications in circulation, reserves, cataloging, etc.

2. Hyperlinked documents are a second way to file share. Such web-based products such as Google Docs, Dropbox, Facebook, Amazon, and many other companies are set up for users with accounts and permissions to share files, e-books, audio, video, and other content via the internet.
3. Distributed peer-to-peer (P2P) networks[6] are the most secure type of file sharing where computers use a P2P program to form a network. P2P file sharing software is configured to address security and other issues in order to keep the network closed to the outside. LSS who work in government, academic, and special libraries may use P2P file sharing for confidential or other sensitive information.

A second method of the internet that is specific to customers of SaaS, PaaS, and IaaS is **vendor hosting**. Libraries use vendor hosting for ILS, discovery, and library platform services. In cloud computing a vendor host is a company or individual who contracts cloud services with libraries who access their software and content remotely. Today, libraries seek vendor host arrangements to support their use of ILS.[7]

Some vendors host both the software (SaaS) and hardware (IaaS) whereby the servers with the library data are maintained and managed in the vendor host data center. Other vendors may host the SaaS but use a third party to maintain the library's local server. Libraries find vendor hosting cost effective because in leasing they have a predictable annual ILS budget. They do not have to purchase the hardware and software nor hire IT staff to manage the ILS.[8]

In addition to internet and vendor hosting, a third type of cloud access is gateways. Gateway connections are reliable, secure, and can move large amounts of data quickly and efficiently. LSS may gain access to a gateway via a unique user password or some other type of identifier. Libraries may have a direct connection or secured **gateway** protocol to the ILS vendor, database supplier, or other critical resource. Z39.50[9] is a protocol originally developed that allows libraries to search each other's online catalogs when the catalogs are provided by different vendors. For example, a local consortium of libraries using one vendor could connect their cataloging module to a national supplier of catalog records from another vendor using the Z39.50 gateway. Today, Z39.50 is the common gateway for libraries to connect to the cloud resources of EBSCO*host* and other database vendors. The internet, vendor hosts, and gateways are primary ways LSS access the cloud with specific resources for libraries.

Having access to cloud computing supports how we learn, work, communicate, and do business. Let's examine some examples of specific ways LSS use the cloud in their daily work.

LSS USE CLOUD COMPUTING

Cloud computing is omnipresent in library operations and services. Throughout any workday, LSS use the cloud in library operations and patrons' services.

ILS Modules and Services

LSS work with all of the modules of an ILS in the operations of circulation, reserves, cataloging, acquisitions, serials, and digital resources. LSS are fully engaged in the work of circulating items, which include entering and using data from the ILS cloud to change status of items, run reports, resolve holds and reserves, and resolve fines. LSS may also use ILS email to send circulation-related messages to patrons.

- Research and Discovery Systems: Discovery systems, most common in academic, school, and special libraries seamlessly allow users to research multiple databases, catalogs, websites, and other online resources simultaneously. LSS knowledgeable of advanced searching, language conversation, peer review, reading level, and publication selection can help patrons research using discovery system clouds more successfully and efficiently.
- E-books and e-magazines: LSS support patrons' use of e-books and e-magazines through a third-party cloud or service. With their library barcode, patrons can transfer electronic reading content from the vendor clouds to their personal devices.
- Streaming Media and Video: In a similar manner, libraries that provide audio and streaming video content instruct and support their patrons' downloading of content from the third-party vendor clouds. LSS who use such third-party services for their own reading, listening, and viewing have experience and will be better able to help patrons.
- Communications: LSS use email, ILS email services, texting, chat, and social media (Instagram, Twitter, etc.) cloud platforms to communicate with supervisors, other library staff, vendors, and patrons. Messages and attachments are uploaded and downloaded via the cloud for access, editing, and storage. LSS should separate personal communications from their work email accounts.
- Administrative Support: Microsoft, Dell, Apple, and other computing companies provide cloud storage and computing for their users. Depending upon the preference and policies of the library, LSS who do administrative work may use the cloud for document collaboration and storage. The cloud may be used to support financial (acquisitions, budget), library operations (building, staff), or reports (statistics, monthly, or annual activities).
- Calendars, Schedules, and Meetings: Libraries operate around staffing schedules. Libraries may choose to use cloud computing to schedule staff hours, common meetings, programming of events, and other types of daily activities.

INFORMED PRACTICES

Cloud computing is an external internet activity and one that requires safe and informed practices. LSS successfully and appropriately use cloud computing when they understand not only the functions and features of SaaS, but also policies in place to minimize problems and concerns. Security and privacy are closely related. Libraries have an ethical obligation to protect users' data and ensure it is both secure and held private. This section will address how LSS can help ensure security and privacy for themselves and library users when using cloud computing.

The more hands involved, the less secure may be the situation. In order for cloud computing to work, it involves excessive amounts of data that often pass through several, if not many, people and companies for storage and handling. Handling, processing, and saving files on a personal hard drive is fairly secure as it is one user to one computer. However, when data is saved in untold networked servers by teams and teams of support handlers in the cloud, despite best efforts, there is greater risk that data could be compromised, tampered with, misplaced, or lost.[10]

Another threat to cloud computing is attacks. On a small-scale it is annoying, on a large-scale it could be devastating to a library and compromise its ILS or other critical systems. In networks, LSS can visualize three levels of attackers: a cohost attacker, an internal attacker, and an external attack.

The cohosted attacker can launch an attack through shared resources. A consortium of four libraries that share an ILS system is an example of a cohosted system whereby their data and SaaS is a unit in a vendor-hosted cloud. Because the four libraries access each other's files in the shared system, security practices would need to be in place to protect the consortium from a cohosted attack. The security risks to cohosted computers is most high because it likely falls on local IT to plan for and manage the risk.

An internal attack would most likely target a vendor-hosted remote server in an internal network. The risk would be medium as there could be teams of expert staff who continually perform risk assessment of their customers' data and plan accordingly to minimize it.

An external network attack could have the least risk. An attack of the internet external network would need to pass through multiple layers of security access and authentication. While not impossible, an attack of the cloud computing accessed through the internet would be less likely because of the protections of the external network.

If LSS suspect something is not correct in the systems they use, they should immediately report it to their supervisor. Often it is the end user who first notices an unusual problem.

Even though there is the Library Bill of Rights that upholds the First Amendment right to privacy, and cloud computing information centers understand and work with libraries to protect users, the privacy of patrons can potentially be breached. While the protections vendor hosts take in the United States to help ensure library patrons' information will remain private, there may be less protection from other countries around the world. Cloud computing is global, and patron data may be moved from United States servers in other countries.

ADVICE FOR USERS

This last section is based on an interview with an expert[11] in many aspects of network (PaaS) and software (SaaS) cloud computing, providing a perspective on how users can minimize potential problems using cloud computing at both the library and at home. When asked, "What recommendations do you have for patrons who use SaaS both inside of the library and remotely from home?" the following recommendations were mentioned as the key concerns LSS should know and share with others:

- Designate a single workstation at home for this purpose or function.
- Set a complex password on the workstation and change it every ninety days.

- Enable the locked screen timeout feature on the workstation for inactivity exceeding three minutes or less. In other words, if you are not actively using the computer, lock the screen.
- Keep the workstation updated with the latest patches and run virus protection software (i.e., Microsoft Security Essentials is robust and free). In addition to being a good practice to have updated virus protection, often cloud applications will check for this and deny access to users who the protection tags as suspect.
- Do not disable browser security features unless explicitly requested by the cloud software (i.e., Active-X and JavaScript pose risks).
- Verify that the site is using HTTPS and do not accept invalid certificates. The "S" in HTTPS identifies the link as a secure site.
- Do not save the cloud password in the browser.
- Look for two-factor authentication (RSA, Symantec tokens, text back codes) when logging into the cloud. Having two factors such as a password and a code will help block attacks.
- While library workstations are often registered with the vendor host, see if the at-home workstation can be registered with the cloud software/application.
- Never click on phishing links in emails or online seeking your username and password. Even though the graphics may look authentic, the link will most likely be slightly different than the real website.
- Postpone downloads to your own devices for when you are on library premises if possible.

These suggestions are not only important for patrons to follow but also for LSS with their personal use of cloud computing.

When asked, "What recommendations do you have for library staff who use the cloud for their work?" these key suggestions were recommended:

- Lower your expectations for integration with local peripheral devices, as cloud software has tradeoffs when connecting to document scanners, printers, fingerprint readers, barcode readers, and the like. In other words, not all peripheral devices will seamlessly work with SaaS.
- Navigation performance (screen switching, keyboard and mouse response) can be affected by the library connection to the internet it has on premises.
- Full-featured custom graphical user interface features may be substituted for the capabilities of an Internet Explorer, Chrome, Safari, or a supported browser.
- Batch or background functions such as long-running reports are likely to run faster from a cloud than a standalone workstation.
- The cloud often provides better response time and delays during peak load and will often run faster or be less noticeable.
- Keep your workstation well maintained and up-to-date.

CHAPTER SUMMARY

LSS who are practiced and knowledgeable users of cloud computing in both their personal lives and daily work are able to assist and train users to operate SaaS library applications, and access library services from the internet, vendor-hosted, and cohosted clouds located in remote locations. LSS are aware of security and privacy issues and follow practices and policy to minimize risk and to protect patrons' data.

DISCUSSION QUESTIONS

1. What are the main functions of the three service models and how does each model support library services?
2. How is SaaS used by LSS in their library work? How is it used by patrons using library services?
3. What are some of the ways LSS can assist and instruct users to help them maintain security and their privacy when accessing library cloud services?

ACTIVITY

Create an inventory of all of the cloud services used by library staff and patrons for the library where you work or frequent. Speak with the IT specialist to research each. Categorize the type of each cloud platform (public, private, or hybrid) and the service model(s) the library obtains from it (SaaS, PaaS, IaaS). Is the cloud web-based, vendor hosted, or accessed via a gateway? What kind of authentication is used for security, and what steps does the vendor take to ensure privacy of patron data? After examining the data you obtained, what recommendations could be made to improve how library staff and/or patrons access and use each of these cloud platforms?

NOTES

1. Sharpened Productions, "Cloud Definition," TechTerms, last modified 2020, accessed May 21, 2020, https://techterms.com/definition/cloud.
2. University of Illinois, "Types of Cloud Computing: Private, Public, and Hybrid Clouds," I Technology Services, last modified 2020, accessed May 23, 2020, https://cloud.illinois.edu/types-of-cloud-computing-private-public-and-hybrid-clouds/.
3. Eric James Keen, email interview by the author, Barrington, RI, May 20, 2020.
4. North Dakota Information Technology Department, "Cloud Computing Terminology," Information Technology Services, last modified May 8, 2020, accessed May 10, 2020, https://www.nd.gov/itd/services/application-brokering/cloud-computing-terminology.
5. Field Tech Now, LLC, "File Sharing," Techopedia, last modified 2020, accessed May 27, 2020, https://www.techopedia.com/definition/16256/file-sharing.
6. Federal Trade Commission, "Peer-to-Peer File Sharing: A Guide for Business," Federal Trade Commission, last modified 2020, accessed May 27, 2020, https://www.ftc.gov/tips-advice/business-center/guidance/peer-peer-file-sharing-guide-business.
7. Marshall Breeding, "Managing Tech and the Impact of Cloud Computing on Libraries," *Computers in Libraries* 39, no. 2 (March 2019): https://search.ebscohost.com/login.aspx?direct=true&db=aph&AN=135486413&authtype=cookie,cpid&custid=csl&site=ehost-live&scope=site.
8. Marshall Breeding, "Up in the Air: Cloud Computing and Library Systems," *Computers in Libraries* 38, no. 10 (December 2018): https://search.ebscohost.com/login.aspx?direct=true&db=aph&AN=133655130&authtype=cookie,cpid&custid=csl&site=ehost-live&scope=site.

9. EBSCO Industries, Inc., "What is Z39.50?" EBSCO Connect, last modified 2020, accessed May 23, 2020, https://connect.ebsco.com/s/article/What-is-Z39-50?language=en_US.

10. Sirisha Potluri and Katta Subba Rao, "Improved Quality of Service-Based Cloud Service Ranking and Recommendation Model," *Telkomnika* 18, no. 2 (June 2020): https://search.ebscohost.com/login.aspx?direct=true&db=aph&AN=143030347&authtype=cookie,cpid&custid=csl&site=ehost-live&scope=site.

11. Eric James Keen, email interview by the author, Barrington, RI, May 20, 2020.

REFERENCES, SUGGESTED READINGS, AND WEBSITES

American Library Association. "Library Bill of Rights and Freedom to Read Statement Pamphlet." American Library Association. Last modified 2020. Accessed May 27, 2020. http://www.ala.org/aboutala/offices/oif/LBOR-FTR-statement-pamphlet.

Breeding, Marshall. "Managing Tech and the Impact of Cloud Computing on Libraries." *Computers in Libraries* 39, no. 2 (March 2019): 9–11. https://search.ebscohost.com/login.aspx?direct=true&db=aph&AN=135486413&authtype=cookie,cpid&custid=csl&site=ehost-live&scope=site.

———. "Up in the Air: Cloud Computing and Library Systems." *Computers in Libraries* 38, no. 10 (December 2018): 9–11. https://search.ebscohost.com/login.aspx?direct=true&db=aph&AN=133655130&authtype=cookie,cpid&custid=csl&site=ehost-live&scope=site.

"Different Ways to Access the Cloud." *Modern Healthcare* 50, no. 10 (March 9, 2020): 20. https://search.ebscohost.com/login.aspx?direct=true&AuthType=cookie,ip,cpid&custid=csl&db=aph&AN=142211009&site=ehost-live&scope=site.

Dropbox. "Share Any File or Folder, Easily, With Anyone." Dropbox. Last modified 2020. Accessed May 27, 2020. https://www.dropbox.com/features/share.

EBSCO Industries, Inc. "What is Z39.50?" EBSCO Connect. Last modified 2020. Accessed May 23, 2020. https://connect.ebsco.com/s/article/What-is-Z39-50?language=en_US.

Federal Trade Commission. "Peer-to-Peer File Sharing: A Guide for Business." Federal Trade Commission. Last modified 2020. Accessed May 27, 2020. https://www.ftc.gov/tips-advice/business-center/guidance/peer-peer-file-sharing-guide-business.

Field Tech Now, LLC. "File Sharing." Techopedia. Last modified 2020. Accessed May 27, 2020. https://www.techopedia.com/definition/16256/file-sharing.

Keen, Eric James. Email interview by the author. Barrington, RI. May 20, 2020. https://www.kingston.com/us/community/articledetail/articleid/29685.

North Dakota Information Technology Department. "Cloud Computing Terminology." Information Technology Services. Last modified May 8, 2020. Accessed May 10, 2020. https://www.nd.gov/itd/services/application-brokering/cloud-computing-terminology.

Potluri, Sirisha, and Katta Subba Rao. "Improved Quality of Service-Based Cloud Service Ranking and Recommendation Model." *Telkomnika* 18, no. 2 (June 2020): 1252–58. https://search.ebscohost.com/login.aspx?direct=true&db=aph&AN=143030347&authtype=cookie,cpid&custid=csl&site=ehost-live&scope=site.

Rackspace US, Inc. "What is SaaS?" Rackspace. Last modified 2020. Accessed May 23, 2020. https://www.rackspace.com/library/what-is-saas.

Salesforce.com, Inc. "What is Salesforce?" Salesforce. Last modified 2020. Accessed May 23, 2020. https://www.salesforce.com/ap/products/what-is-salesforce/.

Sharpened Productions. "Cloud Definition." TechTerms. Last modified 2020. Accessed May 21, 2020. https://techterms.com/definition/cloud.

———. "Drive Definition." TechTerms. Last modified 2020. Accessed May 21, 2020. https://techterms.com/definition/drive.

University of Illinois. "Types of Cloud Computing: Private, Public, and Hybrid Clouds." I Technology Services. Last modified 2020. Accessed May 23, 2020. https://cloud.illinois.edu/types-of-cloud-computing-private-public-and-hybrid-clouds/.

CHAPTER 8

Network Infrastructure

Library Support Staff (LSS) know the general trends and developments in technology applications for library functions and services.

Topics Covered in This Chapter
Background
Internet
  Browsers
  Internet Service Providers (ISP)
  Broadband
Network Infrastructure Equipment
  Firewall and Filter
  Wireless
  Troubleshooting
Technology Learning

Key Terms
Bluetooth: A type of wireless service that uses short-range radio waves. It allows two devices located in close proximity to communicate with each other.
Broadband: This is another term for the various technologies that provide high-speed internet access.
Browser: This is the application or program on a computer that allows library users and staff to access and view websites from the internet.
Hotspot: These are the physical devices or locations where users can connect their mobile devices to the internet.
Internet Service Provider: Also known as ISP, these are the companies that sell or provide free internet access.

Interoperability: This is the property that allows for the unrestricted sharing of resources between different systems and computing devices or components. Libraries strive to provide internet access for all types of user devices and mobile equipment.

Network Infrastructure: The equipment, wiring, software, and other resources needed to move data to and from outside providers of services like the internet or subscription databases to the patron user.

BACKGROUND

Systems are built upon foundations or frameworks called infrastructure. Without infrastructure, a building would collapse; our smartphones would not work. Infrastructure support daily life. Infrastructure could be people-based, item- or component-based, or a combination of both. People we rely on, such as caregivers and sitters, provide infrastructure for family support. Infrastructure, such as highways, bridges, and tunnels, are the components that support transportation.

The previous chapters discussed key technology resources used in libraries: computers, Integrated Library Systems, software, and open source and cloud computing. While each is critical, none would function without a **network infrastructure**. Network infrastructure is the equipment, wiring, software, and other resources, including people, needed to move data to and from outside providers of services like the internet or subscription databases to the patron user. Networks and equipment vary in size according to the location, size, and needs of the library.

This chapter offers practical information for Library Support Staff (LSS) about network infrastructure used to support computing in libraries. Network infrastructure for library computing is a combination of IT components, user content, and technical support. Technology is infused in all aspects of library work, and LSS need to be competent in its use. Responsibility for technology may vary depending upon the size, type, and location of the library. The smaller the library, the more hands-on is the staff. Many public, school, and private libraries do not have municipal IT support. Library staff may have full responsibility for operating and managing its technology. In most medium size libraries, the staff share the responsibility with others but are often on the front line of setting up systems, troubleshooting problems, and administering day-to-day functions. Large academic and public libraries will likely have IT staff or outsourced contracts for Infrastructure-as-a-Service full support. No matter the size or type of library, it is important for LSS to understand its network infrastructure. The more competent LSS are with technology, the more confident and successful they will be in the work of helping patrons. LSS will have varying degrees of responsibility for maintaining and managing all or part of the library network. The internet, the ultimate network of networks, connects the users of billions of computers and devices around the world.

INTERNET

Searching the internet is a vital library service. It is made possible because the internet is a vast network of external hyperlinks to an unparalleled number of hosting computers and other cloud services. Websites provide content that is accessed via the cloud. LSS can be most helpful in guiding patrons to using internet browsers to obtain web resources.

Browsers

A web browser is the application software that allows users to access and view websites from the internet. Without a browser, content in websites could not be searchable as we know it today. Hypertext Markup Language (HTML) is the code used to design or "markup" webpages. Each time a browser loads a web page, it processes or translates the HTML computer language into a native language, such as English, that ordinary people can read and view.[1] A web browser takes us anywhere on the internet. It retrieves information from other parts of the web and displays it on a desktop or mobile device. Users choose their preference of browsers. Those who purchase or lease a PC with Windows OS will have the browser Microsoft Edge installed on it. Apple computers come with its own browser called Safari. Browsers have regular updates, and new versions can be downloaded quickly by the user. LSS may have multiple browsers on their desktops and use more than one to cross-check search results. The most popular browsers, in addition to Edge and Safari, are Mozilla Firefox, Google Chrome, and Opera. Browsers are a matter of personal choice or preference, but most libraries use Chrome, Firefox, Safari, and Edge.

Internet Service Provider

The **Internet Service Provider**, or ISP, is the company that provides the library its internet service. Many libraries' ISP is the same company that provides the library telephone or cable service. In many communities the utility company, if it is an ISP, may provide free internet to the library or school in the town. Some states, such as Minnesota, Kentucky, and Connecticut,[2] are the ISP, connecting academic, school, and public libraries to statewide fiber optic networks. The main types of ISP[3] are:

- Digital subscriber line (DSL) providers
- Copper providers (Business T1/T3 connections)
- Cable
- Fiber internet
- Fixed wireless broadband
- Mobile broadband and LTE (long-term evolution)
- Satellite

In the United States, internet services are predominantly fiber and cable in urban areas and DSL and satellite in rural parts of the country.

Broadband

Broadband[4] is high-speed internet access. Speeds vary depending upon the technology and the level of service. The type of broadband a library uses may depend upon the state in which the library is located, whether it is in an urban or rural location, and the ISP vendors nearby. Broadband typically provides faster download speed (from the

Table 8.1. Libraries Use Five Types of Broadband

Digital Subscriber Line (DSL)	Found in rural areas where other services are not available, transmits data over multiple traditional copper telephone lines already installed in libraries, homes, and businesses. Distance affects the speed of transmission.
Cable	Using the same lines for internet and television service, at the point of entry into the building the cable services split from the modem into routers that send internet to the computers. Improved speed over DSL.
Fiber	Converts electrical signals carrying data to light and sends the light through transparent glass fibers about the diameter of a human hair at speeds far exceeding cable. Fiber provides excellent and reliable video and internet. Networks managed by large companies or state institutions.
Wireless Fidelity (Wi-Fi)	Users connect mobile devices to the local ISP via short-range Wi-Fi technology. Widely available in many libraries. May be slower than either wired or fixed wireless service.
Satellite	May be the best option for libraries in remote areas. Speeds for satellite broadband depend on several factors, including the provider and service package, line of sight to the orbiting satellite, and even the weather. Speeds may be slower than DSL and cable modem

internet to your computer) than upload speed (from your computer to the internet). Broadband transmission is digital, meaning text, images, sound, and video all come across as "bits" of data. The bits travel much more quickly than traditional telephone or wireless connections. Connecting to streaming video is made possible via broadband. As shown in table 8.1, broadband can be provided over five different platforms.[5]

NETWORK INFRASTRUCTURE EQUIPMENT

Depending upon the type and size of library, the network infrastructure varies in speed, equipment, and overall reliability and performance. Regardless of the end user devices such as computers, smartphones, tablets, or peripherals, network infrastructure should have **interoperability**.[6] Interoperability is the property that allows for the unrestricted sharing of resources between different systems. This can refer to the ability to share data between different components or machines, both via software and hardware, or it can be defined as the exchange of information and resources between different computers through LANS (local area networks) or WANs (wide area networks). Broadly speaking, interoperability is the ability of two or more components or systems to exchange information and to use it. Libraries strive to provide internet access for all user devices and mobile equipment.

All networks use cables to connect network equipment externally from the ISP to the network router. Analogous to an old-time switchboard, the router "routes" data between different external networks, such as EBSCO and the library, and to different devices within the library network. If there is a heavy load or group of user devices, such as a computer lab, switches will be added to increase performance. Library wireless is another port with a device on the router that broadcasts wireless radio waves through a designated area.

The standard today are fiber optic and RJ-45 twisted pair Ethernet cables that rapidly transmit digital signals and data. Older networks may still use a modem or modem/router to convert analog data on phone lines to digital data that the computer could interpret. Today, because most data are transmitted digitally, the modem is

Network Infrastructure 77

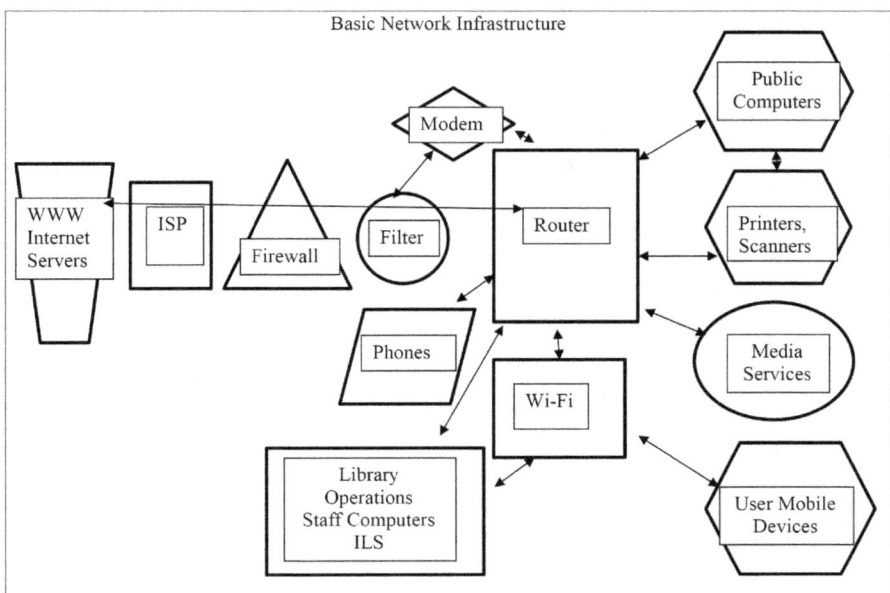

Figure 8.1. Basic Network Infrastructure.

not needed. Figure 8.1 shows a simplistic overview of how the internet moves to the ISP to the router to computing devices in a small to medium sized library.

The double arrows in figure 8.1 represent data coming into the library network from external internet web servers from the ISP to the end users. They also represent the opposite flow of data of the end user leaving the library network and going outside, or externally, to search the web and other internet provided products and services.

The larger the library the more routers, switches, and groups of devices there are. Routers, switches, and hub distribute internet service to computers in the building and regulate performance and speed. Table 8.2 presents the common infrastructure LSS encounter in the library network.

Table 8.2. Network Infrastructure Components

Fiber Optic Cables	Microscopic glass or plastic filaments transmit light beams of rapid pulses of digital data.
Filter	Programs that block certain data and websites from the user.
Firewall	Hardware or software solutions blocking damage by unauthorized users.
Hubs and Switches	Terms used interchangeably, distribute internet services to multiple computers or devices.
Modem	MOdulator/DEModulator—Analog data communications device for transmitting and converting data over DSL to digital.
Peripheral Devices	Equipment connected to a computer such as a printer, scanner, digital camera, or flash drive.
RJ45 Cables	A type of connector commonly used for Ethernet networking.
Router	Device that forwards digital data packets along a network.
Servers	Computers that provide data to other computers over the internet including web servers, mail servers, and file servers.
UPS	Battery power that keeps a network functioning for about a half hour for safe shutdown when power is suddenly lost.

Firewall and Filter

While every piece of equipment on a network is essential, an understanding of firewalls and filters is helpful for library staff who may be asked to explain to patrons why they cannot access certain websites. Every library network should have a firewall to stop unauthorized data or websites that could potentially harm library computers. Firewalls stop corrupted data that may have viruses from entering the local network. A firewall also protects the network from hackers. Library networks need firewalls to protect both equipment and users from intended or unintended harm. Firewalls have a default setting generally to deny all traffic, but rules made by the network administrator will open the firewall to permit appropriate traffic into the network. Firewalls configured properly allow trusted data to flow through it.

As with the need for a firewall, there is also the need for every computer to be filtered. Filters protect the user from obscene or inappropriate content. Filters can be set to allow certain content that is age appropriate. Like firewalls, filters may be devices or software, depending upon the size of the library. Software filtering solutions should be on every computer to work with the firewall to protect from incoming viruses, phishing, and other harmful acts. Phishing is to fraudulently gain online access to users' data and credentials. Filters work by blocking specific websites, phrases, or words. Filters can also block larger amounts of data or content such as pornography or obscenity. Most library administrators rely on the filter product's preselected blocked content and may exempt an occasional site. Since 2000, when the United States enacted the Children's Internet Protection Act, all schools and libraries that receive federal assistance for e-rate internet service are required to use filtered computers for minors (see also chapter 15).

Wireless

The demand for libraries to provide reliable wireless, or Wi-Fi, computing has exploded in the past few years as patrons have acquired more mobile phones, tablets, and laptops. Today, in many libraries patrons can check out the materials, place holds, and search the internet using their mobile phones. Having robust Wi-Fi has been a priority of libraries so that patrons can access the internet and other services when they visit the library from their own devices. Public Wi-Fi using any of the above broadband connectivity encourages patrons to use their own equipment in ways such as:

- Patrons download library apps to their own devices and use library services such as e-books, online catalog, and databases both in and out of the library.
- A library does not need to budget and purchase as many computers when patrons use their own equipment.
- A library does not need to have every model and make of computing devices to satisfy patrons who have a preference in computer platforms.

Wireless broadband connects a home or business to the internet using a radio link between the customer's location and the service provider's facility. Wireless broadband can be mobile or fixed. In remote locations wireless transmissions are boosted with extended antenna and may have intermittent interruptions. Wireless broadband often requires a direct line-of-sight between the wireless transmitter and receiver, thus limiting its range and reliability. In the library building, a wireless router antenna (Wi-Fi or wireless fidelity) may be connected to the router to transmit internet service at a limited range to devices that are adapted to receive Wi-Fi connectivity.

Another type of wireless technology is **Bluetooth**. Using radio waves, Bluetooth is beneficial for providing communication when two Bluetooth compatible devices are close or in short range of each other. For example, a smartphone that has Bluetooth capability and an automobile radio that also has it can communicate with each other via the car's radio speakers and some limited functionality for answering and closing calls. If library devices such as printers and scanners have Bluetooth capability, users may be able to connect with their laptop, tablet, or smartphones.

Hotspots, or mobile wireless broadband subscription services, are becoming increasingly more common for mobile users who need internet "on the go." These services can be purchased on a monthly basis from an ISP. When turned on, the hotspot provides the ISP signal. With proper access information, library users can access the internet using the library's hotspots. Some libraries, especially special, school, and academic, may lend users hotspots who either do not have internet access at home or are traveling to areas with unreliable access. Many libraries lend hotspots for a limited time and specific purposes as a user service.

Troubleshooting

As they are in direct contact with the public, LSS are often the first to learn if there are internet problems. When issues occur, and they will, it is helpful for LSS to get a sense of what is working and what is not.

The first step LSS can take to help diagnose a problem is to check the power supply. Is the computer getting power? What about surrounding computers? Determine if the problem exists with just one computer or is duplicated on several or all computers. The more computers affected, the more likely the problem is occurring closer to the router or even the ISP or external web servers.

If all public computers are working but not the wireless, suspect that the wireless signaling device has failed and may need to be rebooted or have IT support troubleshoot. If all wired and wireless computers are working except for a group, it could be the cabling or power to the switch is loose or the switch needs to be powered down and brought up again. Use the 10-10 rule, which is while holding down the power button, count to 10. Wait ten seconds. Power up. If both wired and wireless computing is down, most likely the problem is with the router or ISP.

Library services are dependent upon many types of hardware, applications software, and network infrastructure. Most LSS do not have formal training in technology, nor are they expected to be experts. The reality is, however, that LSS are often on the front line of technology and often can perform invaluable troubleshooting. In the next section we will look at ways LSS enhance their learning of technology.

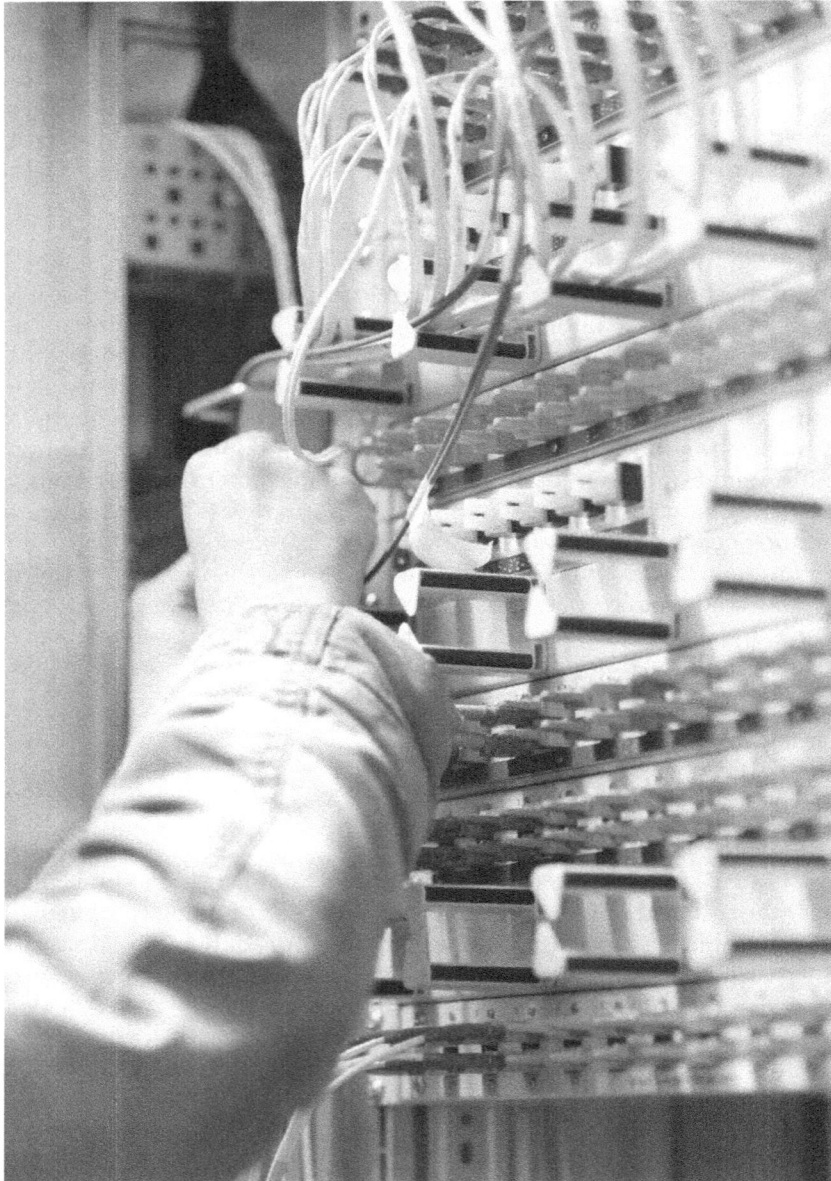

Figure 8.2. Example of Public Library Network Infrastructure. *comptine/E+ via Getty Images*

TECHNOLOGY LEARNING

LSS can provide critical support for functional and reliable library technology. There is no one place to obtain all the technical learning LSS need. Technology is ever changing, and LSS need to think of technology training as life-long learning. There are many ways adults learn:

1. When we compare new ideas to our own past or key experiences
2. Work in an environment (i.e., other library staff, patrons, etc.) that provides challenge, feedback, and support
3. Are self-motivated to keep learning

LSS can enhance their learning to work with and support others' use of new technology. They draw upon their past experiences with technology and compare them to what is new. They expand upon what they already know by seeking help from others either in the library or the technology vendors and specialists who work with library staff. They are motivated to keep learning about technology because they want to be able to help others use library resources with library equipment or patron-owned devices.

For LSS interested in finding technology resources, the Nebraska Library Commission[7] offers many suggestions through its digital literacy guidebook. Divided into six sections such as "Basic Tech Skills" and "Tracking Tech Trends," each topic provides ample links to resources to enhance technology learning. WebJunction,[8] a site for library professional learning through webinars and presentations, offers training in a topic called "Managing Library Computers." The majority of webinars are free, and through them LSS can learn both background and current practices in technology specific to library use and patrons' needs.

LSS can also regularly check technology websites, blogs, and Twitter, and other social media to keep current with library technology issues and solutions. TechSoup[9] is a website that offers technology resources and services to both subscribers and nonsubscribers of nonprofit institutions, including libraries. Any library staff would benefit from following Library Technology Guides[10] maintained by Marshall Breeding, known for his articles published in *Computers in Libraries*. These guides provide network and computing learning specific to libraries through news, reports, documents, vendor, and product links. One thing LSS can depend on is that libraries are and will be depending upon networking services, and it behooves us to continue learning about how they function so that, in turn, we can provide better service and support to patrons.

CHAPTER SUMMARY

In just a few short decades, libraries shifted from being print centric to digital centric. LSS daily work is reliant on a highly functional and reliable network infrastructure. LSS who are attentive to the network and knowledgeable about the basics of how it works can better support its use by patrons.

DISCUSSION QUESTIONS

1. What are the differences between internet browsers and Internet Service Providers?
2. What are the network components for a library network and what is the main function of each?

3. What are the main types of broadband capabilities? What strengths or weaknesses may they have for library users?
4. Why are firewalls and filters important to any library network?
5. What ways can LSS keep current with technology and network infrastructure?

ACTIVITY: CREATE A CONCEPT MAP OF A HOME OR LIBRARY NETWORK

Using PowerPoint or Word, draw a concept map of your home or library network similar to figure 8.1. Use shapes to represent hardware with lines to represent connectivity and flow of data. Be sure to:

- include on the map all phone, TV, and computer systems. These may be separate or integrated;
- include all peripheral devices, that is, printers, scanners, projectors, gaming systems, etc.;
- include the ISP name and what type of service it provides (DSL, fiber, cable, etc.);
- include wireless;
- label all shapes;
- compare the concept map with others and have a discussion about the similarities and differences of the networks.

NOTES

1. Sharpened Productions, "Web Browser," Tech Terms, last modified 2020, accessed May 31, 2020, https://techterms.com/definition/web_browser.
2. Christine Fox and Rachel Jones, *State K-12 Broadband Leadership 2019: Driving Connectivity, Access, and Student Success*, Glen Burnie, MD: SETDA, 2019, 18–30.
3. BROADBANDNOW, "Complete List of Internet Providers in the U.S.," BROADBANDNOW, last modified 2020, accessed June 5, 2020, https://broadbandnow.com/All-Providers.
4. Federal Communications Commission, "Getting Broadband Q&A," Federal Communications Commission, last modified February 5, 2020, accessed June 5, 2020, https://www.fcc.gov/consumers/guides/getting-broadband-qa.
5. Ibid.
6. Techopedia, "Interoperability," Techopedia, last modified 2020, accessed June 6, 2020, https://www.techopedia.com/definition/631/interoperability.
7. Nebraska Library Commission, "Basic Technology Skills & Assessment," Digital Literacy Guidebook, last modified 2020, accessed June 6, 2020, http://nlc.nebraska.gov/Tech/literacy/choosing.aspx.
8. OCLC, "Topic Areas," WebJunction, last modified 2020, accessed June 6, 2020, https://www.webjunction.org/explore-topics.html.
9. TechSoup Global, "TechSoup," TechSoup, last modified 2020, accessed June 6, 2020, https://www.techsoup.org/.
10. Marshall Breeding, "Library Technology Guides," Library Technology Guides, last modified 2020, accessed June 6, 2020, https://librarytechnology.org/index.pl.

REFERENCES, SUGGESTED READINGS, AND WEBSITES

Breeding, Marshall, "Library Technology Guides." Library Technology Guides. Last modified 2020. Accessed June 6, 2020. https://librarytechnology.org/index.pl.

BROADBANDNOW. "Complete List of Internet Providers in the U.S." BROADBANDNOW. Last modified 2020. Accessed June 5, 2020. https://broadbandnow.com/All-Providers.

CEN. "Fiber Map." CEN. Last modified 2020. Accessed June 3, 2020. https://ctedunet.net/fiber-map/#.

———. "Getting Broadband Q&A." Federal Communications Commission. Last modified February 5, 2020. Accessed June 5, 2020. https://www.fcc.gov/consumers/guides/getting-broadband-qa.

Federal Communications Commission. "Getting Broadband Q&A." Federal Communications Commission. Last modified February 5, 2020. Accessed June 5, 2020. https://www.fcc.gov/consumers/guides/getting-broadband-qa.

Fox, Christine, and Rachel Jones. *State K-12 Broadband Leadership 2019: Driving Connectivity, Access, and Student Success*. Glen Burnie, MD: SETDA, 2019.

Hutchings, Jeff. "A Look at AI in the Information Profession." *ARMA Magazine*, 1 (January/February 2019): 12–17. https://search.ebscohost.com/login.aspx?direct=true&AuthType=cookie,ip,cpid&custid=csl&db=lxh&AN=139417686&site=ehost-live&scope=site.

Meyer, Jeffrey. "The Fundamentals of Navigating Computer Networks." *Computers in Libraries* 39, no. 2 (March 2019): 14–17. https://search.ebscohost.com/login.aspx?direct=true&AuthType=cookie,ip,cpid&custid=csl&db=aph&AN=135486415&site=ehost-live&scope=site.

Mozilla Corporation. "What Is a Web Browser?" Mozilla. Last modified 2020. Accessed May 31, 2020. https://www.mozilla.org/en-US/firefox/browsers/what-is-a-browser/.

Nebraska Library Commission. "Basic Technology Skills & Assessment." Digital Literacy Guidebook. Last modified 2020. Accessed June 6, 2020. http://nlc.nebraska.gov/Tech/literacy/choosing.aspx.

OCLC. "Topic Areas." WebJunction. Last modified 2020. Accessed June 6, 2020. https://www.webjunction.org/explore-topics.html.

Sharpened Productions. "Tech Terms: The Computer Dictionary." Tech Terms. Last modified 2020. Accessed June 6, 2020. https://techterms.com/.

———. "Web Browser." Tech Terms. Last modified 2020. Accessed May 31, 2020. https://techterms.com/definition/web_browser.

Techopedia. "Interoperability." Techopedia. Last modified 2020. Accessed June 6, 2020. https://www.techopedia.com/definition/631/interoperability.

TechSoup Global. "TechSoup." TechSoup. Last modified 2020. Accessed June 6, 2020. https://www.techsoup.org/.

CHAPTER 9

Online Meetings, Programming, and Learning

Library Support Staff (LSS) demonstrate flexibility in adapting to new technology. LSS know concepts and issues concerning the appropriate use of technology by different user groups.

> **Topics Covered in This Chapter**
> Online Meetings
>   Expectations of Participants
>   Best Practices
>   Limitless Possibilities
> Online Programming
> Online Learning
>   Webinars
>
> **Key Terms**
> *Participant:* Someone who's invited and has access to a specific online meeting.
> *Programming:* These are the services and events that libraries plan, schedule, lead, or host that engage community involvement and learning.
> *Videoconference:* When libraries conduct a meeting between two or more participants at different sites by using computer networks to transmit audio and video data.
> *Webinar:* Online seminar, workshop, or class that's conducted over the internet for the purpose of instruction and new learning.

In 2020, the world was drastically changed by the pandemic that resulted from the new coronavirus, or COVID-19. Within days countries shut down all but essential economic and social activities in order to contain its spread. Schools and universities closed, and classes moved to online learning. Libraries that were open on a Wednesday were shuttered by Friday. No one could have predicted such unprecedented actions, and Library Support Staff (LSS) with other library staff, grappled with safe ways to provide essential services to patrons.

This chapter will explore three of the main ways librarians supported communications and learning during this time:

1. Online meetings
2. Online programming
3. Online learning

Where once **videoconferencing** was substandard because of the limitations of the technology, such is not the case today. However, what the pandemic has shown is that there is much to be learned about how users plan for and interact with each other with the technology. LSS who work with and participate in online conferencing, programming, and learning are supportive to others in these endeavors. How libraries use online environments to foster communications, offer services, and support learning is in its infancy. What is certain is that online technologies, products, and processes will improve as users creatively develop new and effective online uses. LSS who are knowledgeable and practiced in hosting and participating in videoconferencing will provide professionalism and efficiency to online meetings.

ONLINE MEETINGS

What once was a cumbersome and expensive process, initiating and participating in online conferences are now straightforward and simple. With the ease of clicking on a link and typing a password, people from around the globe can simultaneously participate in online meetings. Online or videoconferencing enhances personal, professional, and business communications. The person who created the meeting or is leading the meeting is known as the host. Those who attend may be known as **participants** or attendees. Invitations from the host to participate in a specific meeting most likely are received through email. Just as with any invitation, they warrant a response so that the host can plan for meeting attendance. The host is mainly responsible for managing participants by adding or removing them from the meeting, controlling participants' ability to speak during the meeting by muting or unmuting individuals, opening (unlock) and closing (lock) the meeting, if desirable, recording the meeting, and at the end terminating the meeting.

Hosts and participants must use devices with the vendor product application (app) installed. These apps can be obtained at no cost with a quick download from the vendor site or an app store. To initiate a meeting, the host follows the simple steps of the product, scheduling the date, time, estimated length of the meeting, and number of participants. If it is a paid subscription, other resources such as chat and presentation supports are scheduled. The host receives email confirmation of the scheduled meeting with a unique URL of the meeting for one-click access, the meeting ID, and password. If the meeting can be dialed in for audio, domestic and international phone numbers will be included. If the product does not have automatic distribution to registered participants, the host forwards the meeting information to participants.

Expectations of Participants

Just as in a traditional meeting, there are certain expectations[1] of protocol and behavior during online meetings. LSS who participate in work-related meetings should be prepared for the meeting and any role they may have, be informed about the background and topics of the meeting, and be adept at using the technology. LSS should identify themselves with their full name at login similar to having a name tag or name plate in a professional meeting setting. This is important because how you identify yourself will be the name the other participants will see from their screens under your image. Turn on your video and audio feed so that others can see and hear you. Once you are connected, introduce yourself so the host can check your attendance as well as the clarity of your audio and resolution of your video. While others are joining the meeting acquaint yourself with the features you may be expected to use, such as being able to mute/unmute your microphone and how to toggle full screen view of the host or some or all of the participants simultaneously. If you will be sharing documents from your screen, be sure you can switch your camera between the shared screen view and your image. Look to see if there is a raised hand image or icon that, if clicked, lets the host or presenter know that you have a question or would like to say something. Being familiar with the product features not only will make you more confident during the meeting but it also shows others that you are competent with the technology.

Online meetings simulate the functions and behaviors of face-to-face meetings. The host or leader is responsible for the meeting being run efficiently and remaining on topic. Library online work meetings may be around a goal or objective that needs planning, execution, or resolution. They may also be administrative or management meetings, such as department, committee, or board meetings. Online meetings may

Figure 9.1. Online Meeting. *filadendron/E+ via Getty Images*

also be between other libraries or organizations. If invited to participate in a meeting, be prepared for the role that is assigned to you.

Many library meetings follow the protocol of Robert's Rules of Order.[2] Robert's Rules provides specific guidelines on appropriate protocol of meetings so that they are conducted in a manner that is fair, expedient, and inclusive. Robert's Rules also provide direction for getting work done. Librarians are expected to know the basics of Robert's Rules so that they are equipped to participate professionally in meetings. Robert's Rules are just as, if not more, important to guide online meetings because of the guidance they provide both the host and participants to meet the objectives of the meeting.

Just as we would not take personal calls or do other unrelated work during a face-to-face meeting, when participating in an online meeting LSS should not try to multitask other work at the same time. A contributing member of the meeting is one who is fully engaged and listens actively to others. Knowing some of the best practices of online meetings supports such expectations.

Best Practices

A result of the pandemic of 2020, millions of people turned to online videoconferencing as an alternative to face-to-face. Best practices of how to both host and participate in online meetings were rapidly learned and shared. Table 9.1[3] offers many practical ideas and suggestions on how to make the most of these interactions as well as some mistakes to avoid.[4]

One of the key advantages of online conferencing is its convenience. A disadvantage is that the meetings require functioning technology. Some key advantages of online meetings[5] are:

- Attendees from multiple locations "sit" in the meeting as if all were in one location
- Saves cost of travel, meals, and hotel accommodations
- Saves time spent to travel thus increasing work productivity
- Participants can engage across time from any location in the world
- Saves time and expense of planning and hosting in-person meetings and conferences

While online meetings have gained great popularity out of necessity, they will never replace the human touch of face-to-face meetings. Some disadvantages of online meetings are:

- Participants may miss out on visual cues from other people's body language causing miscommunication
- Videoconferencing taking place in personal settings may take away from the professional aspect of the meeting
- A lack of informal conversation, shaking hands, and personal contact.
- Technology cannot be always trusted by libraries and educational facilities who use free or inexpensive videoconferencing platforms. The lack of technical sup-

port personnel makes it much more difficult for participants who are unskilled in videoconferencing.
- People might find it harder to concentrate on the communication because of the remoteness of the video screen
- There is a chance security is breached and meetings could be intercepted

LSS should be aware of both the advantages and disadvantages of online meetings and prepare beforehand with their supervisors to mitigate any potential problems.

Table 9.1. Best Practices for Online Meetings

Before the Meeting

Have a clear purpose for the meeting and prepare agenda.
Select a conferencing software that is available and easy for attendees
Use a scheduling tool for the meeting.
Enable advanced end-user security settings, such as waiting rooms and attendee passwords. Lock meeting when all present.
Agenda should follow Robert's Rules.
If unfamiliar with software features, test meeting beforehand.

During the Meeting

Minimize distractions, stay present and engaged.
If host, adjust settings to automatically mute attendees. Attendees unmute to speak.
Set camera at eye level. Consider a virtual background.
Begin meeting with introductions. Actively move discussions along and manage time.
Share tasks of timekeeper, presenter, note taker, etc.
To accomplish work use breakout sessions.
Deal with topics in a sequential manner according to agenda.
Record the meeting for future viewing. Let participants know in advance the meeting will be recorded.
Invite contrary opinions. Unlike face-to-face meetings, some participants may hold back their opinions in an online meeting format.
Set the date and time for any follow-up meetings.

After the Meeting

Conclude with clear action items. Be disciplined about ending meetings at their designated stop times, reserving five minutes for wrap-up and next steps. All attendees should ensure they understand any assigned action items and delivery timelines.
Share meeting notes with participants and others of any decisions or action items.

Limitless Possibilities

Where once online meetings were reserved for the exceptional situation, today online meetings among library staff have become commonplace. A librarian can attend multiple online meetings scheduled on the same day where, if travel were required, perhaps only one meeting could have been attended.

It is possible that with multiple meetings LSS may need to switch from one online product to another. A morning meeting may be in Zoom while an afternoon meeting may be in Teams.

An important word of advice when switching from one product to another is to be sure to shut down your computer between sessions. Problems may occur if the audio and video settings created in the first meeting product are not the same with the second. It is best to always shut down your computing device to clear it of previous meeting settings and start afresh with a new meeting.

LSS participate in local, regional, and national online meetings. At the local level, libraries that share an Integrated Library System (ILS) or other common interests have reason to form committees and assign staff to work together on initiatives such as finding ways to better use a system or refine a process. LSS may also participate in regional and state library organizations and will be expected to meet with others online. LSS may serve their professional organizations at the state or national level. There are myriad reasons LSS need to be confident and competent in their use of online meeting products and technology in order to perform their work and support their professional interests.

Libraries have adapted online meetings for staff use. Some libraries have also made online meetings available for patrons. For example, a library acquired a paid subscription to Zoom and allows its patrons with a library card to use the account to schedule weekday business meetings[6] that do not exceed two hours. A library staff member is on hand just prior to the start of a meeting to address technical questions and hand over meeting controls before exiting the room, and IT staff are also on standby.

A majority of state libraries and state library associations turned to online annual meetings in 2020 when large conventions were not possible. The Washington State's Washington Library Association[7] declared "the online format allows the conference to remain accessible. We also hope to reach library professionals who may have never had the opportunity to attend a WLA conference." In addition to attending meetings, LSS support library online programming and online learning.

ONLINE PROGRAMMING

Librarians plan, schedule, perform or invite others to lead programs. **Programming** is a core service of libraries. LSS are key to the success of their libraries' programs for the work they do to prepare and support the daily activities that engage patrons and other users in library services and new learning. Having the knowledge, experience, and using tools of technology, librarians and their staff are more prepared than other professionals to turn to online programming as a solution to bring their services to the communities of users.

All the protocols and processes of online meetings can apply to online programming. Programming may be recorded live during the event to be shared in future times. The library may choose to share its programs from its YouTube archive, its TV cable channel, or other means of streaming.

Just as there is for online meetings, there are limitless possibilities for online programming. The Vermont Department of Libraries suggests:

- Synchronous and asynchronous online book clubs
- Online art gallery

- Online craft hangout: knit, quilt, etc. while socializing online
- Online trivia nights
- DIY programs from your kitchen (e.g., green cleaners, cooking, etc.)
- Local organizations cohost events on important community topics
- Parent online support groups
- Celebrate poetry month online

Similarly, there are countless ideas for online programming for youth and children around themes[8] of story times, literacy, play-at-home, and academic support. Guest speakers and performers may agree to be recorded to be later shared with the community. Examples of successful online programs for teens are:[9]

- Teen clubs: *Dungeons and Dragons* and other thematic video games
- Digital escape rooms: Create a Harry Potter (or other literary characters) escape room with Google forms
- Summer reading and crafts: Around a reading theme, lead participants in weekly craft activities.
- Demonstrations: Endless possibilities for programs that provide "how to" instruction

Programming is highly linked with learning. LSS support online learning for patrons and enhance their knowledge and skills by engaging in it themselves.

ONLINE LEARNING

Libraries with free and available materials and programming are centers for learning. Libraries subscribe to databases, software, and other technologies to support education both within the library and remotely. As their responsibility to support education expands, libraries may seek software solutions in order to offer courses and programs.

One early distributor of courses that was available for libraries to subscribe to was Lydia.com, now LinkedIn Learning. It has more than fifteen thousand courses in the areas of technology, business, graphical design, photography, etc. Many universities make LinkedIn Learning available to students to augment their planned academics. Libraries may also consider In Learning or the alternative Gale product Udemy.[10] Udemy's focus is primarily on business and technology, including marketing, software, and design. Courses are on CPR, sign language, Japanese conversation, and more. LSS who have access to an online course product and are familiar with offerings can recommend specific classes to patrons or suggest to supervisors that a class be used as part of instruction or programming.

Online learning can also be accomplished using virtual classrooms. While there are virtual classroom programs uniquely designed for K-12 and higher ed with built-in class rosters, attendance tools, gradebooks, and so forth, librarians who do not work in academic institutions can create a simplified version of a virtual classroom using the online meeting videoconferencing products. This was demonstrated during the pandemic of 2020 when schools across the world, out of necessity, closed and students continued their learning from teachers who hosted online meetings. Much was learned from that experience including these practical suggestions[11] for instructors for classroom control:

1. After all are present, lock the meeting so that no one else may join without the host permission. Enable the waiting room feature.
2. Control screen sharing.
3. Lock down chat.
4. Remove a participant who is disruptive.

While it is likely most LSS will not encounter these situations, it is useful to know these controls exist to support instructors who may encounter the need to apply these measures.

Webinars

Webinars are different from classes in that they are planned and formal presentations without an open "give and take" exchange with students that occur in a classroom. A webinar is an online seminar, workshop, or class that is conducted over the internet for the purpose of instruction. First-time webinars are live online educational presentations that are a type of synchronous learning. Webinars[12] are ideal for large audiences. Typically, webinar attendees do not interact with one another. The host controls all aspects of the webinar including the ability to mute and disable video of the participants. The viewers during the live session can submit questions and comments either by voice, email, or chat, depending upon the preference of the

Figure 9.2. Learning by Webinar. *vgajic/E+ via Getty Images*

presenter and the capability of the videoconferencing program. Most webinars are planned to be shown again to future learners and are recorded for asynchronous viewing at future times. Webinars are an excellent source of content for LSS to learn about the library profession.

Synchronous webinars with the live presenter often require advanced registration and payment. State library or other organization host some webinars at no cost for its libraries. Archived or preserved webinars of previous presentations most often are able to be viewed without cost.

Webinars can accommodate hundreds of viewers. The New England Technical Services Librarians (NETSL), when faced with cancelling its annual conference in April 2020, asked speakers if they would be willing to give their presentations in a webinar format. With their willingness to do so, NETSL returned registration fees and held a free webinar conference to librarians around the globe. One session alone had approximately five hundred attendees. Presentations were made from speakers' homes with a NETSL volunteer host providing technical and management support. In this case the webinar was a logical and successful alternative for library professional learning.

CHAPTER SUMMARY

LSS demonstrate flexibility in adapting to new technologies of online meetings, programming, and learning. As both hosts and participants, LSS can expect to attend online meetings with local, regional, and national library staff on topics related to their work. LSS may also meet online in committees and roundtables. LSS support programming services created for their library community. They also enhance their knowledge and skills by attending online classes and webinars. LSS who are confident in the protocols and competent of the processes and technology of online meetings present themselves as professionals to peers and others.

DISCUSSION QUESTIONS

1. What are the roles of the host of an online meeting? What are the expectations of the participants of the meeting?
2. What are the basics of online meetings? What protocols are expected or participants?
3. Why should LSS be skilled with online programming and online learning?

ACTIVITY

The objective is for LSS to gain professional practice in using two different online conferencing products such as Zoom, Teams, WebEx, etc.

1. Download two of the most popular (free of charge) online meeting applications on your computing device. Have a friend or colleague do the same.

2. Go to the vendor website and read or watch tutorials/instructions to learn about the features of the product.
3. Be the host for each of these products and invite your friend to a meeting.
4. During each meeting experiment with features and functions. Keep notes and compare each product. What are each one's strengths? What do you see as problems or weaknesses?
5. Share your results with your supervisor. Discuss with your supervisor the online product used by the library. Ask if you can repeat this activity with others on the staff so that they will gain similar experience in using online meeting products.

NOTES

1. Tufts University, "Meeting Room Basics," Technology Services, last modified 2020, accessed June 30, 2020, https://it.tufts.edu/guides/audio-and-virtual-conferencing-webex/meeting-room-basics.

2. Robert's Rules Association, "The Official Robert's Rules of Order Web Site," The Official Robert's Rules of Order Web Site, last modified 2020, accessed July 1, 2020, https://www.robertsrules.com/.

3. Georgia Institute of Technology, "Best Practices for Virtual Meetings," Georgia Tech Professional Education, last modified 2020, accessed July 1, 2020, https://pe.gatech.edu/blog/future-work/virtual-meetings.

4. Howard Tiersky, "Five Mistakes NOT to Make When Holding Online Meetings: Avoid These Mistakes If You Want to Hold Successful Online Meetings," *Advisor Today*, May/June 2020, https://search.ebscohost.com/login.aspx?direct=true&AuthType=cookie,ip,cpid&custid=csl&db=mfi&AN=143427519&site=eds-live&scope=site.

5. Boston University, "Will Video Conferencing Become the Preferred Communication Tool?," College of Communication: Center for Mobile Communication Studies, last modified 2020, accessed June 22, 2020, https://sites.bu.edu/cmcs/2017/11/16/will-video-conferencing-become-the-preferred-communication-tool/.

6. Mary Bakija, "Libraries Offer Virtual Meeting Rooms on Zoom," *Library Journal*, April 3, 2020, accessed July 3, 2020, https://www.libraryjournal.com/?detailStory=libraries-offer-virtual-meeting-rooms-on-zoom.

7. Washington Library Association, "WLA2020 to Be Held Online," Washington Library Association, last modified 2020, accessed July 3, 2020, https://www.wla.org/.

8. New York Public Library, "Kids," New York Public Library, last modified 2020, accessed July 3, 2020, https://www.nypl.org/education/kids.

9. Anne Ford, "Pandemic Forces Programs to Move Online: Libraries Adapt Quickly to the Crisis," *American Libraries* 51, no. 6 (June 2020): https://search.ebscohost.com/login.aspx?direct=true&AuthType=cookie,ip,cpid&custid=csl&db=aph&AN=143591347&site=ehost-live&scope=site.

10. Craig Letteroff, "Gale Presents: Udemy," *Booklist* 116, no. 18 (May 15, 2020): https://search.ebscohost.com/login.aspx?direct=true&AuthType=cookie,ip,cpid&custid=csl&db=aph&AN=143240407&site=ehost-live&scope=site.

11. Zoom Video Communications, Inc., "Best Practices for Securing Your Virtual Classroom," Zoom Blog, last modified 2020, accessed July 3, 2020, https://blog.zoom.us/best-practices-for-securing-your-virtual-classroom/.

12. Zoom Video Communications, Inc., "Meeting and Webinar Comparison," Zoom Help Center, last modified 2020, accessed June 25, 2020, https://support.zoom.us/hc/en-us/articles/115005474943-Meeting-and-Webinar-Comparison.

REFERENCES, SUGGESTED READINGS, AND WEBSITES

Bakija, Mary. "Libraries Offer Virtual Meeting Rooms on Zoom." *Library Journal*, April 3, 2020. Accessed July 3, 2020. https://www.libraryjournal.com/?detailStory=libraries-offer-virtual-meeting-rooms-on-zoom.

Boston University. "Will Video Conferencing Become the Preferred Communication Tool?" College of Communication: Center for Mobile Communication Studies. Last modified 2020. Accessed June 22, 2020. https://sites.bu.edu/cmcs/2017/11/16/will-video-conferencing-become-the-preferred-communication-tool/.

Ford, Anne. "Pandemic Forces Programs to Move Online: Libraries Adapt Quickly to the Crisis." *American Libraries* 51, no. 6 (June 2020): 14–15. https://search.ebscohost.com/login.aspx?direct=true&AuthType=cookie,ip,cpid&custid=csl&db=aph&AN=143591347&site=ehost-live&scope=site.

Georgia Institute of Technology. "Best Practices for Virtual Meetings." Georgia Tech Professional Education. Last modified 2020. Accessed July 1, 2020. https://pe.gatech.edu/blog/future-work/virtual-meetings.

Letteroff, Craig. "Gale Presents: Udemy." *Booklist* 116, no. 18 (May 15, 2020): 10. https://search.ebscohost.com/login.aspx?direct=true&AuthType=cookie,ip,cpid&custid=csl&db=aph&AN=143240407&site=ehost-live&scope=site.

New York Public Library. "Kids." New York Public Library. Last modified 2020. Accessed July 3, 2020. https://www.nypl.org/education/kids.

Robert's Rules Association. "The Official Robert's Rules of Order Web Site." The Official Robert's Rules of Order Web Site. Last modified 2020. Accessed July 1, 2020. https://www.robertsrules.com/.

Stromberg, Meghan, and Mary Hammon. "All We Do Now and in the Future, Will Be Informed by This Experience." *Planning* 86, no. 6 (June 2020): 28–33. https://search.ebscohost.com/login.aspx?direct=true&AuthType=cookie,ip,cpid&custid=csl&db=aph&AN=143582233&site=ehost-live&scope=site.

Tiersky, Howard. "Five Mistakes NOT to Make When Holding Online Meetings: Avoid These Mistakes If You Want to Hold Successful Online Meetings." *Advisor Today*, May/June 2020, 26–27. https://search.ebscohost.com/login.aspx?direct=true&AuthType=cookie,ip,cpid&custid=csl&db=mfi&AN=143427519&site=eds-live&scope=site.

Tufts University. "Meeting Room Basics." Technology Services. Last modified 2020. Accessed June 30, 2020. https://it.tufts.edu/guides/audio-and-virtual-conferencing-webex/meeting-room-basics.

University of California - Berkeley. "Video Conferencing." Berkeley Technology. Last modified 2020. Accessed June 29, 2020. https://technology.berkeley.edu/video-conferencing.

Vermont Department of Libraries. "Virtual (and Non-Virtual) Programming Ideas and Resources for Adults." Agency of Administration. Last modified 2020. Accessed July 3, 2020. https://libraries.vermont.gov/covid19/virtualprogram_adult.

Washington Library Association. "WLA2020 to Be Held Online." Washington Library Association. Last modified 2020. Accessed July 3, 2020. https://www.wla.org/.

Zoom Video Communications, Inc. "Best Practices for Securing Your Virtual Classroom." Zoom Blog. Last modified 2020. Accessed July 3, 2020. https://blog.zoom.us/best-practices-for-securing-your-virtual-classroom/.

———. "Meeting and Webinar Comparison." Zoom Help Center. Last modified 2020. Accessed June 25, 2020. https://support.zoom.us/hc/en-us/articles/115005474943-Meeting-and-Webinar-Comparison.

CHAPTER 10

Social Media

Library Support Staff (LSS) are able to assist and train users to operate public equipment, connect to the internet, use library software applications, and access library services from remote locations.

LSS know concepts and issues concerning the appropriate use of technology by different user groups.

Topics Covered in This Chapter
Terminology
    Social Networks, Platforms, and Channels
Library Policies
    Library of Congress
    K–12 School Library Media Centers
Usage
    Behaviors

Key Terms
Analytics: The measurement of a social media and how it is used provides insight to library administrators about its success as a communication and collaboration tool for the library.
Channels: Folders or unique places within the social network created around a special topic or for a particular audience or group to have better focus of conversation and collaboration.
Metrics: Statistics that measure the performance of posts, clicks, likes, etc. that help libraries understand how their social network accounts are being used.
Platform: The computer programming software unique to each social network to make it function.

> *Social media:* Forms of electronic communication such as websites for social networking and microblogging through which users create online communities to share information, ideas, personal messages, videos, and other content.
>
> *Social networks:* Dedicated website or other application that enables users to communicate with each other by posting information, comments, messages, images, etc.

Libraries purposefully use **social media** as a way to communicate with patrons and potential users. Social media can strengthen the bond between the needs of the community and library services. For many patrons, social media has become a primary means to keep track of family and friends, to obtain news, to become informed about events, and to share their own personal and professional experiences. An effective approach to promoting library services is to create a library presence on social media that will respond to the needs of users.

Social media is a way to feel and become connected. A study published in 2018, conducted jointly by Psychology departments of four universities in the United States, found that some people who are socially disconnected or ostracized form relationships through Twitter. On Twitter, behavior may be particularly revealing as it allows individuals to create one-way communications that may help fulfill unmet affiliation needs.[1] Libraries that use social media may be able to reach people who otherwise would be reluctant to come into the library. Social media offers an alternative to face-to-face services. During the COVID-19 pandemic many libraries were able to creatively continue to offer patrons virtual programming and reference services using their social media networks.

TERMINOLOGY

There is a vocabulary of social media terms to aid in its use. Some words are repurposed from other applications, such as the word "metrics," a standard of measurement. In social media, **"metrics"** could be the monthly number of followers, engagement rate, and number of links, clicks, etc. to determine which content has most appeal to patrons. The following are terms[2] with definitions Library Support Staff (LSS) may encounter when creating or helping patrons with various library social media:

- Avatar: a small image that represents a user on a social network
- Boosted post: different than an advertisement, this is a post on Facebook that costs money in order to reach targeted audiences
- Channel: an account from which one can make content available to others using the service
- Chatbox: an artificial intelligence program that provides customer service, answers questions, etc.
- Clickbait: manipulative content that encourages clicking on a specific link
- Cross-channel: marketing messages that appear across several or all of a user's social media platforms
- Crowdsourcing: using a group to generate ideas, services, or content

- Dark social: web traffic coming from social media that is difficult to track
- Feed: the stream of content from other users that functions as a homepage
- Hashtag (#): connect posts to other posts on the same subject or trending topic
- Platform: software used on a social network
- Social listening: gather mentions, comments, hashtags, and relevant posts from across social media
- Targeting: select potential audience for ads based on age, location, gender, interests, etc.
- Trending topic: a topic, subject, or event that has a sudden surge in popularity
- Viral: content that spreads exponentially on social media creating a snowball effect

Social Networks, Platforms, and Channels

These three important social media terms—**social networks**, **platforms**, and **channels**—are closely related and often used interchangeably. Figure 10.1 illustrates the relationships, social network, and channels of Slack, a collaboration space aimed for both personal and business use. Slack is a social network website that enables people to communicate with each other by posting and leaving messages, sharing documents and photos, scheduling meetings, etc. Each unique social network, such as Facebook, Pinterest, or Slack, has its own specialized and customized software platform. A platform is the computer programming software that is unique to and makes, in the example Slack, function. Confusion may arise because the platform is the same name as the social network. Be clear about the distinction: Is the discussion about the social network tool and how it is being used or is it about the functionality of the software programming platform?

Most social networks have two-way communication for collaboration. A library presents an event on a topic of local interest on Facebook, and people respond with their opinions or ideas about it. Similar to a TV channel, a social media channel is created around a special topic or for a particular audience or group to provide better focus and organization of the conversations and collaborations. Channels can

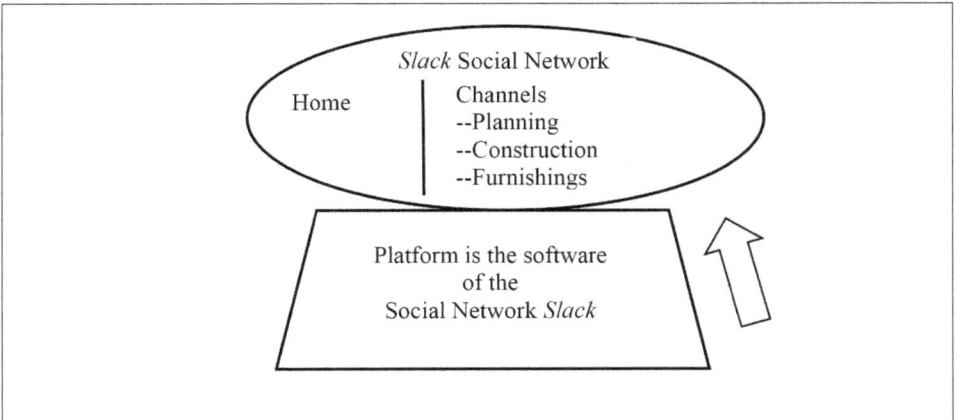

Figure 10.1. Relationship among Platforms, Social Network, and Channels.

be thought of as folders or subfolders of a particular social network. An academic library planning a large renovation may use Slack with channels around topics such as "planning," "construction," "furnishings," etc. to keep staff informed about the project. Channels may be private or open but are not interchangeable nor able to cross over with other social networks.

LSS can follow their library social media to determine if channels could be an effective means for organizing focused discussions. For example, LSS may recommend a separate and unique channel for weekly book discussions. Library policy should guide staff and patrons' use of social media.

LIBRARY POLICIES

Social media is not without its controversy as it most often requires the user to provide some amount of personal information. Libraries, bastions of guarding patrons' right to privacy and freedom of speech, must tread carefully with social media. By design, social media is meant to be shared.

There is no one social media policy for all libraries. Academic libraries may have different purposes and guidelines than K–12 school libraries. Public libraries may select and target social media for specific departments, such as teen services or adult reference. School libraries align social media with guidelines from national and state departments of education as well as with local board of education policy. Special libraries adapt guidelines from its corporate or parent institution. It is important that LSS, regardless of the type of library they work in, read and understand the Library of Congress (LOC) and the American Library Association policies and guidelines, as well as their local institutional policy. LSS align their practices with such rules and are able to explain to patrons the guidelines around how the library chooses content for its social media.

Library of Congress

Relatively few people have the opportunity to visit the LOC, but everyone can access it remotely through its free and available social media and websites. The LOC welcomes comments on its blogs, from those who participate in its webinars and on its public forums, and on its other social media platforms. The LOC hosts many different types of social media around the content of its collections and archives. With its wide breadth of expertise, the LOC has developed a practical and usable Comment and Posting[3] policy that others, including LSS, can emulate and follow. While the LOC is clear that it does not discriminate against any views, it does monitor user-generated content and reserves the right to remove content for any reason without consent. Highlights of the LOC policy are:

- Stay on topic
- Content will be removed, and users may be blocked for:
    - abusive, vulgar, offensive, racist, threatening, or harassing content, personal attacks of any kind, or offensive terms that target specific individuals or groups;

Figure 10.2. Library Social Media. *filo/DigitalVision Vectors via Getty Images*

- spam, the promotion of services or products, or political campaigning or lobbying;
- copyright infringing material;
- content from children twelve and under.

- Legal disclaimers:
  - Communications made through social media posts, email, webinars, and messaging systems will in no way constitute a legal or official notice or comment to the Library of Congress or any official or employee of the Library for any purpose.
  - All user-generated content is released into the public domain unless the participant clearly states otherwise.

The LOC is both clear and practical in its policy. The overarching concept of respectful civil discourse guides its rules. This is a concept LSS can support to help make social media usage in their libraries successful.

K–12 School Library Media Centers

Library social media policy is created to ensure hosted networks are used in a purposeful way. It is also created to protect participants and set guidelines for expected behaviors. K–12 schools are entrusted with the development and education of children. LSS are members of the educational team responsible for students' well-being, and as such, both personally abide by social media policy as they guide children to use it appropriately.

Librarians must be careful when they create social media accounts and protect children from any undue harm. LSS have an obligation to guide students' use and to report any suspicion of misuse to supervisors. When LSS know the intended purpose of school endorsed social media, they can better support the school rules of use.

The International Society for Technology in Education, or ISTE, is a dynamic society of educators whose research and leadership promote best practices of integrating technology into curriculum and instruction. From an ISTE blog,[4] the following are ways students' learning can be enhanced through social media:

- Sharing tools and resources for research, projects, and assignments
- Gathering survey data for research and writing
- Collaborating with peers over their learning
- Participating in group work for special projects
- Communicating with teachers outside of the school day about their learning
- Researching careers and subjects to make college and work decisions
- Meeting with mentors and experts to support new learning
- Showcasing student work to the school communities

Aligning library social media networks with student learning supports the mission and values of the school. Students learn from educators to use social media in purposeful ways that are different than personal use. Teachers and library staff have the opportunity to guide and teach students appropriate and safe practices for using school social. In a similar way, public libraries can adapt school library policy for their underage patrons.

School and academic libraries are departments within a larger institution and typically follow their institutional social media policy. LSS should seek a copy of the social media policy and discuss its implications with their supervisor to be clear about the role LSS have and how to implement the policy in their day-to-day work. For example, if LSS overhear students talking about not using library social media as intended, LSS may ask the students to remain seated and immediately report what was heard to their library supervisor or the classroom teacher. LSS are educational staff and have a professional responsibility to support appropriate use of social media.

Figure 10.3. Facebook—Groton Public Library, Groton, CT.

Training in writing social media policies is available from many state libraries and state education departments. WebJunction[5] surveys libraries about their social media policies and encourages libraries to share policies with others on its website.

USAGE

Social media accounts for some of the phenomenal and expediential explosion of information each year. People grapple with how much time it takes to be active followers and participants and how to manage all their subscribing feeds. LSS can help manage their own feeds and help others with these timely suggestions and tools:[6]

1. Use Twitter List Copy tool to copy Twitter lists that others have made to your account. When you see a Twitter account that you like, see if it is linked to a list that you may also want to follow.
2. If you want to use or share a Facebook post, click on the time stamp to get a permalink that you can then copy and share.
3. Instagram is owned by Facebook so Instagram content shared to Facebook will contain all the details (location, hashtag, etc.).
4. Instagram and Twitter are not necessarily compatible. Tweet Instagram as native photos to Twitter for easier sharing.
5. Use image cropping to get the best part of the photographs before posting.
6. Facebook automatically adds keyword text description to photos that account managers can change.
7. Flickr automatically adds tagging to photos. You can control the searching of photos by adding your own metadata.

Another helpful tool is **analytics**, which is the measurement of a product and how it is used. This analysis is made through data collection and interpretation of

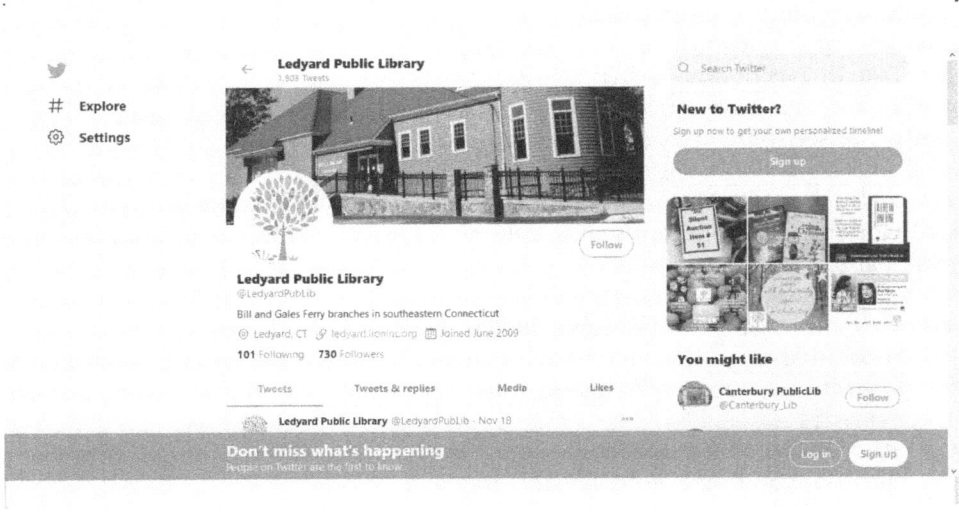

Figure 10.4. Twitter—Ledyard Public Library, Ledyard, CT.

statistics. Candidly speaking, social media are marketing devices, and platforms are written to include programming to collect information about what followers do on the social media network and how they collaborate with others. Account managers can run reports to collect data on how followers use library social media. For example, if the library has a Facebook business account, the tool Facebook Audience Insights provides information about followers' locations, demographics, purchases, likes, and so forth. As social media is an investment of time and staff, it is to the benefit of library administration to know how social media is being used to get the greatest connection to its community with it.

LSS who master these, and other, built-in platform tools may find they are essential to the success of the library's social media.

Behaviors

Schools and school districts can obtain guidance for social media policy from their state or city departments of education. Successful adherence to policy comes when students understand it and believe in its importance. Important advice is offered by the New York City Department of Education[7] for children age twelve and under who use school social media:

- Keep a good online image and reputation.
- Be positive.
- Know who you are talking to.
- It is a responsibility to post.
- Be mindful of your audience.
- Communicating online is different than in person.
- Talk with your family about posting and their expectations.
- Follow your school rules.
- Consider the consequences of your actions.
- Be safe.
- Know your privacy settings.
- Keep passwords private.
- Take threats of cyberbullying seriously.
- Treat others how you would like to be treated.
- If you see something, say something.

The New York City Department of Education also has social media policy for its staff working with children[8] that should be followed for their own safety and professional practice:

- Maintain separate professional and personal email addresses.
- School-based professional social media sites should be designed and limited to addressing reasonable instructional, educational, or extracurricular program matters.
- Staff should treat professional social media space and communication like a classroom and/or a professional workplace.

Social Media

- Exercise caution, sound judgment, and common sense when using professional social media sites.
- Consider the intended audience and the level of privacy, specifically, whether the site should be a private network limited to a particular class or grade within a school or a public network where anyone within the school or an external group can participate.
- It is recommended that professional social media sites be private networks.
- Staff should use privacy settings to control access to their professional social media sites so that professional social media communications only reach the intended audience.
- Private communication published on the internet can easily become public. Social media sites can change their current default privacy settings and other functions.
- In order to maintain a professional and appropriate relationship with students, staff should not communicate with students on personal social media sites.

Parents and family rightfully are concerned when a member demonstrates an addiction to social media. By our nature we want to belong, and social media provides such outlets that require little of the social norms and anxieties of meeting new people and making friends.[9] LSS can recognize some of the common signs of addiction in patrons or staff:[10]

- Spending more than one hour daily at social media sites.
- Checking social media sites whenever possible.
- Oversharing: A possible reason for this is to gain approval or acknowledgment from peers. This is sometimes called the need for social affirmation.
- Interference with work, school performance, or your offline social life.

Figure 10.5. Instagram—Groton Public Library, Groton, CT.

- Withdrawal symptoms if you try to cut down on the time you spend on social media
- Escapism: If you are using your time on social media to avoid conflicts or problems that are occurring in your real life
- Losing sleep to go on social media. Staying up late is one characteristic of those who overuse social networking sites, according to some studies.

Research studies affirm the need to curb time on social media. The Pew Research Center[11] found more than half (54%) of teens believe they spend too much time on their cell phones while 36 percent of adults also feel the same. Forty-one percent of teens say they spend too much time on social media, and more than half admit they are trying to cut back.

Being unable to control social media usage is an addiction. Social media addiction is an unhealthy dependence on interactive platforms such as Facebook, Twitter, and Instagram. The difference between casual use and addiction is the inability to do without and to let go. LSS observe many who use library computers to check or participate in their social media. LSS, especially those who work with teens and young people, may feel uncomfortable when they suspect addictive behaviors. Here are some steps they may take:

- Education: Initiate a brief discussion with the person about your observations of their use. Share with them the library social media policy.
- Caring: Let the patrons know you care. Is the time they are spending taking away from other aspects of their lives? Let them know that you will be sharing your concerns with your supervisor.
- Referral: Privately and confidentially share your concerns with your supervisor. Ask that the librarian intervene with the patron.

LSS who notice or are told about these behaviors should share their information with supervisors. In academic and school libraries, students with these signs could quickly descend to failure. It is important that those with social media addictions receive professional help.

CHAPTER SUMMARY

Social media supports the library presence in its community. LSS should be knowledgeable of policies and trained in the functions in order to assist and support patrons' use of library social media networks and platforms. Social media connects patrons as it provides remote access to library information and services.

LSS recognize issues concerning the purpose and appropriate use of social media by different age and user groups and alert supervisors when rules are not being followed or behaviors warrant intervention.

DISCUSSION QUESTIONS

1. Why is social media important to libraries and the communities they serve?
2. Why should libraries have social media policies?

3. What are the most popular social media used by libraries? Why so?
4. What behaviors should LSS be aware of that indicate a patron may have a social media addiction? What should they do when this is observed?

ACTIVITY

Access the LOC's "Connect with the Library of Congress," found at https://www.loc.gov/connect/. Find ten social media networks offered by the LOC that you are unfamiliar with, such as the *Music Performing Arts* blog, the Facebook Veteran's History Project, or the Medium of great stories. Keep a list of the LOC resources from your investigation you would like to share with others. Meet with the library supervisor to show these resources and discuss ways they could be linked to the library social media or website. Continue to explore the LOC and other institutional social media sites to find quality information to share with staff and patrons.

NOTES

1. Nicole E. Ionnone et al., "Connecting in the Twitterverse: Using Twitter to Satisfy Unmet Belonging Needs," *Journal of Social Psychology* 158, no. 4: https://search.ebscohost.com/login.aspx?direct=true&AuthType=cookie,ip,cpid&custid=csl&db=f5h&AN=129717232&site=eds-live&scope=site.

2. Maxwell Gollin, "The 65 Social Media Terms & Definitions to Know in 2020," Falcon, last modified 2020, accessed July 10, 2020, https://www.falcon.io/insights-hub/topics/social-media-management/social-media-terms-buzzwords-definitions-marketers-need-to-know/#c.

3. Library of Congress, "Comment & Posting Policy," Comment & Posting Policy, last modified 2020, accessed July 8, 2020, https://www.loc.gov/legal/comment-and-posting-policy/.

4. Michael Niehoff, "9 Ways Real Students Use Social Media for Good," ISTE blog, last modified 2020, accessed July 13, 2020, https://www.iste.org/explore/Digital-citizenship/9-ways-real-students-use-social-media-for-good.

5. OCLC, "Social Media Policy Examples," WebJunction, last modified January 17, 2018, accessed July 14, 2020, https://www.webjunction.org/news/webjunction/social-media-policies.html.

6. Jessamyn West, "Mastering Social Media Metadata," *Computers in Libraries* 39, no. 2 (March 2019): https://search.ebscohost.com/login.aspx?direct=true&AuthType=cookie,ip,cpid&custid=csl&db=aph&AN=135486414&site=ehost-live&scope=site.

7. New York City Department of Education, "Social Media Guidelines: 12 and Younger," NYC Department of Education, last modified 2020, accessed July 14, 2020, https://www.schools.nyc.gov/school-life/school-environment/digital-citizenship/social-media-guidelines-for-students-12-and-younger.

8. New York City Department of Education, "Social Media Guidelines for DOE Staff," NYC Department of Education, last modified 2020, accessed July 14, 2020, https://infohub.nyced.org/working-with-the-doe/current-employees/social-media-guidelines-for-doe-staff.

9. Nicole E. Ionnone et al., "Connecting in the Twitterverse: Using Twitter to Satisfy Unmet Belonging Needs," *Journal of Social Psychology* 158, no. 4: https://search.ebscohost.com/login.aspx?direct=true&AuthType=cookie,ip,cpid&custid=csl&db=f5h&AN=129717232&site=eds-live&scope=site.

10. David Squires, "The Cause and Effects in Social Media," Digital Technology & Culture, last modified 2020, accessed July 14, 2020, https://scalar.usc.edu/works/everything-you-always-wanted-to-know-about-social-media-but-were-too-afraid-to-ask/the-cause-and-effects-in-social-media-1.

11. Brooke Auxier, Monica Anderson, and Madhu Kumar, "10 Tech-Related Trends That Shaped the Decade," FactTank, last modified December 20, 2019, accessed July 14, 2020, https://www.pewresearch.org/fact-tank/2019/12/20/10-tech-related-trends-that-shaped-the-decade/.

REFERENCES, SUGGESTED READINGS, AND WEBSITES

American Library Association. "Social Media Guidelines for Public and Academic Libraries." Issues & Advocacy. Last modified 2020. Accessed July 7, 2020. http://www.ala.org/advocacy/intfreedom/socialmediaguidelines.

Auxier, Brooke, Monica Anderson, and Madhu Kumar. "10 Tech-Related Trends That Shaped the Decade." FactTank. Last modified December 20, 2019. Accessed July 14, 2020. https://www.pewresearch.org/fact-tank/2019/12/20/10-tech-related-trends-that-shaped-the-decade/.

Esser, Sven. "Cross-Channel vs. Platform Strategy." Cross-Channel vs. Platform Strategy. Last modified 2020. Accessed July 11, 2020. https://esser.me/cross-channel-vs-platform-strategy/.

Freudenberge, Erica. "Programming Through the Pandemic." *Library Journal* 145, no. 5 (May 2020): 14–16. https://search.ebscohost.com/login.aspx?direct=true&AuthType=cookie,ip,cpid&custid=csl&db=aph&AN=142941943&site=ehost-live&scope=site.

Gollin, Maxwell. "The 65 Social Media Terms & Definitions to Know in 2020." Falcon. Last modified 2020. Accessed July 10, 2020. https://www.falcon.io/insights-hub/topics/social-media-management/social-media-terms-buzzwords-definitions-marketers-need-to-know/#c.

Ionnone, Nicole E., Megan McCarty, Sara Branch, and Janice Kelly. "Connecting in the Twitterverse: Using Twitter to Satisfy Unmet Belonging Needs." *Journal of Social Psychology* 158, no. 4: 491–95. https://search.ebscohost.com/login.aspx?direct=true&AuthType=cookie,ip,cpid&custid=csl&db=f5h&AN=129717232&site=eds-live&scope=site.

Johnston, Joyce P. "Can Facebook Steal My Stuff? Your Students' Intellectual Property Rights on Social Media." *Computers in Libraries* 40, no. 3: 32–36. https://search.ebscohost.com/login.aspx?direct=true&AuthType=cookie,ip,cpid&custid=cs.

Library of Congress. "Comment & Posting Policy." Comment & Posting Policy. Last modified 2020. Accessed July 8, 2020. https://www.loc.gov/legal/comment-and-posting-policy/.

———. "Connect with the Library of Congress." Connect with the Library of Congress. Last modified 2020. Accessed July 8, 2020. https://www.loc.gov/connect/.

New York City Department of Education. "Social Media Guidelines for DOE Staff." NYC Department of Education. Last modified 2020. Accessed July 14, 2020. https://infohub.nyced.org/working-with-the-doe/current-employees/social-media-guidelines-for-doe-staff.

———. "Social Media Guidelines: 12 and Younger." NYC Department of Education. Last modified 2020. Accessed July 14, 2020. https://www.schools.nyc.gov/school-life/school-environment/digital-citizenship/social-media-guidelines-for-students-12-and-younger.

Niehoff, Michael. "9 Ways Real Students Use Social Media for Good." ISTE Blog. Last modified 2020. Accessed July 13, 2020. https://www.iste.org/explore/Digital-citizenship/9-ways-real-students-use-social-media-for-good.

OCLC. "Social Media and Libraries Survey Summary." WebJunction. Last modified February 13, 2018. Accessed July 14, 2020. https://www.webjunction.org/news/webjunction/social-media-libraries-survey.html.

———. "Social Media Policy Examples." WebJunction. Last modified January 17, 2018. Accessed July 14, 2020. https://www.webjunction.org/news/webjunction/social-media-policies.html.

Squires, David. "The Cause and Effects in Social Media." Digital Technology & Culture. Last modified 2020. Accessed July 14, 2020. https://scalar.usc.edu/works/everything-you-always-wanted-to-know-about-social-media-but-were-too-afraid-to-ask/the-cause-and-effects-in-social-media-1.

West, Jessamyn. "Mastering Social Media Metadata." *Computers in Libraries* 39, no. 2 (March 2019): 12–13. https://search.ebscohost.com/login.aspx?direct=true&AuthType=cookie,ip,cpid&custid=csl&db=aph&AN=135486414&site=ehost-live&scope=site.

CHAPTER 11

Mobile Technologies

Library Support Staff (LSS) are able to assist and train users to operate public equipment, connect to the internet, use library software applications, and access library services from remote locations.

Topics Covered in This Chapter
Internet
Devices
   Circulation
   E-readers
   Hotspots
Apps

Key Terms

Cellular: Technology facilitates mobile device communications, especially with smartphones, over a specific area of coverage using transceivers on towers for sending and receiving data.

E-readers: Portable hardware devices designed for reading digital publications.

Hotspot: Typically a small boxlike device, it is part of a cell phone data plan that converts cellular service into Wi-Fi internet. Many libraries lend hotspots to provide patrons portable internet service.

Mobile devices: Also known as smart devices, these are handheld tablets, smartphones, or other computing equipment that is portable, lightweight, and compact.

Smart device: Another term for a small, portable computer such as a smartphone, smart watch, etc.

Synchronization: When a device can transfer and receive data from applications from another device or computer so that both have the same information.

Transceiver: A device that can both transmit and receive communications, such as a combined radio transmitter and receiver.

Mobile technology has changed library operations and services. Where once patrons only used computers from the library inventory on site, today patrons have a wide array of devices with expectations that they work flawlessly with library databases and other content from almost anywhere. Library Support Staff (LSS) are expected to work with and support a variety of mobile technologies that are both library and patron owned. One of the challenges is competition and great profit for companies to continually improve on devices. Similar to automobiles, mobile devices are identified by model and date, with consumers buying into the idea that newer is better. How can LSS keep up?

Key components of mobile technology are the internet, mobile devices, and apps. The speed, reliability, and availability of the internet are essential to the function of mobile technology. Mobile devices are portable computers. Apps are computer programs written specifically to work on them. Supporting mobile devices and apps are now standard library services as patrons acquire smaller and more powerful technology in their everyday lives. LSS who are curious users of mobile technologies learn how to successfully apply them in their work. As LSS become personal users, they are able to guide and help patrons who may be grappling to make their own mobile devices work with library services. LSS can become proficient in mobile technologies so that they, in turn, can help others.

THE INTERNET

Robust, high speed internet service is essential to the success of mobile devices. The internet is designated by generations or "Gs." The 4G system is slowly being replaced by 5G. The 4G system made **cellular** service possible which, in turn, boosted the proliferation of mobile devices. Two types of 4G internet service, cellular and Wi-Fi, enable people to connect to the internet "on the go." Broadcast from cell towers, every station has **transceivers** to transmit and receive data to and from mobile devices. The first mobile phones were called cell phones because they received telephone transmission from the towers. Today, 4G cellular networks support smartphones.[1]

Mobile devices also may connect to an Internet Service Provider (ISP) using Wi-Fi. Once a mobile device is connected to the library Wi-Fi, it swaps the session from the patron's ISP to the library ISP, thus eliminating any additional cost to the patron. LSS can help patrons locate and connect to the library Wi-Fi. Key differences between using cellular and Wi-Fi in a library are:[2]

- Service range: Wi-Fi limited to library premises while cellular range is extensive
- Cost to user: Library Wi-Fi is free while patron pays for cellular service
- Data plan: Unlimited data use to patrons on library Wi-Fi while data is limited by cellular plan.
- Speed: Library Wi-Fi should be faster than cellular service

There is great competition among developers of mobile devices. There is a fast turnover in products with new innovative features and functions each year as a way to contend for larger market share. Today, some smartphones have powerful artificial intelligence (AI) chips that can perform limitless operations per second and use significantly less power. With AI, these devices provide features from face identification to augmented reality. It is predicted customers will want all the personal and compelling experiences AI will provide, significantly growing smartphone ownership.[3]

Mobile devices embedded with AI chips require better data transceivers and faster internet service. Depending upon where the library is located, especially if it is in a major city, it may already be receiving 5G internet service. By 2025, most of the world is expected to have 5G as its internet service.

To be 5G, a device must have these functions:[4]

- Integrated with inbuilt technology that supports network connections that cause a device to operate
- Ability to communicate with other devices with Wi-Fi or Bluetooth
- Sensors that provide useful information

The 5G system will access many smaller wireless points of service than 4G. Transmission between more access points allows more devices to simultaneously connect to a network with seamless performance to the user.[5] The 5G system meets the growing demands for data from both consumer and industrial users. Streaming, facial identification, and virtual reality applications will expand as 5G internet supports a growing number of mobile devices and potentially changing how we work.

The work that LSS do and how they perform it will change with 5G. Many manual tasks will be automated freeing LSS to have a sharper focus on customer service. As new mobile devices that use 5G are deployed in libraries, the need for LSS to be capable users of the new technologies will be great so that they can assist patrons.

DEVICES

Mobile devices are handheld computers[6] that are portable, lightweight, and compact. They are also known as **smart devices** for their computing capabilities. New data storage, processing, and display technologies have allowed small devices to do nearly anything and more than larger personal computers. Mobile devices most used by patrons are smartphones, tablets, and laptop computers, smart watches, e-readers, and handheld gaming consoles. Below are examples of how LSS can assist patrons with smart devices:

- Smartphones: LSS demonstrate how to download the online catalog app so that patrons can search and reserve library materials from their phones.
- Tablets: LSS offer to assist patrons to take a user satisfaction survey on a library tablet. Data will be analyzed as part of the library planning process.
- Laptop computers: School LSS circulate laptop computers on wheels in carts to classrooms.
- Smart watches: LSS encourage patron to check the schedule of library events from his smart watch.
- E-readers: LSS help patron download an e-book onto a library e-reader to be checked out for home use.
- Handheld gaming consoles: Teen LSS host a weekly night of gaming on library mobile devices.

Figure 11.1. Working with Smart Devices. *Westend61 via Getty Images*

Responding to the trends and needs of patrons, libraries also found themselves diverting from long-range technology plans consisting of mostly wired PC desktops to supporting mobile devices. With patrons using their own mobile technologies, libraries do not have to acquire large numbers of one-to-one computers. Patrons prefer to use their own devices to search and do other types of work in the library. Bring Your Own Device (BYOD) has greatly reduced hardware expenses for libraries.

For those who do not BYOD many libraries acquire mobile devices. Libraries have a dual mission with smart devices. One purpose is to acquire them for staff and patrons to use in the library to support information seeking and other activities. The second purpose is to circulate or lend devices to patrons to use outside the library for a defined amount of time. By lending smart devices, libraries support technology use in homes for those that may not be able to acquire or afford technology, providing equal opportunities for all users. Not that long ago it was not feasible for libraries to circulate computers, but today, lending tablets and e-book readers are a common service. K–12 school and academic libraries are the hubs of technology and often manage the daily scheduling of mobile devices to classrooms. By investing in tablets, Chromebooks, or laptops, acquiring large numbers of computers becomes affordable for schools.

Circulation

While special and academic libraries serve a limited and defined group of users, public libraries, however, have a different relationship with their patrons whom they may or may not see on a regular basis. Regardless of the type of library, there needs to be a circulation policy with regulations and consequences for lending mobile devices to ensure inventory is available, shared, and returned in good working order. LSS are key to circulating library materials and equipment. Often when circulating a device, LSS are most helpful when they spend a few extra minutes with the patron explaining its basic functions. It is also a time for the LSS to emphasize all aspects of the lending policy and the expectations about handling and care. LSS may receive questions about downloading programs, etc. that, if not in the policy, should be addressed with a supervisor before check-out. When the device is returned, just as LSS do with other resources, it should be inspected to ensure it is in good working order before used or lent to another patron. LSS can have a returns checklist to help ensure all the conditions have been met, adding that it be charged before the next user acquires it. LSS can discuss with their supervisor ways the ILS or another management system could be used to track use by patrons of library-owned mobile devices. Below are considerations for libraries lending mobile devices:

1. One device per (household, student);
2. Defined lending time period (three days, one week, two weeks) TBD by library;
3. Location of equipment (where patron obtains it and subsequently returns it);
4. Deny circulation of mobile devices to patrons who abuse equipment or repeatedly have late returns;
5. Library is not responsible for any liability, damages, content accessed, or expense resulting from use or misuse of the device, connection of the device to other electronic equipment, or data loss resulting from use of the device;
6. Patron accepts full responsibility for the device while it is checked out to them and will not tamper or change any settings;
7. Device will be returned only to the [name of library] circulation desk and not be placed in the book drop or any other location;
8. Post the daily financial penalties for late return;
9. Patron is responsible for full replacement cost of device or any parts TBD by library administration if lost, stolen, damaged, or otherwise not returned. If patron fails to pay costs, the library may engage a collections service.

One academic library[7] categorizes its lending policy of mobile devices into common user-friendly questions:

1. Who can borrow a mobile device?
2. How long can it be checked out?
3. What's loaded?
4. What about my liability?
5. What are the fines or fees for late or damaged mobile devices?

This format presents itself in a readable document that can be posted and displayed both in the library and electronically. If the brief answers to each question are written in clear and simple language, the policy will be unambiguous and easy for all to understand.

E-readers

One of the first mobile devices libraries acquired were **e-readers**. Prior to tablets, and still used by many today, e-readers are mobile and downloadable devices for a new type of digital resource called an e-book. An e-reader, or e-book reader, is a portable device designed for reading digital publications such as e-books, electronic magazines, and digital versions of newspapers. Since textual data does not require a lot of storage space, most e-readers can store thousands of books, articles, or other publications.[8] At that time there were several competing e-readers. Leading the pack was the Kindle, created for e-books and purchased through Amazon. Amazon supported the many developments of the Kindle as it claimed the largest market share for the e-book format. As people became accustomed to purchasing and using e-books from Amazon, they now wanted libraries to offer e-book collections. Another problem developed because patrons who did not own e-book readers may not have access unless their library also provided a lendable device. In addition, because some publishers eschewed Amazon, other e-book providers and publishers began to offer their own proprietary devices. Libraries who purchase from many publishers had to acquire several brands of e-book readers in order to match a variety of content.

As rapidly as the competition among e-book readers started, it abruptly came to a halt with the introduction of the tablet. Tablets offered viewing in color (Kindle screens were only black-and-white), and they recognized many file formats, including HTML, PDF, and TXT that are commonly used for e-books. Amazon realized if it were to continue being a giant distributor of e-book content, it would have to offer books in other formats than its proprietary AZW Kindle file type. In response, Amazon began to offer a new device, the tablet-like Fire, in an attempt to replace the traditional Kindle market that had slumped.

Libraries suddenly did not have to invest in many brands of e-readers because patrons preferred to own a more versatile tablet than an e-reader. Tablets are portable, lightweight, and compact, meeting all criteria of a mobile device. Many people substitute their tablet for a smartphone or laptop, as many of the functions of these can be done on a tablet. Today, there is a wide variety of tablets and hybrid laptops that include the iPad, Chromebook, Amazon Fire, Surface, Galaxy, and many others. Many libraries have invested in lendable tablets to offer patrons computing and reading support.

Hotspots

Hotspots are a popular mobile device many libraries lend to patrons who do not have Wi-Fi internet access at home or when traveling. A patron may have a smartphone, but without Wi-Fi they cannot reap the benefits of turning it into a computer with low or no cost internet. The hotspot is a small boxlike device with a cell phone data plan for internet service that is portable and usable in any location where the cell phone plan reaches. When the hotspot dials in and connects to the cell towers, the user has a small area of range of internet service. Like other library-owned circulating devices, hotspots fall under a lending policy for users.

APPS

Mobile devices are computers that require software programs in order to perform some sort of task or work. Software programs for mobile devices are commonly referred to as apps, an abbreviation for applications. Some apps are developed specifically for devices while others are modifications to software programs more commonly used on desktop or stationary computers. In this case apps make a better display on the mobile device than a full program would. An example of this is the app for the library ILS for searching the catalog on mobile devices.

The term "app" was popularized by Apple with its "App Store" in 2008, a year after the first iPhone was released. The term "app" became the standard way to refer to mobile applications for android and Windows phones as well. Mobile apps can only be obtained by downloading them from an online app store.[9] Many apps are free, such as the library catalog. Others are fee-based in the one to three dollar range, although some gaming and other special apps can be more costly. If the library obtains twenty-five new tablets, LSS may be asked to download apps from the appropriate Apple, Windows, Amazon, Galaxy, or other brand of device app store. Apps typically have less features than full software programs. Apps are intended to be used in a mobile environment and for a smaller touchscreen display than a full keyboard.

For technology to be mobile, it must be small, have sufficient amounts of memory to run, and be able to store all the data of app programming. The solution is cloud computing services, key enabling app functionality. When LSS download an app for

Figure 11.2. Using Library App Remotely. *Oscar Wong/Moment via Getty Images*

personal or work purposes, he is downloading the app from a cloud service. There is no media, that is, a disc or other hard copy of the app or program. Apps can be considered SaaS, or Software-as-a-Service, where the program is downloaded from an external cloud source and then installed or uploaded onto the smart device.

Think of the Apple App Store, Samsung Galaxy Apps Store, Amazon, or Microsoft Apps Store as cloud services. Smart devices are registered with the app store account. Along with registration is a credit card or other type of payment that is automatically billed if an app is purchased. Many of the apps libraries use or promote to patrons are free because they support a product or service the library has already purchased or subscribed to.

Synchronization of mobile devices takes place in proprietary clouds. The mobile device communicates through apps to the computer or server. Clouds linked to owners' devices transfer and receive data from applications so that owners' devices have the same information. A common example of this is with photos and contact lists. Photos on one device, if synchronized, will appear on other devices by the same vendor registered to the user. Likewise, the contact list on an iPhone is in the cloud and is shared with the other Apple devices, such an iPad or iWatch. Debit and credit cards can be synchronized to a store account. People are rapidly becoming comfortable with not carrying cash and using their smartphone apps to make payments. Some of the many benefits to library users of synchronization are:

1. Data, photos, and files found on one device are also available on other devices that are registered to the account.
2. Data, photos, and files are backed up to the cloud and not solely on a device.
3. Data, photos, and files can be assigned levels of security and access in the cloud.
4. It saves time as access to files is quick and not dependent on one device.
5. It increases library staff productivity as more than one staff member can work on a shared document.
6. It ensures data consistency when multiple staff share or have access to work files.
7. With proper security it allows transactions to take place between or among accounts.
8. It improves customer service by having data available.

Mobile technologies are here to stay and have enormous potential to not only explode in numbers, but more importantly, to change the way people live and work, including how libraries conduct their services. An academic library[10] suggests library experiences are enhanced with smart mobility:

1. Mobile optimization: Libraries respond to the smaller size of users' screens by seeking and promoting apps that make online catalogs, e-books, databases, and other sources usable and viewable.
2. Mobile applications and catalogs: Libraries should have apps for their online catalogs so that patrons can borrow, renew, reserve, and otherwise self-serve remotely with their smart devices.
3. Implement mobile library instruction: Patrons use apps to learn about resources of the library.

4. Create new services: Ask a Librarian service can be a chatbot or robotic voice computer program found on the library website or through an app for a two-way conversation.
5. Use social media: Mobile technologies have developed around social media such as Facebook and Twitter that support quick interaction with others.

Mobile devices improve the library experience. As mobile technology continues to grow and change, so do our libraries. The future of mobile technologies is dependent upon the next generation of the internet. These are exciting times, promising many new innovations to improve library experiences and services.

CHAPTER SUMMARY

Advancements in internet service, the innovation of mobile devices, and apps that support information seekers enable LSS to assist and train users to operate public equipment, connect to the internet, use library software applications, and access library services from remote locations. LSS who are knowledgeable and experienced users of mobile devices both personally and professionally are more successful in helping patrons with new technologies that expand services from the library into the home and beyond.

DISCUSSION QUESTIONS

1. What are the relationships and differences between cellular and Wi-Fi services?
2. What should libraries consider when creating lending policies for mobile devices?
3. How are apps growing in their importance to improve library services? Provide a few examples.

ACTIVITY

Create a list of all the library databases and programs that have corresponding apps such as the online catalog, EBSCO or other databases, digital reading libraries, calendar, reservations, social media, etc. Using the appropriate app store, download the app for as many of the library software programs on your list. Access each of these library products on both your PC using the full program and the smart device using the app. Make a chart and compare any differences between the two experiences. For example, when accessing the online catalog via the app, were you able to get all functions of the full program? If not, what functions or features were missing?

NOTES

1. Techopedia, Inc., "Cellular," Techopedia, last modified 2020, accessed July 29, 2020, https://www.techopedia.com/definition/6412/cellular.

2. Connectify, "What Is the Difference Between Wi-Fi and Cellular Connections?," Speedify Desktop, last modified 2020, accessed July 27, 2020, https://support.speedify.com/article/257-difference-between-wifi-cellular-connection-avoid-connection-interruptions.

3. AITHORITY, "AI: Increasing the Intelligence on Smartphones," AITHORITY, last modified April 21, 2020, accessed July 29, 2020, https://aithority.com/guest-authors/ai-increasing-the-intelligence-on-smartphones/.

4. Software Testing Help, "18 Most Popular IoT Devices in 2020 (Only Noteworthy IoT Products)," Software Testing Help, last modified June 30, 2020, accessed July 29, 2020, https://www.softwaretestinghelp.com/iot-devices/.

5. Sara Brown, "5G, Explained," Ideas Made to Matter, last modified February 13, 2020, accessed July 22, 2020, https://mitsloan.mit.edu/ideas-made-to-matter/5g-explained.

6. Techopedia, Inc., "Mobile Device," Techopedia, last modified March 30, 2018, accessed July 31, 2020, https://www.techopedia.com/definition/23586/mobile-device.

7. University of Pittsburgh, "Owen Library Mobile Device Lending Program," University Library System, last modified 2020, accessed July 31, 2020, https://www.library.pitt.edu/owen-library-mobile-device-lending-program.

8. Sharpened Productions, "E-reader," Tech Terms, last modified 2020, accessed July 31, 2020, https://techterms.com/definition/ereader.

9. Sharpened Productions, "App Definition," Tech Terms, last modified 2020, accessed July 31, 2020, https://techterms.com/definition/app.

10. University of Southern California, "How Mobile Technology Changes the Library Experience," USC Marshall School of Business, last modified 2020, accessed August 2, 2020, https://librarysciencedegree.usc.edu/blog/how-mobile-technology-changes-the-library-experience/.

REFERENCES, SUGGESTED READINGS, AND WEBSITES

AITHORITY. "AI: Increasing the Intelligence on Smartphones." AITHORITY. Last modified April 21, 2020. Accessed July 29, 2020. https://aithority.com/guest-authors/ai-increasing-the-intelligence-on-smartphones/.

Brown, Sara. "5G, Explained." Ideas Made to Matter. Last modified February 13, 2020. Accessed July 22, 2020. https://mitsloan.mit.edu/ideas-made-to-matter/5g-explained.

Connectify. "What Is the Difference Between Wi-Fi and Cellular Connections?" Speedify Desktop. Last modified 2020. Accessed July 27, 2020. https://support.speedify.com/article/257-difference-between-wifi-cellular-connection-avoid-connection-interruptions.

Federal Communications Commission. "Keep Americans Connected." FCC Initiatives. Last modified July 8, 2020. Accessed August 28, 2020. https://www.fcc.gov/keep-americans-connected.

Gao, Ya Jun, Yan Quan Liu, and Arlene Bielefield. "The Provision of Mobile Services in US Urban Libraries." *Information Technology & Libraries* 37, no. 2 (June 2018): 78–93. https://search.ebscohost.com/login.aspx?direct=true&AuthType=cookie,ip,cpid&custid=csl&db=aph&AN=130397497&site=ehost-live&scope=site.

Hazlett, Denice Rovira. "Open Safe." *Library Journal* 145, no. 8 (August 2020): 20–22. https://search.ebscohost.com/login.aspx?direct=true&AuthType=cookie,ip,cpid&custid=csl&db=aph&AN=144664638&site=ehost-live&scope=site.

Indiana University. "Archived: For Mobile Devices, What Is Synchronization?" Knowledge Base. Last modified August 6, 2018. Accessed July 22, 2020. https://kb.iu.edu/d/alkc.

Journal of Broadcasting & Electronic Media 64, no. 2 (May 2020). https://search.ebscohost.com/login.aspx?direct=true&AuthType=cookie,ip,cpid&custid=csl&db=aph&AN=144475189&site=eds-live&scope=site.

Lane, Rob. "Devices Bring Ideas to the Table." *AV Magazine*, February 2020, 74–76. https://search.ebscohost.com/login.aspx?direct=true&AuthType=cookie,ip,cpid&custid=csl&db=mfi&AN=141499595&site=ehost-live&scope=site.

Sharpened Productions. "App Definition." Tech Terms. Last modified 2020. Accessed July 31, 2020. https://techterms.com/definition/app.

———. "E-reader." Tech Terms. Last modified 2020. Accessed July 31, 2020. https://techterms.com/definition/ereader.

———. "Internet Definition." TechTerms. Last modified 2020. Accessed July 29, 2020. https://techterms.com/definition/internet.

Software Testing Help. "18 Most Popular IoT Devices in 2020 (Only Noteworthy IoT Products)." Software Testing Help. Last modified June 30, 2020. Accessed July 29, 2020. https://www.softwaretestinghelp.com/iot-devices/.

Techopedia, Inc. "Cellular." Techopedia. Last modified 2020. Accessed July 29, 2020. https://www.techopedia.com/definition/6412/cellular.

———. "Mobile Device." Techopedia. Last modified March 30, 2018. Accessed July 31, 2020. https://www.techopedia.com/definition/23586/mobile-device.

University of Pittsburgh. "Owen Library Mobile Device Lending Program." University Library System. Last modified 2020. Accessed July 31, 2020. https://www.library.pitt.edu/owen-library-mobile-device-lending-program.

University of Southern California. "How Mobile Technology Changes the Library Experience." USC Marshall School of Business. Last modified 2020. Accessed August 2, 2020. https://librarysciencedegree.usc.edu/blog/how-mobile-technology-changes-the-library-experience/.

PART III

Education and the Future

CHAPTER 12

STEM/STEAM and Makerspaces

Library Support Staff (LSS) are able to assist and train users to operate public equipment, connect to the internet, use library software applications, and access library services from remote locations.

Topics Covered in This Chapter
STEM/STEAM
   The Arts
Makerspaces
   Staffing
   Training
   Management and Safety
   Volunteers
Equipment
   3-D Printers
Projects and Programs

Key Terms

3-D Printers: Computer-driven machines used to create models and parts by layering and building up plastic or other materials to make a specific shape.

Circuit Kits: Found in library makerspaces, these are popular plastic kits that allow users to connect circuits of electricity to provide energy to lights, small motors, and other devices by snapping together appropriate parts rather than soldering.

CNC Machine: Machines that make parts out of plastic, metal, aluminum, wood, and many other hard materials for almost every industry. The abbreviation "CNC" stands for Computer Numerical Control. It is the process of using a computer-driven machine tool to produce a part out of solid material in a different shape.

Digitization: The process of converting information and other data into bits and bytes so that it can be understood and used by computers.

Inclusive Learning: A learning environment where all participants are fully respected and are open to ideas, perspectives, and ways of thinking that are distinct from their own.

Makerspace: A designated work or lab area where library users are invited to innovate, create, problem-solve, and enhance their STEAM knowledge and skills in self-paced, collaborative, hands-on ways.

Materials Safety Data Sheets: Also known as MSDS, these are safety documents required by the Occupational Safety and Health Administration (OSHA) that contains data about the physical properties of a particular hazardous substance.

STEAM: In addition to STEM areas of study, both visual and practical arts are included as essential courses.

STEM: The acronym for four areas of education: science, technology, engineering, and mathematics.

Supply Chain: A process that involves a series of steps to get a product or service to the customer.

STEM/STEAM

At the turn of the twenty-first century, the US government, through concerted efforts of the National Science Foundation, Department of Education, and other agencies, created a focused integration of **STEM** education. STEM is an acronym for science, technology, engineering, and mathematics. Prior to STEM, these subjects were rarely taught in coordination with each other. It was more happenstance that K–12 students "found" careers that used these areas of knowledge rather than learned the four subjects in a way that would advance their future academic and career choices in these areas. Often falling short in one or more of the subjects, students lacked confidence and skills to pursue careers in higher paying careers in the sciences, engineering, or computer technologies. Today, with STEM subjects integrated and complementing each other, high school graduates are able and ready to choose from a wider variety of fulfilling career choices. STEM enables all students, including underserved and disadvantaged, to be better prepared for professional careers.

The Arts

STEM education successfully has influenced a generation of learners, but, as most things, it could be improved upon. In recent years STEM has evolved to **STEAM** whereby the "A," for Arts, is an equal partner of necessary skill sets required for modern society. The fine and practical arts should be taught in an interdisciplinary manner along with science, technology, engineering, and mathematics.

STEAM takes STEM to another level through combining innovation, design, and aesthetics. While certainly delving into problems around engineering and technology, Library Support Staff (LSS) who mentor teens in a robotics competition have to also have them work through the artistic issues of design and aesthetics. The elements and experiences of design (How does it function?) and aesthetics (How does it look?) are critical to the success of any scientific, engineered, or technology-based project. STEAM engages in interactive, hands-on learning by experiencing and doing. STEAM also connects learning across subjects through functionality and appeal. Students uncover new possibilities when they connect ideas from STEAM subjects. For example, high school students discovered that an elementary student wanted to play the violin but could not hold the bow in her hand due to a disability. They designed and 3-D printed a prosthesis to make it possible for the student to hold a bow and play the violin.[1] LSS who work in libraries with **3-D printers** may be supportive with the technology in such a STEAM project.

Libraries can create STEAM services and programs in ways that stir users' interests and boost their learning.[2] Libraries promote STEAM learning when their programs promote the following important elements:

- Open-ended exercises
- Offer some level of competition with prizes
- Users have a say in planning and selecting the library STEAM programs
- Users take pride and ownership in library STEAM programs
- Librarians keep current with what the schools are teaching and what type of STEAM programs are offered in the area
- Technology is not the focus of the STEAM program but rather it is a tool
- STEAM library programs can augment learning rather than adding to an already busy schedule

Many libraries have set aside resources and space to accommodate STEAM learning in labs called **makerspaces**.

MAKERSPACES

Makerspaces are purposeful work areas where library users are invited to innovate, create, solve problems, and enhance their STEAM knowledge and skills in self-paced, collaborative, hands-on ways. In many communities there is no other public place where all people have equal and free access to build upon and apply STEAM learning.

While not a new concept, makerspaces continue to evolve to fit the needs of the library community. For example, during the COVID-19 pandemic in 2020 when personal protective equipment (PPE) was in high demand and short supply, the Los Angeles Public Library offered its Octavia Lab makerspace to print 3-D face shields for the county hospitals.[3] The makerspace lab staffers produced the headbands and bottom pieces for an approved PPE face shield model. In addition, library staff coordinated a drive with other libraries who had 3-D printers to also print shields to their specifications.[4]

Staffing

Successful makerspaces have skilled and supportive LSS. Makerspaces house expensive and complex equipment. They also need to be well-supplied. It should be accessible for most, if not all of the library hours, to benefit users. LSS have an important role managing and maintaining the purpose and services of makerspaces.

Take the initiative to become involved with the library makerspace. One LSS who learned the library was planning a makerspace offered to visit surrounding libraries and talk to their staff about what worked, what did not, and what would they do differently. He not only became a viable member of the planning team, but his job description was expanded to be the manager of the new makerspace.

What subjects of STEAM hold your interest? LSS may be skilled in visual and practical arts or be excited about the environment and nature. LSS can offer expertise in their outside interests and develop makerspace activities and programs. LSS have expertise they can share with others. They also participate in makerspace training.

Training

Training can be obtained in many ways. Vendor training often is part of the package of acquiring a new piece of equipment. Similar to purchasing a new car, companies may arrange to have a representative provide staff training shortly after equipment purchase. Ask if training or technical support is ongoing, and if so, how it can be acquired. Often with a new piece of equipment there is a learning curve, and for the first few weeks it may be necessary to seek help. Find training materials online, such as instruction sheets or videos. These will be helpful as others will need to be trained on the operation of the makerspace equipment. The American Library Association[5] has a robust site called Makerspaces, Tools, Publications, & Resources that freely shares information about many aspects of successful makerspaces. YouTube[6] yields

Figure 12.1. Makerspace. *Pekic/E+ via Getty Images*

a plethora of informative videos on the success of makerspaces from the theory behind STEAM education to practical applications and programs.

LSS learn from each other as well as their patrons. One of the main purposes of makerspaces is that they provide opportunity for collaborative learning. Collaborative learning is when people help and learn from each other. By sharing knowledge, skills, and experiences, LSS develop a learning environment with colleagues as they establish and grow an important new service for the community.

LSS may attend professional roundtables and conferences where topics about makerspaces are presented. Pay attention to regional and state library educational opportunities. If LSS work in a K–12 school library, they may be able to participate in educational presentations about STEAM curriculum and learning. LSS may contact colleagues in the local K–12 school districts with makerspaces to explore future collaborations between the school and public libraries. Using the model of the makerspace, LSS have many opportunities to enhance their learning as they practice skills that they, in turn, may be able to share with staff and patrons.

Management and Safety

In many libraries LSS are responsible for the makerspace and manage its use and resources. As such, LSS need to have open and regular communication with their supervising librarian about both the successes of programs and usage as well as issues that are certain to arise. A well-managed service with expectations of behavior is one that people want to use. LSS need to be attentive to ensuring people feel welcomed, safe, and can obtain the help they may need. This may include monitoring the numbers of people at any one time in an enclosed area and providing enough space for social distancing.

Safety is paramount to the users of the makerspace. Consider the makerspace an industrial lab with standards and requirements for such things as wiring, eye protection, and chemical disposal and control. OSHA safety signs should be posted wherever appropriate. **Materials Safety Data Sheets** (MSDS)[7] should accompany any chemical or potentially hazardous material. An MSDS is a document that contains information related to a potentially hazardous material that is found in a workplace and the remedies for safety. Companies that use, create, sell, ship, or store any type of potentially hazardous material or equipment need to have its MSDS sheet. LSS work with supervisors to identify and prepare ways to create a safe environment for users. Not only storage of potential equipment and materials must be considered but also their disposal.

Library makerspaces need to have appropriate accommodations and modifications for disabled or special-needs users. If participants may be unsafe under normal staffing in the lab, LSS should immediately contact the supervisor who can reallocate staff to help in the accommodations. Public spaces have a legal obligation to make them accessible. Most likely modifications can resolve the impediment. The following are ways makerspaces can be modified to be **inclusive learning** labs:[8]

1. Secure all equipment, wires, and component parts. Lock down main power when closing so that equipment cannot be turned on inadvertently.

2. Design and layout should be user friendly to people with disabilities including such things as appropriate signage, flexible and movable worktables, variable-height chairs and tables, wide aisles, push buttons to accommodate those in wheelchairs, safety guards always in place, no sharp angles or edges.
3. Consider each user on a case-by-case basis as to the safety, modifications, and appropriateness of their using power and cutting tools, etc. Lend support and guidance with additional staff.
4. Place shaped- and color-coded hazard signs at eye level.
5. Use tactile materials such as clay for prototyping for those who do not have fine motor skills for drawing, etc.
6. Scaffold instruction with step-by-step points or introduce new material in "chunks" with guided practice.

Volunteers

Many libraries have volunteers who monitor and assist in the makerspace. Volunteers need training and should never be left alone without close-by staff supervision. LSS can offer to coordinate volunteers, creating a makerspace schedule of staffing. LSS can also assess the volunteer skill sets to determine how best they can be used to support the center. Volunteers can inventory supplies, create templates, organize workspaces, etc. They can greet new users and provide a scripted overview of the purpose of the makerspace. Training for volunteers should be ongoing as new equipment and purposes arise. Volunteers should also be made aware of ongoing projects and programs involving the makerspace so that they, like users, are more engaged in the purpose of this library service.

EQUIPMENT

An important goal of the makerspace is to provide opportunities to freely explore and work with materials. Makerspaces support our multiple intelligences when we learn by interacting with others and ourselves, helping us build strong neuro connection between our brains and hands. Table 12.1 lists many of the more common pieces of equipment[9] found in library makerspaces.[10] Not all equipment needs to be had. Most important is to engage new users in ways to explore ways to be innovative as they probe for new designs as well as solve problems.

Some of the equipment listed in table 12.1 would not typically be found in a library. Makerspaces create an unusual environment where people are introduced to equipment that they would not necessarily find elsewise. For example, **CNC machines** are used mostly in manufacturing where these computer-driven machines tool materials into different shapes and sizes. "CNC" stands for Computer Numerical Control. It is the process of using a computer-driven tool to produce a part out of solid material into a different shape. CNC machines can cut a perfect circle, in any size, with a hole directly in the center. It can also cut complex shapes, letters, pockets, insets, gears, or anything else. As users imagine and create shapes, the CNC machine is the tool for making them. CNC machines make parts for almost every industry out of plastic, metal, aluminum, wood, and many other hard materials.

Table 12.1. Types of Makerspace Equipment

Machines connected to computers	Laser cutters, 3-D printers, scanners, vinyl cutters, CNC
Computers/software	iMAC, AutoCAD, and Adobe Creative Cloud
Textiles	Sewing, quilting, and embroidery machines and tools
Robotic kits	LEGO Mindstorms
Circuit kits	SparkFun Inventor, LilyPad, Arduino, LittleBits, STEAM Student, Snap Circuits, Makey kits
Photography/video tools	Cameras, lens, SD storage card, LED lights, tripod, screen projector, backdrop
Music	Stratocaster and electric guitars, midi keyboard, microphones, audio interface, GarageBand and Logic Pro
Digital art	Drawing and graphics tablets, Adobe Illustrator, Clip Studio Paint, and CorelDRAW.
Digitization	Equipment to digitize VHS and audio cassettes, LPs, photographs, slides, negatives, and 8 mm film
Crafts	Cutters for paper, cardstock, vinyl, and fabric; 3-D stamp maker, heat press, button maker, scrapbooking, jewelry making, stamping, weaving, knitting, and crocheting.
Bicycle repair	Bicycle repair stand, truing stand, and tools for tune up.
Tools and safety	Such as assorted wrenches, pliers, screwdrivers, gaffers tape, soldering station, fire extinguisher, first aid kit, and multimeter for testing circuits.
Other	Tabletop easel; tracing light box; artist's paper, pencils, and pastels; board games; puzzles

Many makerspaces offer users snap **circuit kits**. These are plastic kits that allow users to connect circuits of electricity to provide energy to lights, small motors, and other devices by snapping together appropriate parts rather than soldering them. The idea is the same, and people can learn about and use electricity creatively in relatively safe ways.

Digitization is the process of converting analog to digital. Makerspaces may have digitization equipment where analog audio and video recordings can be converted to digital.

3-D Printing

Makerspaces are often synonymous with 3-D printing. Three-dimensional printing is taking a 3-D digital image and printing it as an actual object. The image is originally designed on a computer or scanned from models. Printing involves building the object with small successive layers of material such as plastic, titanium, plaster, etc. Today, 3-D printing has many world applications, including prosthetics. Bioengineered ears, tracheas, and tissue can be printed and used to restore a patient's health.[11]

Three-dimensional printing became affordable to libraries and educational institutions in a relatively short amount of time. Three-dimensional printers are now smaller, less expensive, and higher performing. Today, they are used in elementary school libraries to the largest of special libraries to create solutions to real-world problems.

Figure 12.2. 3-D Printer. *vgajic/E+ via Getty Images*

PROJECTS AND PROGRAMS

There are four principles of makerspaces: projects, passions, peers, and play.[12] Easy to remember, the four Ps serve as guides to successful makerspaces:

1. Projects are broad enough that allow for personalization and creativity
2. Passion and motivation spur the user to see the project to its conclusion
3. Peers work in a collaborative environment where they learn from each other
4. Play makes learning fun and without fear of making mistakes

Videos have great utility when instruction is needed. Simple step-by-step instruction sheets can be next to each piece of equipment as well as posted on the library website. Checklists are useful as there is typically an order to operating equipment. LSS can ensure instructions for operation and projects are accurate and available.

There is a need for oversight of a **supply chain**. A functional supply chain is the process in which a company has the resources and materials in hand and on time in order to manufacture a product. LSS can offer to assume responsibility for the makerspace supply chain that entails daily checking of supplies on hand. Did the last person use up all the scrap fabric for quilting? LSS can create an inventory list of all the supplies needed for the equipment, expanding the list to account for supplies that are purchased and supplies that are donated or otherwise acquired. Keep two-thirds of any supply in storage. When supplies dwindle by half or one-third, it is time to either order or acquire replacements. Discuss with the supervisor ways the makerspace can be more self-efficient, such as fundraisers or donor drives. Make community connections for donations of craft and other items.

One way to introduce new users to the makerspace is to create short, quick demonstration projects. Did you know you could make a golf ball marker or (fill in the blank) in just twenty minutes with the 3-D printer at the library makerspace at no cost? At the same time, the patron will be learning how to use the equipment. LSS can create several small projects with instructions that both introduce and teach skills. These demonstration projects are also helpful to train volunteers and, later, for them to use with new patrons.

School and public libraries in the same town may coordinate makerspace programs and activities. An example of school and public library collaboration occurred when a public librarian reached out to a high school computer class to invite them to "Build a Better Book."[13] Build a Better Book is an organization that works with school and public library makerspaces to design and create accessible picture books for visually impaired children. The four Ps were there: students quickly engaged in this meaningful project with passion and after a pilot, the collaboration grew with other agencies and schools, including a school for the blind in another state.

LSS can do much to integrate the library makerspace as a gateway to lifelong learning and community service.

CHAPTER SUMMARY

LSS may ask, "Did I sign up for this when I was hired?" when the library acquires its makerspace. First thought as an unusual library service, today makerspaces complement a national desire to prepare citizens for the competitive world where STEM and STEAM learning and skills are deemed necessary. LSS who enhance their learning of STEAM and are curious about using practical skills, when trained, are able to assist and support users to operate makerspace equipment, supervise and manage the lab, and encourage the development of new STEAM projects and programs.

DISCUSSION QUESTIONS

1. What are STEM and STEAM? What are their similarities? Differences?
2. Why are the arts now considered essential to STEM learning?
3. Why are libraries appropriate places for makerspaces? What can LSS do to support a makerspace?
4. What kinds of training do LSS need to manage makerspaces and their users?

ACTIVITY: PLANNING OR ENHANCING A LIBRARY MAKERSPACE

Either in-person or by looking at library websites, evaluate the makerspaces at five libraries. Make an inventory of major or important equipment found in each makerspace. Next to the equipment describe how it is being used by patrons. Look for collaborative and community projects. Make note of them in a separate column. Are there restrictions about using the makerspace? If so, what are they? Of the five libraries, how do their audiences differ? What other strengths can be found by either visiting or looking at libraries' makerspace websites? Provide a narrative summary of your data with recommendations how to improve or initiate a makerspace.

NOTES

1. Fairfax County Public Schools, VA, "STEAM," Academic Overview, last modified 2020, accessed August 29, 2020, https://www.fcps.edu/academics/academic-overview/steam.

2. Wayne D'Orio, "Teen-Led STEM," *School Library Journal* 66, no. 6 (June 2020): https://search.ebscohost.com/login.aspx?direct=true&AuthType=cookie,ip,cpid&custid=csl&db=aph&AN=143323061&site=ehost-live&scope=site.

3. Alison A. Trotta, "News Desk," *Computers in Libraries* 40, no. 5 (July/August 2020): https://search.ebscohost.com/login.aspx?direct=true&AuthType=cookie,ip,cpid&custid=csl&db=aph&AN=144661588&site=ehost-live&scope=site.

4. City of Los Angeles, "Octavia Labs: Creativity within Reach," Los Angeles Public Library, last modified 2020, accessed September 1, 2020, https://www.lapl.org/labs.

5. American Library Association, "Makerspaces," Tools, Publications, & Resources, last modified 2020, accessed September 2, 2020, http://www.ala.org/tools/atoz/makerspaces.

6. Google, "YouTube," YouTube, last modified 2020, accessed September 2, 2020, https://www.youtube.com/results?search_query=makerspace.

7. Creative Safety Supply, "What Does MSDS Stand For?," Hazcom Questions and Answers, last modified 2020, accessed September 2, 2020, https://www.creativesafetysupply.com/qa/hazcom/what-does-msds-stand-for.

8. Tyler Love, Ken R. Roy, and Matthew Marino, "Inclusive Makerspaces, Fab Labs, and STEM Labs: How Can Instructors Make Appropriate Accommodations and Modifications While Maintaining a Safer Teaching and Learning Environment for All Students and Themselves?," *Technology & Engineering Teacher* 79, no. 5 (February 2020): https://search.ebscohost.com/login.aspx?direct=true&AuthType=cookie,ip,cpid&custid=csl&db=aph&AN=141301044&site=ehost-live&scope=site.

9. Nebraska Library Commission, "Library Makerspaces - Common Items and Tools," Nebraska Library Commission, last modified 2020, accessed September 2, 2020, http://nlc.nebraska.gov/libraries/maker/items.aspx.

10. Wallingford Public Library, "Collaboratory Equipment," Wallingford Public Library, last modified 2020, accessed September 2, 2020, https://www.wallingford.lioninc.org/collaboratory/collaboratory-equipment/.

11. National Institutes of Health Libraries, "3D Printing Service," NIH Library Services, last modified 2020, accessed September 2, 2020, https://www.nihlibrary.nih.gov/services/3d-printing-service.

12. Kurt Salisbury and Nicholas T. Phillip, "School Makerspaces: Beyond the Hype," *Phi Delta Kappan* 101, no. 8 (May 2020): https://search.ebscohost.com/login.aspx?direct=true&AuthType=cookie,ip,cpid&custid=csl&db=aph&AN=143320231&site=ehost-live&scope=site.

13. Kara Yario, "Collaboration Makes a Difference," *School Library Journal* 66, no. 2 (February 2020): https://search.ebscohost.com/login.aspx?direct=true&AuthType=cookie,ip,cpid&custid=csl&db=aph&AN=141392136&site=ehost-live&scope=site.

REFERENCES, SUGGESTED READINGS, AND WEBSITES

American Library Association. "Makerspaces." Tools, Publications, & Resources. Last modified 2020. Accessed September 2, 2020. http://www.ala.org/tools/atoz/makerspaces.

City of Los Angeles. "Octavia Labs: Creativity within Reach." Los Angeles Public Library. Last modified 2020. Accessed September 1, 2020. https://www.lapl.org/labs.

Creative Safety Supply. "What Does MSDS Stand For?" Hazcom Questions and Answers. Last modified 2020. Accessed September 2, 2020. https://www.creativesafetysupply.com/qa/hazcom/what-does-msds-stand-for.

D'Orio, Wayne. "Teen-Led STEM." *School Library Journal* 66, no. 6 (June 2020): 34–36. https://search.ebscohost.com/login.aspx?direct=true&AuthType=cookie,ip,cpid&custid=csl&db=aph&AN=143323061&site=ehost-live&scope=site.

Fairfax County Public Schools, VA. "STEAM." Academic Overview. Last modified 2020. Accessed August 29, 2020. https://www.fcps.edu/academics/academic-overview/steam.

Fontichiaro, Kristin. "Makerspace Tune-Up 2.0: Looking into the Future." *Teacher Librarian* 46, no. 5 (June 2019): 43–45. https://search.ebscohost.com/login.aspx?direct=true&AuthType=cookie,ip,cpid&custid=csl&db=aph&AN=138838619&site=ehost-live&scope=site.

Google. "YouTube." YouTube. Last modified 2020. Accessed September 2, 2020. https://www.youtube.com/results?search_query=makerspace.

Love, Tyler, Ken R. Roy, and Matthew Marino. "Inclusive Makerspaces, Fab Labs, and STEM Labs: How Can Instructors Make Appropriate Accommodations and Modifications While Maintaining a Safer Teaching and Learning Environment for All Students and Themselves?" *Technology & Engineering Teacher* 79, no. 5 (February 2020): 23–27. https://search.ebscohost.com/login.aspx?direct=true&AuthType=cookie,ip,cpid&custid=csl&db=aph&AN=141301044&site=ehost-live&scope=site.

National Institutes of Health Libraries. "3D Printing Service." NIH Library Services. Last modified 2020. Accessed September 2, 2020. https://www.nihlibrary.nih.gov/services/3d-printing-service.

Nebraska Library Commission. "Library Makerspaces - Common Items and Tools." Nebraska Library Commission. Last modified 2020. Accessed September 2, 2020. http://nlc.nebraska.gov/libraries/maker/items.aspx.

Snelling, Jennifer, "The Tech Edge." *School Library Journal* 65, no. 4 (May 2019). https://search.ebscohost.com/login.aspx?direct=true&AuthType=cookie,ip,cpid&custid=csl&db=aph&AN=136192021&site=ehost-live&scope=site.

Trotta, Alison A. "News Desk." *Computers in Libraries* 40, no. 5 (July/August 2020). https://search.ebscohost.com/login.aspx?direct=true&AuthType=cookie,ip,cpid&custid=csl&db=aph&AN=144661588&site=ehost-live&scope=site.

Wallingford Public Library. "Collaboratory Equipment." Wallingford Public Library. Last modified 2020. Accessed September 2, 2020. https://www.wallingford.lioninc.org/collaboratory/collaboratory-equipment/.

Yario, Kara. "Collaboration Makes a Difference." *School Library Journal* 66, no. 2 (February 2020): 10–11. https://search.ebscohost.com/login.aspx?direct=true&AuthType=cookie,ip,cpid&custid=csl&db=aph&AN=141392136&site=ehost-live&scope=site.

CHAPTER 13

Coding and Robotics

Library Support Staff (LSS) know the role and responsibility of libraries for introducing relevant applications of technology, including digital literacy, to the public. LSS demonstrate flexibility in adapting to new technology.

Topics Covered in This Chapter
Coding
   Encoding and Decoding
   Librarians Code
Robotics
   Robotics Competition
LSS as Facilitators
   Professional Learning
Coding and Robotic Resources
   Beginning or Entry Level
   Basic Level
   Advanced Level

Key Terms

Coding: The creation of taking ideas in everyday language and converting them into a specific set of forms or symbols that will be understood by either another person or interpreted by a computer or machine.

Peer collaboration: Library Support Staff (LSS) work together in teams in order to accomplish tasks, using the suggestions and recommendations of others to improve the quality of their work. Likewise, LSS's knowledge and skills of coding and robotics is enhanced when they learn together with others.

Robotics: The result of applying computer code to instruct a device to perform a task or take an action.

Two areas associated with STEAM (science, technology, engineering, arts, and mathematics) education are computer coding and robotics. Where once these highly complex topics required developers with advanced degrees and experience, today, with new ways of teaching STEAM, materials and resources are available to even the youngest learners. Today, libraries offer such opportunities. This chapter explores ways that Library Support Staff (LSS) who work in such libraries can provide support to both the staff who are teaching and the patrons who are discovering how to develop and apply basic coding and robotics.

CODING

Code is a system of letters, numbers, or symbols that represent information. For example, Morse code, once used by militaries to convey strategies and secrets, represented numerals, alphabet letters, or punctuation, depending upon the use of dots, dashes, and spaces. Coaches of some sports, such as football, use hand signals and other movements as code to communicate with their players on the field. Software developers use various programming languages such as Java or C+ to code instructions for the computer to perform. Today, many libraries support patrons' learning how to write the code of software instructions to have computers perform specific tasks.

The action of writing and using computer code is expressed in the verbs **coding**, encoding, and decoding. These words are often interchanged as the subtle differences among them may not be apparent.[1]

- *Coding* is putting ideas into the form or symbols of a code.
- *Encoding* is converting something, such as a body of information, from one system of communication into another especially to convert a message into code.
- *Decoding* is converting something, such as a coded message, into intelligible form.

Coding is the creation of taking ideas in everyday language and converting them into a specific set of forms or symbols that will be understood by either another person or interpreted by a computer or machine. The act of writing a new computer program is coding.

Encoding and Decoding

Encoding deals with volumes of data and often is done through a process or program specific to the task. Examples of encoding include media files, such as audio, video, and images that are compressed in order to save disk space. Encoded media files are typically similar in quality to their original uncompressed counterparts but have much smaller file sizes such as a WAVE audio file converted to a MP3 to reduce it to one-tenth its size. Typically, in encoded compression the quality of the media file is not noticeably compromised. Encoding processes are deliberate and most often done to enhance computer performance or to use the data on other systems.[2]

If encoding is the conversion process from one language or code to another so that the computing device can work with it, then decoding is going in the opposite direction. Decoding is similar to "breaking the code" in order to put the data back into its original or understandable form. Decoding takes place constantly when people use their computers. The data and programs have been encoded into binary 0s and 1s. Computers read binary code—humans do not! Binary must be decoded into one of the understandable global languages such as English, Chinese, Spanish, etc. so that people can read and use the computer. Encoding and decoding is a constant computing process. LSS use encoding and decoding every time they operate a digital device and interact with its content.

Librarians Code

When we think of careers in coding, librarian may not immediately come to mind. Computer programmers primarily work as software engineers designing systems and related services. Smaller percentages of programmers work for financial and manufacturing institutions.[3] However, librarians do perform coding in many ways. Traditionally, they use codes to classify information. The standard classification codes are either the Library of Congress or the Dewey Decimal classifications. LSS "see" the library in classification codes. They guide patrons to specific locations to find exact book titles, using the coding system of the library. In this example coding simplifies the arrangement of a library by ensuring that books on similar topics will be shelved together, increasing the opportunity for patrons to find materials on a topic.

LSS also use programming codes when they catalog books and other materials. Collections are coded in two or three letters to represent general fiction, teen mysteries, children's picture books, etc. Related to computing coding, LSS code when they catalog in MARC 21. The framework of MARC 21 is in tags, fields, and subfields. In the first tagline, the 008, data is coded about the item. The code in the 008 tag creates the correct template for the item's information to be properly displayed in the online catalog. The number "1" may indicate in a certain character space that the book has an index. The letter "g" in another specific character space indicates the item is for a general audience. LSS catalogers learn these codes and input them appropriately.

LSS may also code as they set up parameters of a customized report in the Integrated Library System (ILS). If they work in an open source library, they may learn how to reproduce or modify programming code in specific lines to accomplish a certain task. For example, there may be a need to modify the name of the report or only select data about certain types of activities in circulation. With training, LSS may perform tasks that require changing lines of code. LSS who are adept in doing such tasks may also be interested in learning more about coding in order to help facilitate patrons learning to code.

ROBOTICS

Robotics is the result of applying computer code to instruct a device to create actions or movements. Coding alone does not produce actions. Along with coded instructions and commands, there are devices to interpret the code in order for it to do its work. These devices, appliances, and machinery, with specific coding, perform the work of humans. While the idea of robots doing our work seems somewhat far-fetched, look around your home and library and you may be surprised how robotics is employed. Automation and robotics are closely linked. Auto, meaning "self" automation, is the process of making an apparatus, process, or even a system appear to work on its own. Automation can be mechanical, such as a windmill, or computer-driven robotics. Self-driven vacuums, pool cleaners, grass clippers, and experimental cars are examples of robotics. The UBTECH humanoid robot Lynx[4] that combined with Alexa, can be programmed to do numerous personal services, including security, in the home.

NAO and Pepper are autonomous programmable humanoid robots offered by SoftBank Robotics.[5] These programmable robots are developed for both educational teaching tools and personal uses. Wide price ranges reflect capabilities as found with a simple web search. Robotics and coding are at the core of twenty-first-century living and will continue to influence how we live and work. The affordability of NAO robots now makes it possible for libraries to consider acquiring one to show robotics in use and encourage patrons to participate in computer-related workshops where learning is both fun and intriguing.

Libraries are also using robotics to augment work. The following examples[6] describe some uses of robotics in libraries today:

- The Chicago Public Library, partnering with Google Chicago provided five hundred Finch Robots for checkout and in-house use. The robots feature a robust set of input mechanisms, such as accelerometers and light, temperature, and obstacle sensors. They can output complex behaviors, including motion, light, sound, and drawing.
- Connecticut's Westport Library has two humanoid child-sized NAO robots, named "Nancy" and "Vincent," that are programmed to activate video cameras, directional microphones, tactile sensors, etc. to have a complex range of motion to exhibit humanlike behaviors. They turn heads to look at people who speak to them, identify and manipulate objects, and retrieve internet information to add to a conversation. Nancy and Vincent are charismatic machines, and they attract curious public into the library.
- Automatic materials handling machines are coded to check-in and sort large volumes of returned library books and other circulating resources by scanning radio frequency identification tags that are embedded in materials. Using this robotic process streamlines the return of library materials to shelves for faster turnaround time for patrons.
- In some academic libraries, Library Retrieval Systems with robotic cranes tend to thousands of closely packed bins of books. When a patron requests a stored book from the online catalog, a crane retrieves the appropriate bin and brings it to an employee who retrieves the requested book.

Robotic Competitions

A successful way that schools have spurred student interest in coding and robotics is through competitions. Similar to competing in sports, robotic teams led by teachers and community adults form healthy competition both intra- and interscholastically. *FIRST* (For Inspiration and Recognition of Science and Technology) was founded

Figure 13.1. Building a Robot. *fstop123/E+ via Getty Images*

in 1989 to inspire young people's interest and participation in science and technology.[7] FIRST supports robotic teams from inception to global competitions offering resources, including scholarships, to its members. LSS interested in learning about robotic competitions should explore FIRST.

Robotic competitions can take place on a much smaller scale as well, such as between groups within or between local schools or libraries. LSS can be part of the team to help others learn coding and robotics when they, themselves, are intrigued by and motivated to learn new ways of using technology.

LSS AS FACILITATORS

The majority of LSS did not train to be computer programmers. Yet most jobs, including working in libraries, require knowledge and skills using technology that includes codes. Here is what one study[8] found about librarians who were willing to run or participate in successful coding programs:

- They were willing to try something new
- They were not afraid to fail (for themselves or in front of others)
- They could make changes on the fly
- They were okay with not being an expert
- They identified and capitalized on peer-based learning among participants

LSS experience **peer collaboration** when people learn from each other. Truth be told, many young adults have a higher level of computer expertise than older adults, and with guidance, they can be encouraged to help support coding classes. The key to success is that LSS and other library staff take a risk to offer coding, even when they are not experts in the topic themselves, are motivated, willing to try something new, are adaptable, and willing to be peer collaborators and willing to support coding workshops.

Professional Learning

In addition to the aforementioned characteristics, LSS can learn the fundamentals of coding and robotics and be familiar with resources such as software, kits, etc. that will be used in the makerspace or workshops. There is a plethora of supporting materials. For example, a simple YouTube search of "Scratch programming," a popular instructional coding software developed by MIT for both young and old, yields numerous videos of basic instruction.

LSS, similar to teachers and paraprofessionals, may obtain instruction and practice in computational thinking, robotics, and coding from educational and professional organizations, websites, tutorials, journals, and, of course, peer collaboration. LSS may also attend webinars, workshops, and classes. Nonprofits offer training tutorials, materials, and other resources. The specific coding software and robotic kits the library purchases or freely subscribes to likely offer training materials on their products. Local, regional, or state level organizations that sponsor robotic competitions may also offer training.

The American Library Association sponsors a website and program called Libraries Ready to Code.[9] The Ready to Code Collection provides resources and strategies for coding and computational thinking activities that are grounded in research, aligned with library core values, and support broadening participation. The National Institute of Museum and Library Services[10] sponsored a grant program called Coding at Every Library: Empowering Kids in Rural Communities across the Country. Just one of its numerous programs, Code Club, is designed to teach children computer programming skills. More than one hundred small libraries participated in the program. LSS can obtain a list of these libraries and search their websites and make contact for more information on how to initiate coding programs in their libraries.

The majority of state libraries support coding and robotics through webinars, instructional and program materials, and videos. Many state libraries, such as North Dakota (Coding at Every Library) and California (ROBO DOJO) offer grants to fund coding and robotics clubs and projects. Check your state library website to see what it may offer to help establish coding and robotics in your library.

ISTE, the International Society for Technology in Education, has a site dedicated to Coding and Robotics.[11] This site offers articles, blogs, and connections to other social media on topics of teaching coding and robotics such as a recent post on teaching robotics through dance and music. Reading ISTE posts can spur ideas that LSS can share with library staff to help plan a coding and robotics program or workshop. The Massachusetts Institute of Technology (MIT) developed the popular coding program Scratch. Accessing its MIT Media Lab[12] LSS explore exciting videos, articles, news, and shared stories about innovation and changes taking place through these technologies. MIT's Scratch for Educators[13] site provides a wide variety of examples of projects and professional learning on using this free coding application software. Many other universities and colleges also offer free professional learning.

Many nonprofits believe that young people should and can learn computer science skills. Code.org aims to provide free or minimal cost training for educators with no background in computer science. CSforALL,[14] supported by the National Science Foundation and other leading institutions and companies, is an initiative to empower all students in the United States, from kindergarten through high school, to learn computer science and be equipped with the computational thinking skills they need to be active citizens in our technology-driven world. To this end, CSforALL is a rich resource for anyone involved in early computer science projects, teaching, and programs. In the next section many of the more commonly used coding and robotic programs used in schools and libraries are discussed.

CODING AND ROBOTIC RESOURCES

Many programs developed for the classroom for differing grades and ages can also be used in libraries. Students may want the same programs available to them in school also in their public libraries so they can continue programming after school hours. In this section examples of coding and robotic resources[15] are designated by beginner, basic, and advanced levels.

Beginner Level

There are a number of robot toys that teach beginner programming skills using brief commands. Fun with building an object and coding it with action and movement are found in Lego Boost, Think Fun Gravity Maze, Cozmo Coding, and Wonder Workshop Dash. Many accessories are available for Dash **robots**. Toys are an effective way for LSS to demonstrate beginning coding to young people in a way that will hold their interest and bring enjoyment.

Libraries can reinforce learning when they emphasize foundational math concepts and coding. Bee-Bot, Ozobot, Edison, Cubelets, and Dash are programming tools that can be used to reinforce numbers, shapes, counting money, and other mathematical concepts.[16]

Basic Level

At a basic level the robot processes the users' coding to perform tasks. The programmer imagines ways to automate the robot. LSS need to learn entry level programming skills to support this level. Scratch, Python, Ruby,[17] and MakeCode are all excellent starter languages for authentic computer coding.

Scratch is a free entry programming language developed and supported by MIT. Users "snap" together blocks of commands that the computer can carry out. Interactive stories, games, and animations can be created and written and shared with others in the online community.

Python reads like normal speech. Python provides a basic grasp on how to think like a programmer, yet it is easy to transfer ideas into instructions that a device can interpret.

Ruby requires little explanation of its code as much of it is self-explanatory.

Figure 13.2. Learning to Code. *Ariel Skelley/DigitalVision via Getty Images*

Microsoft's MakeCode editor is a way to create with the BBC micro:bit.[18] The color-coded blocks are familiar to anyone who's previously used Scratch and yet powerful enough to access all the features of this tiny computer.

Advanced Level

Once people gain experience in basic computer languages, learning the professional languages of C++ and Java[19] should come more readily because of the early practice in computational thinking skills.

C++ programming language can look a bit like math and might discourage students from learning to code. Once the basic fundamentals of programming are understood, however, C++ can open many doors into the world of programming. Many of today's most successful programmers started learning to code with C or C++.

Java, which has been around for two decades, is harder to learn than the other languages. There are many online resources, toolkits, and tutorials that can guide you to create virtually anything from the ground up using Java. Java looks similar to C and C++ but offers more functionalities, thereby enabling students to create more robust programs.

Once one or both of these languages are acquired, robotic devices can be manipulated and instructed to do work. Some devices, referred to as software robots, have built-in ready inputs for programs. An example of programming a software robot can be coding a motion sensor that is connected to a camera on the front door that will activate and take a picture of anyone there. Next, you can code it to scan the image and compare it to a specific set of features in your library of faces. If there is a match, open the door. If not, take another action.[20]

CHAPTER SUMMARY

The purpose of this chapter is to remove some of the mysteries behind coding and robotics and to provide LSS concrete ways they can use to begin to become involved in supporting libraries' entry into these fields of computer science. LSS that know the role and responsibility of libraries for introducing relevant applications of technology, including coding and robotics, to the public, demonstrate flexibility in adapting to new technology.

DISCUSSION QUESTIONS

1. What is the relationship between coding and robotics? How do they support each other?
2. What steps can LSS take to become familiar with coding and robotics? How can they support others?
3. In being a member of a team planning a new coding and robotics workshop, what steps can LSS take to ensure the instruction and materials are appropriate for the participants?

ACTIVITY

Many links are provided for free or low cost programming, such as Scratch, Python, MakeCode, and Ruby. As a beginner programmer, access these sites and learn to program in one of these languages, using the excellent resources and tutorials provided.

NOTES

1. "Dictionary," in *Merriam-Webster*, online ed. (Merriam-Webster, 2020), last modified 2020, accessed September 27, 2020, https://www.merriam-webster.com/.

2. Sharpened Productions, "Encoding," Tech Terms, last modified 2020, accessed September 27, 2020, https://techterms.com/definition/encoding.

3. "Computer Programmers," in *Occupational Outlook Handbook*, 2020 ed. (Washington, DC: U.S. Bureau of Labor Statistics Office of Occupational Statistics and Employment Projections, 2020), accessed September 27, 2020, https://www.bls.gov/ooh/computer-and-information-technology/computer-programmers.htm#tab-3.

4. UBTECH Robotics, Inc, "Lynx," UBTECH, last modified 2020, accessed October 4, 2020, https://ubtrobot.com/products/lynx-with-amazon-alexa?ls=en.

5. SoftBank Robotics, "NAO," NAO, last modified 2020, accessed October 5, 2020, https://www.softbankrobotics.com/emea/en/nao.

6. "Robotics and the Human Touch in Libraries and Museums," *Unbound* (blog), entry posted 2020, accessed October 4, 2020, https://slis.simmons.edu/blogs/unbound/2015/04/06/robotics-and-the-human-touch-in-libraries-and-museums/.

7. For Inspiration and Recognition of Science and Technology (FIRST), "Vision and Mission," FIRST, last modified 2020, accessed October 5, 2020, https://www.firstinspires.org/about/vision-and-mission.

8. Crystle Martin, "Libraries as Facilitators of Coding for All," *Knowledge Quest* 45, no. 3 (January/February 2017): [Page 50], http://search.ebscohost.com/login.aspx?direct=true&AuthType=cookie,ip,cpid&custid=csl&db=aph&AN=120539471&site=ehost-live&scope=site.

9. American Library Association, "Libraries Ready to Code," Libraries Ready to Code, last modified 2020, accessed October 3, 2020, http://www.ala.org/tools/readytocode/home.

10. Institute of Museum and Library Services, "Code Club," Coding at Every Library, last modified 2020, accessed October 3, 2020, https://www.imls.gov/grant-spotlights/coding-every-library-empowering-kids-rural-communities-across-country.

11. International Society for Technology in Education, "Coding & Robotics," ISTE, last modified 2020, accessed October 4, 2020, https://www.iste.org/explore/topic/coding-robotics.

12. Massachusetts Institute of Technology, "News and Updates," MIT Media Lab, last modified 2020, accessed October 4, 2020, https://www.media.mit.edu/.

13. Massachusetts Institute of Technology, "Scratch for Educators," Scratch for Educators, last modified 2020, accessed October 4, 2020, https://scratch.mit.edu/educators.

14. CSforAll, "CSforAll," About CSforALL, last modified 2020, accessed October 4, 2020, https://www.csforall.org/about/.

15. Dawn Nelson, "Robots—From Playthings to Applied Learning Tools," *Computers in Libraries* 40, no. 4 (May/June 2020): http://search.ebscohost.com/login.aspx?direct=true&AuthType=cookie,ip,cpid&custid=csl&db=lxh&AN=143605886&site=ehost-live&scope=site.

16. Amy Sokoll et al., "Preparing Elementary Teachers to Incorporate Coding in Math and Science," *Elementary STEM Journal* 24, no. 2 (December 2019): http://search.ebscohost.com/login.aspx?direct=true&AuthType=cookie,ip,cpid&custid=csl&db=aph&AN=144250200&site=ehost-live&scope=site.

17. CoderZ, "5 Best Programming Languages for Kids," CoderZ, last modified 2020, accessed October 5, 2020, https://gocoderz.com/blog/5-best-programming-languages-kids/.

18. Micro:bit Educational Foundation, "Create, Learn, Code," BBC Micro:bit, last modified 2020, accessed October 5, 2020, https://microbit.org/.

19. CoderZ, "5 Best Programming Languages for Kids," CoderZ, last modified 2020, accessed October 5, 2020, https://gocoderz.com/blog/5-best-programming-languages-kids/.

20. Dawn Nelson, "Robots—From Playthings to Applied Learning Tools," *Computers in Libraries* 40, no. 4 (May/June 2020): http://search.ebscohost.com/login.aspx?direct=true&AuthType=cookie,ip,cpid&custid=csl&db=lxh&AN=143605886&site=ehost-live&scope=site.

REFERENCES, SUGGESTED READINGS, AND WEBSITES

American Library Association. "Libraries Ready to Code." Libraries Ready to Code. Last modified 2020. Accessed October 3, 2020. http://www.ala.org/tools/readytocode/home.

California State Library. "ROBO DOJO." Robo Dojo (formerly Coding with the Robot). Last modified 2020. Accessed October 3, 2020. https://www.library.ca.gov/services/to-libraries/copycat-grants/the-journey-begins/.

Chun, Traci. "Coding, Computational Thinking, and Collaboration." *Teacher Librarian* 47, no. 5 (June 2020): 8–11. http://search.ebscohost.com/login.aspx?direct=true&AuthType=cookie,ip,cpid&custid=csl&db=lxh&AN=145727037&site=ehost-live&scope=site.

CoderZ. "5 Best Programming Languages for Kids." CoderZ. Last modified 2020. Accessed October 5, 2020. https://gocoderz.com/blog/5-best-programming-languages-kids/.

"Computer Programmers." In *Occupational Outlook Handbook*, 2020 ed. Washington, DC: U.S. Bureau of Labor Statistics Office of Occupational Statistics and Employment Projections, 2020. Accessed September 27, 2020. https://www.bls.gov/ooh/computer-and-information-technology/computer-programmers.htm#tab-3.

CSforAll. "CSforAll." About CSforALL. Last modified 2020. Accessed October 4, 2020. https://www.csforall.org/about/.

"Dictionary." In *Merriam-Webster*, Online ed. Merriam-Webster, 2020. Last modified 2020. Accessed September 27, 2020. https://www.merriam-webster.com/.

For Inspiration and Recognition of Science and Technology (FIRST). "Vision and Mission." FIRST. Last modified 2020. Accessed October 5, 2020. https://www.firstinspires.org/about/vision-and-mission.

Institute of Museum and Library Services. "Code Club." Coding at Every Library. Last modified 2020. Accessed October 3, 2020. https://www.imls.gov/grant-spotlights/coding-every-library-empowering-kids-rural-communities-across-country.

International Society for Technology in Education. "Coding & Robotics." ISTE. Last modified 2020. Accessed October 4, 2020. https://www.iste.org/explore/topic/coding-robotics.

Martin, Crystle. "Libraries as Facilitators of Coding for All." *Knowledge Quest* 45, no. 3 (January/February 2017): 46–53. http://search.ebscohost.com/login.aspx?direct=true&AuthType=cookie,ip,cpid&custid=csl&db=aph&AN=120539471&site=ehost-live&scope=site.

Massachusetts Institute of Technology. "News and Updates." MIT Media Lab. Last modified 2020. Accessed October 4, 2020. https://www.media.mit.edu/.

———. "Scratch for Educators." Scratch for Educators. Last modified 2020. Accessed October 4, 2020. https://scratch.mit.edu/educators.

Micro:bit Educational Foundation. "Create, Learn, Code." BBC Micro:bit. Last modified 2020. Accessed October 5, 2020. https://microbit.org/.

Nelson, Dawn. "Robots—From Playthings to Applied Learning Tools." Computers in Libraries 40, no. 4 (May/June 2020): 32-36. http://search.ebscohost.com/login.aspx?direct=true&AuthType=cookie,ip,cpid&custid=csl&db=lxh&AN=143605886&site=ehost-live&scope=site.

"Robotics and the Human Touch in Libraries and Museums." *Unbound* (blog). Entry posted 2020. Accessed October 4, 2020. https://slis.simmons.edu/blogs/unbound/2015/04/06/robotics-and-the-human-touch-in-libraries-and-museums/.

Robotics.net. "How to Program a Robot: Beginner's Guide." Robotics. Last modified November 29, 2019. Accessed October 5, 2020. https://robots.net/robotics/how-to-program-a-robot/.

Sharpened Productions. "Encoding." Tech Terms. Last modified 2020. Accessed September 27, 2020. https://techterms.com/definition/encoding.

SoftBank Robotics. "NAO." NAO. Last modified 2020. Accessed October 5, 2020. https://www.softbankrobotics.com/emea/en/nao.

Sokoll, Amy, Tammera Mittlestet, Amanda Thomas, and Kelly Buchjheister. "Preparing Elementary Teachers to Incorporate Coding in Math and Science." *Elementary STEM Journal* 24, no. 2 (December 2019): 9–11. http://search.ebscohost.com/login.aspx?direct=true&AuthType=cookie,ip,cpid&custid=csl&db=aph&AN=144250200&site=ehost-live&scope=site.

UBTECH Robotics, Inc. "Lynx." UBTECH. Last modified 2020. Accessed October 4, 2020. https://ubtrobot.com/products/lynx-with-amazon-alexa?ls=en.

CHAPTER 14

Digital Media Technologies

Library Support Staff (LSS) are able to perform basic troubleshooting of technical problems and resolve or refer those problems as appropriate.

Topics Covered in This Chapter
Digital Audio
   Podcasts
   Digital Music
Digital Video
   Streaming Video
   Tutorials
   Programming
   Public Access
   Media Labs

Key Terms

Digital Audio Workstation: Also referred to as a DAW, the station supports creating and editing digital music.

Podcasts: The word is derived from a combination of *iPod* and *broadcast*. These are digital recordings of interviews or informative discussions about a topic or theme.

Public access: Cable companies are required by law to provide educational and local municipal channels for the community.

Streamed: This is a method to transmit or receive audio and video data over a computer network as a steady, continuous flow that allows playback to start while the rest of the data is still being received.

Streaming video: Rather than purchasing DVDs, libraries subscribe for the rights to allow patrons to view on their own devices movies, programs, and documentaries via a network.

DIGITAL AUDIO

In 2001, Apple launched its first digital music device, the iPod, which quickly gained favor for its size and lack of moveable parts over the digital CD. Apple was the first company to shift listeners' mindsets from owning pieces of music they could touch to having lifetime rights to use digital music that **streamed** from a proprietary network called the Apple Store. The iPod and the Apple Store revolutionized how people listen to music, with Amazon and others soon joining the fray with their own audio streaming devices and options.

Audio file formats of WAV, MP3, and others listed in Textbox 14.1[1] are used today to stream audio for music, entertainment, e-books, and information such as news and podcasts. Most common audio file formats that Library Support Staff (LSS) may encounter are MP3, Dolby, AA, and WAV.[2]

TEXTBOX 14.1: AUDIO FILE FORMATS

AAC (bitrates from 8 to 320Kbps)
HE-AAC (bitrates from 8 to 320Kbps)
Protected AAC (from the iTunes Store)
ALAC (Apple Lossless)
MP3 (bitrates from 8 to 320Kbps)
MP3 VBR (Variable Bitrate)
Dolby Digital (AC-3)
Dolby Digital Plus (E-AC-3)
AA (Audible formats 2, 3, 4) / Audible Enhanced Audio / AAX / AAX+
WAV (Waveform Audio File Format)
AIFF (Audio Interchange File Format)

Podcasts

The word "podcast" is derived from a combination of *iPod* and *broadcast*. **Podcasts** are interviews or informative discussions about a topic or theme. LSS can identify weekly or monthly sources of professional podcasts that library users may be interested in and vet the information with library supervisors. The sources found in Table 14.1[3] are reputable podcasts.

Table 14.1. Examples of Podcasts Sources

NPR Podcasts	The majority of NPR programming is available as podcasts.
Science Podcasts	American Association for the Advancement of Science (AAAS) podcasts its programs.
The MOTH	The MOTH Podcast feature stories are true by live storytellers.
Google Play Music	Podcasts are free to download or stream with no subscription.
iTunes Podcasts	Free podcasts for Apple devices and TV.
Listen Notes	Search the whole internet's podcasts and curate podcast playlists.
PodcastRE	Links to over 150,000 files, from over 1,000 different podcast feeds.
Spotify: Podcasts	Thousands of podcasts directly from the Spotify app.

In addition to helping patrons find podcasts for their personal or research information, LSS may help others create podcasts. Adapting suggestions from an academic library,[4] LSS can learn how to create and edit a digital audio podcast as follows:

1. Develop a well-defined topic or theme for the podcast.
2. Envision the target audience.
3. Plan the content:
    a. Factual information
    b. Interviews
    c. Discussion group
4. Plan an outline of the podcast. Line by line, from start to finish, list each subtopic, the amount of time it will take to speak about it, and focus notes to guide the speakers.
5. Locate an appropriately quiet room and test equipment prior to making the podcast. Speak into the microphone and adjust volume or distance.
6. The equipment needed is a microphone, computer with digital editing recording software, and output capability.
7. If using a MAC, GarageBand is a free and versatile digital audio recording and editing program used for creating podcasts. If using a PC, Audacity is also a highly reputable, free, and versatile digital audio editing program.
8. Know the functions of the editing tools. Cut out any unnecessary material such as long moments of silence, coughs, sneezes, etc.
9. Use a host server to store and provide access to the podcast. If the podcast is made as a library program, speak with the library IT professional who will identify the correct library server or outsource provider to use.

LSS become confident and comfortable helping others make podcasts when they make one themselves. Using the steps above, refine technique with practice. A makerspace is an ideal place to introduce podcasting to others. Upcoming library programming, such as summer reading, can be enhanced with podcasting, such as creating podcasts with local authors, book discussion groups, and subject matter experts on content of selected books, etc. Library podcasts can be cataloged similar to other online resources with active links to the content.

Many libraries offer makerspace or other space in support of a digital music program, curriculum, or just for patrons to explore their musical talent or interests.

Digital Music

Today, both professionals and amateurs can create and optimize digital sound recordings using a **digital audio workstation** (DAW).[5] A DAW can be as simple as having a program installed on their computer or a larger setup of software, mixer, synthesizer, musical instruments, and other audio components in a digital media lab. GarageBand software has a sound library of instruments, presets for guitar and voice, drummers and percussionists, amps and effects, and loops of music genres

Figure 14.1. Digital Audio Workstation. *Zero Creative/Cultura via Getty Images*

to build from. Users have the option to plug in a guitar or mic to add their own original music and voice.

Not unlike copying and moving data from one file to another when writing a report, creating music on DAW is taking bits of data from numerous sources within GarageBand, Audacity, or another digital audio source and arranging it in a way that creates a desired sound and sequence. Digital audio has revolutionized how music is composed on both the professional and personal level.

DAW supports the technology and arts of STEAM. Those who have background knowledge and interest of music may find working with DAW an outlet expression. Creating music on DAW can be an exploratory, learning experience.

LSS can do much to support the library obtaining DAW and how patrons will use it. Identify a computer that would be appropriate for use as a recording studio. This could be a computer in the makerspace, a computer lab, or even a dedicated laptop that could be carried to a conference room. Upload GarageBand if it is an iMAC, or Audacity if it is a PC with Windows. Patrons may prefer to use their own mobile device and need only to borrow a portable MIDI controller keyboard and synthesizer from the library to create music.

There is a plethora of free YouTube and Apple videos and instructional tutorials on Garageband and Audacity. LSS who work in libraries with DAWs become familiar with the software and peripherals so that they can help new users. They may also enjoy the experiences themselves with DAWs becoming a personal source of learning, entertainment, and satisfaction. Table 14.2 lists sources of DAWs instruction.

Table 14.2. Sources of DAWs Tutorials

GarageBand	The GarageBand Guide https://thegaragebandguide.com/
	How to Use GarageBand: A Step-By-Step Guide https://www.makeuseof.com/tag/download-guide-to-garageband/
	The Basics of GarageBand https://ds.bc.edu/the-basics-of-garageband/
	GarageBand—University of Texas Libraries legacy.lib.utexas.edu › media-labs › GarageBand essential tutorial
Audacity	Audacity Manual https://manual.audacityteam.org/#
	Basic Editing with Audacity https://diglibarts.whittier.edu/tutorial-basic-editing-with-audacity/
	Basic Recording with Audacity https://libguides.wooster.edu/c.php?g=719097&p=5134800
	Audacity https://www.xavier.edu/teachingwithtech/a-z/audacity

DIGITAL VIDEO

Similar to digital audio, digital video is the process of computers interpreting and translating pictures into binary coded data. When one makes a digital video with their phone, computer, or camera, the images and sounds are immediately coded into data of "0s" and "1s." When the video is played, the data is translated back again into pictures and sounds.

DVDs, which stands for digital versatile disc, have proven a reliable means for storing data, especially high-quality digital video. Because of the popularity, affordability, and ease of use, libraries acquired large numbers of DVDs that quickly replaced VHS tapes. Circulating collections were sought by patrons as DVDs could be played on relatively inexpensive home devices.

Streaming Video

Libraries that provide streaming video content services provide the downloading of content from third party vendor clouds to their patrons. There are many vendors of **streaming video**. Cable, satellite, and other TV and internet providers offer home users packages of video services from vendors such as Netflix, Amazon Prime, Hulu, Disney, and Peacock, to name just a few. Video streaming is in its infancy, and there is much competition for users. Academic libraries offer educational video streaming services with a focus on curriculum topics to faculty and staff. For example, there are Kanopy, Hoopla Digital, Academic Video Online, or Films on Demand. Academic libraries offer subject specific streaming video services on science, history, literature, and other subjects.

Home video streaming services can be costly to the family budget. In 2020 Kiplinger's found people are spending more on video subscription services. Not only have more consumers signed up for video-streaming services during the COVID pandemic of 2020, but the average streamer pays for more services than ever.[6] As libraries reduce in size or even eliminate purchasing DVDs in favor of acquiring video steaming subscription services, LSS who have direct contact with patrons can do much to promote these services by providing information and support from their firsthand experience.

Home users often have the option of subscriptions versus pay-per-view. Pay-per-view is a one-time cost for watching a specific video or film. If the person is an occasional viewer, pay-per-view may be a better option. Libraries that are negotiating video streaming services should also weigh the cost of subscriptions versus pay-per-view, especially if the service has content that would only occasionally be used. Libraries can also look into the option of bundling video services, something that is done for residential customers. If it is not against library policy, staff can investigate if a bundled streaming service with advertisements would cost less than a bundled service without advertising. Libraries can also see if they are eligible for free trials for services that they may be interested in acquiring.

LSS who use video streaming services for their own reading, listening, and viewing have firsthand experience and are better able to help patrons new to a library subscription service. If LSS do not use their library's streaming services as a patron, they should register to access the accounts so that they can be familiar with all steps involved for library patrons to be successful users.

Tutorials

Librarians create digital video tutorials on a variety of topics with practical information for when they may not be present or have time to individually instruct patrons. Digital video works well because the actions of the presenter performing the task and their verbal instructions are captured and can be played using most any computing device and at the time and place of the user's choice. Tutorials can be viewed in full unlimited times or just the segments that need repeating.

Tutorials were popular during the Covid-19 pandemic when face-to-face library programming was not available. Librarians used their knowledge, skills, and ingenuity to create meaningful instruction such as "Librarians Learn."[7] In less than ten minutes a local expert teaches two or three staff members how to do something. Topics include oil pastels, TikTok dancing, karate board chopping, jumping rope, applying make-up, and learning the ukulele. The tutorials can be found on YouTube and Facebook. The popularity far exceeded all expectations with thousands of views, and the staff will continue to create tutorials on interesting topics after the pandemic. Not only do viewers learn new skills, but just as important, they make the connection that the library is a place where life-long learning on myriad topics is free and available.

When creating a video, a concern academic librarians have is whether users will actually watch how-to videos or other points of need. Is there a better way to design videos to ensure maximum interest and engagement? Results of a comprehensive study[8] found whether a video is selected for inclusion by an instructor or viewed after it is noticed by a student depends on the following factors:

- Information should be presented in a trustworthy manner by a credible presenter.
- Length should be brief, no longer than four minutes.
- Keep a focus on the content and instruction, do not try to be overly entertaining.
- Voice quality makes a difference. It should be pleasant, even, and clear.
- Tutorials should include an example scenario, no matter how brief, to ground the viewer in the task.

LSS can suggest, plan, script, and present in instructional tutorials about library processes and use of equipment and services. We do not have to be accomplished actors, but rather credible people who know how to communicate the task at hand. With others, identify potential topics for instruction and begin the process of planning a tutorial. Create a prototype as a draft to show to others for their feedback and suggestions. Creating a tutorial can be a rewarding and fun experience and can save hours of staff time while encouraging patron independence. Remember to keep tutorials short and focused, and speak pleasantly. The first successful tutorial will lead to many more!

Programming

In addition to tutorials, libraries create and use videos around programming on health, people and culture, commemorative events, and so forth. YouTube hosts more than one billion videos, and many agencies and institutions use YouTube to reach viewers. For example, if LSS wanted to find videos on Veterans Day, the U.S. Department of Veterans Affairs has hundreds in a dedicated YouTube channel vetted through the agency. With more than thirty million channels, LSS can selectively join channels to follow topics of particular interest to the library programming. Another video service, TikTok, should be explored. With more than one million videos, TikTok has an international focus.

TED[9] (Technology, Entertainment and Design) Talks are another source of video that can complement a library program. TED is a nonprofit devoted to spreading ideas, usually in the form of short, powerful talks of around eighteen minutes or less covering topics from science to business to global issues in more than one hundred languages. LSS can search TED videos by topics as a way to introduce an important world, health, or environmental issue at a library program.

Public Access

Some libraries have video production departments that are responsible for internal or external programming. Internal video programming includes broadcasting announcements, school news, and special events. Public libraries may also create video announcements that are shown within the building.

External programming are broadcasts to the community using the internet or television capabilities. **Public access** under the 1984 Cable Act[10] requires cable operators to provide channels, some equipment, and often facilities for public, educational, or governmental (PEG) use. Operators are not permitted to control the content of programming on PEG channels. Some municipal libraries are designated PEG sites for public access, and LSS may be involved in supporting such

Figure 14.2. Creating a Library Announcement. *bjones27/E+ via Getty Images*

programming from greeting participants to working with the video librarian in aspects of production and archival.

Patrons use libraries so that they can locate and view a wide variety of video content. Students seek to use library digital media equipment and instructional support in planning, directing, presenting, and producing assignments. To this end, many libraries acquire digital media labs.

Media Labs

There is never enough space in libraries, but a dedicated digital media lab ranks equally with all other services. Libraries that have already established makerspaces more than likely included digital media equipment, using the makerspace or part of it as its lab. Digital media labs are primarily used to record and edit sound and video. They are places where work takes place to produce media. Table 14.3[11] contains the necessary type of software options for a digital media lab.

While this table is not extensive, it provides a reasonable start for planning the type and level of audio and video editing envisioned for the digital media lab.

Hardware equipment for a digital media audio[12] and digital video workstation[13] is listed in Table 14.4. Some duplication of hardware will be required for multiple workstations.

Some of the audio equipment, such as microphones and headsets, may be also used in video editing. While these lists are not meant to be all inclusive or to endorse any product, they serve to give LSS an overview of the software choices and hardware inventory for digital media labs.

Table 14.3. Digital Media Lab Software Considerations

Audio Recording and Editing	MAC	PC
Audacity—free, open source audio editing tool	Yes	Yes
GarageBand—free with sophisticated mixing options, digital musical instruments and sounds.	Yes	No
Adobe Audition—professional editing tool to record, mix, and restore audio.	Yes	Yes
QuickTime Pro—export any file playable in QuickTime Player.	Yes	Yes
Video Recording and Editing	**MAC**	**PC**
iMovie—novice video editing. Import and enhance video clips, images, and audio. Directly record voice-overs. Add text and transitions.	Yes	No
Adobe Premiere—professional editing for film, TV, and the web. Adobe Sensei crafts polished films and videos.	Yes	Yes
Davinci Resolve—a free video editor somewhat similar to Adobe Premiere.	Yes	Yes
Final Cut Pro—professional editing. Requires a lengthy learning curve.	Yes	No
Final Cut Express—a better software package for iMac without complexity.	Yes	No
PowToon—free version for video stories and projects with pre-drawn cartoon figures and animation. Uploads YouTube, Vimeo, or linked from PowToon.	Yes	Yes
QuickTime Pro 10—performs core functions of video editing such as recording and capturing footage, trimming clips, and exporting them. QuickTime Pro 10 media can be exported in a wide variety of file formats including .mov and .m4v.	Yes	Yes
Adobe Spark—free and offers many (not all) iMovie features. Add video, images, and audio from external files, search for royalty free images and audio within the program, voice-over audio and text to slides. Minor editing/clipping of video files.	Yes	Yes

Table 14.4. Digital Media Lab Equipment Considerations

Audio Equipment (in addition to the desktop computer or laptop)

Fender Stratocaster and handcrafted electric guitars
USB audio interface to convert analog audio signals (i.e., your voice) into digital signals for the computer.
MIDI keyboard
Snowball iCE USB microphone
Electronic sound synthesizer to generate and modify sounds
Input mixer
Speaker system
Studio headphones
Cables

Video Equipment (in addition to the desktop computer or laptop)

Microphones, such as lapel clip, table, multidirectional
Cameras (various types)—DSL camera; camcorder; FlipHD camera; GoPros
Digital audio recorder to create voice-over video (added voice to video)
SD cards for storage
Digital camera and/or SONY Bloggie touch
Tripods (various sizes)—mounted plate; bendable, etc.
Cables

CHAPTER SUMMARY

Libraries have evolved from repositories of print to exciting collaborative workplaces with the onset of many types of digital media hardware and software. LSS who are interested and motivated to learn digital media technologies are able to perform basic troubleshooting of technical problems and resolve or refer those problems for others, making patrons more willing to experiment with and use makerspaces and digital media labs.

DISCUSSION QUESTIONS

1. What is a podcast and why should LSS promote the use of them to patrons?
2. What are some of the benefits of video streaming and how has it changed how libraries support patrons viewing film?
3. Why is the selection process of digital audio and digital video editing software critical to the success of the makerspace or digital media lab?
4. What ways can LSS support digital media technologies in the library?

ACTIVITY

1. Create a three-minute or less screencast tutorial on how to locate, access, and listen to a podcast on a specific topic of your choosing from one of the sources of podcasts found in Table 14.1. Write notes with step-by-step instructions.
2. Practice a few times and then film your presentation.
3. Have someone view it and follow your instructions. What feedback can they give about the tutorial? Was it effective and helpful? What changes will you make the next time you create one?

NOTES

1. Lifewire, "IPod File Format Compatibility Guide," iPods & MP3 Players, last modified 2020, accessed October 11, 2020, https://www.lifewire.com/ipod-file-format-compatibility-guide-1999462.

2. Yale University, "Audio Timeline," Irving S. Gilmore Music Library, last modified 2020, accessed October 10, 2020, https://web.library.yale.edu/cataloging/music/audiotimeline.

3. Babson College, "Finding Podcasts," Horn Library, last modified 2020, accessed October 11, 2020, https://libguides.babson.edu/podcasts.

4. University of Nevada Las Vegas, "Audio Production: Podcasting," UNLV University Libraries, last modified August 20, 2020, accessed October 11, 2020, https://guides.library.unlv.edu/c.php?g=838501&p=5989328.

5. A. Rothstein, "What Does a Digital Audio Workstation (DAW) Do?" *IPR Institute of Production and Recording* (blog), entry posted February 14, 2020, accessed October 12, 2020, https://www.ipr.edu/blogs/audio-production/what-does-a-digital-audio-workstation-daw-do/.

6. Emma Patch, "A Guide to Streaming Services," *Kiplinger's Personal Finance* 74, no. 10 (October 2020): http://search.ebscohost.com/login.aspx?direct=true&AuthType=cookie,ip,cpid&custid=csl&db=aph&AN=145196290&site=ehost-live&scope=site.

7. Facebook, "Librarians Learn Oil Pastels," Groton Public Library, last modified August 11, 2020, accessed October 12, 2020, https://www.facebook.com/grotonpubliclibrary/videos/librarians-learn-oil-pastels/954997518350245/.

8. Amanda S. Clossen, "Trope or Trap? Roleplaying Narratives and Length in Instructional Video," *Information Technology & Libraries*. 37, no. 1 (March 2018): http://search.ebscohost.com/login.aspx?direct=true&AuthType=cookie,ip,cpid&custid=csl&db=tfh&AN=128636639&site=ehost-live&scope=site.

9. TED Conferences, "Our Organization," TED, last modified 2020, accessed October 12, 2020, https://www.ted.com/about/our-organization.

10. Federal Communications Commission, "Cable Television," Federal Communications Commission, last modified 2020, accessed October 12, 2020, https://www.fcc.gov/media/engineering/cable-television.

11. Trinity University, "Tech Tools and Tips," Coates Library, last modified 2020, accessed October 13, 2020, https://libguides.trinity.edu/tools/video.

12. Betha Gutsche, "Shoestring Digital Media Lab: How One Little Underfunded Library Made It Happen," WebJunction, last modified September 7, 2017, accessed October 13, 2020, https://www.webjunction.org/news/webjunction/shoestring-digital-media-lab.html.

13. Vanderbilt University, "Browse by Type of Equipment," Jean & Alexander Heard Libraries, last modified 2020, accessed October 13, 2020, https://www.library.vanderbilt.edu/technology/hardwaresoftware/type.php?category=Audiovisual.

REFERENCES, SUGGESTED READINGS, AND WEBSITES

ALSC. "Digital Media Resources." Digital Media Resources Page. Last modified 2020. Accessed September 25, 2020. http://www.ala.org/alsc/digital-media-resources.

Babson College. "Finding Podcasts." Horn Library. Last modified 2020. Accessed October 11, 2020. https://libguides.babson.edu/podcasts.

Clossen, Amanda S. "Trope or Trap? Roleplaying Narratives and Length in Instructional Video." *Information Technology & Libraries*. 37, no. 1 (March 2018): 27–38. http://search.ebscohost.com/login.aspx?direct=true&AuthType=cookie,ip,cpid&custid=csl&db=tfh&AN=128636639&site=ehost-live&scope=site.

"Digital Media and Library Instruction." *Library Technology Reports* 55, no. 5 (June 2019): 1–25. http://search.ebscohost.com/login.aspx?direct=true&AuthType=cookie,ip,cpid&custid=csl&.

Facebook. "Librarians Learn Oil Pastels." Groton Public Library. Last modified August 11, 2020. Accessed October 12, 2020. https://www.facebook.com/grotonpubliclibrary/videos/librarians-learn-oil-pastels/954997518350245/.

Federal Communications Commission. "Cable Television." Federal Communications Commission. Last modified 2020. Accessed October 12, 2020. https://www.fcc.gov/media/engineering/cable-television.

Gutsche, Betha. "Shoestring Digital Media Lab: How One Little Underfunded Library Made It Happen." WebJunction. Last modified September 7, 2017. Accessed October 13, 2020. https://www.webjunction.org/news/webjunction/shoestring-digital-media-lab.html.

How Stuff Works. "How Tape Recorders Work." How Stuff Works. Last modified 2020. Accessed October 10, 2020. https://electronics.howstuffworks.com/gadgets/audio-music/cassette.htm.

Lamb, Annette. "Digital Media Part 1: Standards and a Culture of Reading." *Teacher Librarian* 46, no. 1 (October 2018): 52–57. http://search.ebscohost.com/login.aspx?direct=true&AuthType=cookie,ip,cpid&custid=csl&db=lxh&AN=132655299&site=ehost-live&scope=site.

Lifewire. "IPod File Format Compatibility Guide." iPods & MP3 Players. Last modified 2020. Accessed October 11, 2020. https://www.lifewire.com/ipod-file-format-compatibility-guide-1999462.

Patch, Emma. "A Guide to Streaming Services." *Kiplinger's Personal Finance* 74, no. 10 (October 2020): 66–71. http://search.ebscohost.com/login.aspx?direct=true&AuthType=cookie,ip,cpid&custid=csl&db=aph&AN=145196290&site=ehost-live&scope=site.

Rothstein, A. "What Does a Digital Audio Workstation (DAW) Do?" *IPR Institute of Production and Recording* (blog). Entry posted February 14, 2020. Accessed October 12, 2020. https://www.ipr.edu/blogs/audio-production/what-does-a-digital-audio-workstation-daw-do/.

TED Conferences. "Our Organization." TED. Last modified 2020. Accessed October 12, 2020. https://www.ted.com/about/our-organization.

Trinity University. "Tech Tools and Tips." Coates Library. Last modified 2020. Accessed October 13, 2020. https://libguides.trinity.edu/tools/video.

University of Nevada Las Vegas. "Audio Production: Podcasting." UNLV University Libraries. Last modified August 20, 2020. Accessed October 11, 2020. https://guides.library.unlv.edu/c.php?g=838501&p=5989328.

Vanderbilt University. "Browse by Type of Equipment." Jean & Alexander Heard Libraries. Last modified 2020. Accessed October 13, 2020. https://www.library.vanderbilt.edu/technology/hardwaresoftware/type.php?category=Audiovisual.

Yale University. "Audio Timeline." Irving S. Gilmore Music Library. Last modified 2020. Accessed October 10, 2020. https://web.library.yale.edu/cataloging/music/audiotimeline.

CHAPTER 15

Cybersecurity and Appropriate Use

Library Support Staff (LSS) know basic principles and best practices to ensure the integrity of data and the confidentiality of user activities.
LSS know concepts and issues concerning the appropriate use of technology by different user groups.

Topics Covered in This Chapter:
Cybersecurity
Appropriate Use
   Filters
Technology Cyber Threats
Integrity and Security of Data

Key Terms

Appropriate Use Policy: Specifies, for both staff and patrons, appropriate and inappropriate behaviors that are agreed to prior to using library technologies.

Children's Internet Protection Act: Federal legislation that requires libraries and schools that receive internet funding to have filters on all computers being used by children under the age of eighteen years old.

Cybersecurity: A combination of people, policies processes, and technologies libraries and other institutions use to protect their information and operational technologies.

Filters: Hardware, such as firewalls, or software, such as programs that read and manipulate the input data coming into a network to compare it to what is an appropriate pattern. If it is not appropriate, it removes or blocks the data before it comes to the user.

Information nonrepudiation: When Library Support Staff have assurance that the sender of information is provided with proof of delivery and the recipient is provided with proof of the sender's identity, so neither can later deny having processed the information.

Phishing: Fraudulent attempts using email to get personal or sensitive information.

CYBERSECURITY

Cybersecurity is the combination of people, policies, processes, and technologies employed by an enterprise to protect its cyber assets.[1] Cybersecurity includes information technology (IT) and operational technology (OT). In libraries IT are email, databases, programs and software, patron and circulation data, websites, sound and video recordings, e-books, archives, administrative files, users' content, and many other digital information data. Operational technology is the hardware. Libraries have much OT in their inventories including computers and computing devices, sound and video equipment, printers, copy machines, scanners, networks, Wi-Fi, e-readers, projectors, smartboards, and electronic bulletin boards.

APPROPRIATE USE

Behind any breach of technology security is human behavior. Expectations of patrons' behavior and appropriate use of library technology are founded in respect, responsibility, and legality.

When Library Support Staff (LSS) see something, they should say something. Alert supervisors to any suspicion of misuse of technology. LSS need to be familiar with their library policy. Every library should have an **Appropriate Use Policy** (AUP) that governs the behavior of technology users. LSS are often the staff who interact and observe how patrons use library services. If staff are not knowledgeable of the AUP, they may over- or underreact to what they see, thus potentially placing both patrons and the library in peril. LSS cannot rely only on their own values or judgment when it comes to appropriate use. They must be knowledgeable of and trained in the processes and procedures of the library AUP that has had legal review.

Depending upon the library and its purpose, libraries are required by state law or governing boards to have an AUP. Most state and federal technology grants require the library's AUP for application. AUP is a contract or plan of action for how patrons accept their responsibility to use library computers that is strictly enforced by library staff. AUPs may include or reference laws or local rules.

Filters

The Children's Internet Protection Act (CIPA)[2] of 2001 requires that in exchange for federal funding of internet services, all schools and public libraries must provide filtered internet for children under age eighteen. CIPA was created with the intent of protecting minors from obscene and other material considered harmful. The act requires every library computer to be filtered, but it does not legislate to what degree the filter must be set. **Filters** can be hardware, such as a firewall, or software, such as a program that reads and compares data coming into the network. Filters do not make judgments; they are programs that search for words or patterns to compare that will either allow the file or page into the computer or not. Filters can be set to allow certain content that is age appropriate. Software filters are often imbedded in internet services such as the provider or browser. Filters are also features of local computer security programs such as Kaskersky, McAfee, Norton, etc. Filters work by blocking specific websites, phrases, or words. Filters can also block larger amounts of data or content such as pornography or obscenity. Most library administrators have the ability to exempt an occasional site. Filters help to protect a computer from incoming viruses and hackers. Library Wi-Fi networks also have filters so that children and adults who use their own devices on the library network are protected. The network manager should ensure that library patrons cannot disable its filters and to designate children and YA computers from adult because these have a more robust degree of filtering.

The AUP is the basis for determining what computer behaviors are appropriate and what are not. It should be clear to all users that if they want to use library computing services, they must abide by the AUP. Not doing so may cause loss of computing and network access. Depending upon the library, such as K–12 school media centers, patrons (and parents) may be expected to sign the AUP each year. Oher libraries may have the AUP on the website with other library policies. Table 15.1 compares examples of appropriate and inappropriate usage of library technology.

Table 15.1. Use of Library Computers

Appropriate Use	Inappropriate Use
Appropriate communications from email, blogs, etc. when using library computers	Bullying, obscene language, threats, or other unkind or illegal communications.
Educational or informational use of library computers	Use computers for gambling, Ponzi schemes, or participating in other illicit or illegal use.
Accept and use filtering software	Use virtual private networks (VPN) or other means to by-pass library content filters.
Adhere to copyright laws and library licensed agreements	Violation of law copyright or database license agreements.
Respect for other patrons' privacy and work	Trespassing or taking another's files or folders.
Abiding by rules of password security	Acquiring or using others' passwords.
Careful use of library technology equipment	Breakage or other damage to equipment.

While appropriate use is a common goal, there are differences among public, school, and academic libraries to be aware of, such as:

Public libraries: Public libraries serve all people. What is appropriate use for an adult may not be appropriate use for a child. While children and teen computers must always have filters, adults have the right to ask library staff to disable the filter during their use. Libraries strive to guarantee adults' First Amendment rights of confidentiality and freedom of speech. This does not mean obscenity or pornographic materials are tolerated in the library, but adults should be provided an element of privacy while they are using the internet.

K–12 schools: Because the majority of children in K–12 schools are underage, parents are required to cosign the child's AUP. States may require or strongly encourage schools to adopt AUPs and have them signed each year as an annual contract among the child, parent, and school. AUP is used as a way to educate children and their families about the internet and expected behaviors. Teachers and school librarians are obligated to protect children from harm while they are in school.

Academic libraries: College and university students are not underage and therefore CIPA does not apply, and computers do not legally have to be filtered to block content. Academic libraries strive to offer free and unfiltered internet to enhance learning, research, and teaching. Students and faculty should have access to controversial information and all rights protected by the First Amendment. AUPs should guarantee their freedom of information when using academic computers or Wi-Fi.

In addition to the library AUP for patrons and staff, the library staff handbook should provide procedures and guidelines for LSS to follow when there is a breach, and a supervisor is not available. It is important to have written procedures not only to ensure patrons are treated fairly and equally but also to protect LSS from taking actions that may be second-guessed if they do not adhere to library policy.

TECHNOLOGY CYBER THREATS

LSS perform their work with IT and OT and are apt to be one of the first to hear about or spot something that is not quite right. This places LSS in a key position of being a first responder to help minimize cyber threats on library IT. As first responders (or second or third), LSS should immediately report to designated staff when they suspect something is not right. Remember: *if you see something, say something!* If not already in place, LSS should advocate with supervisors the need for procedures and protocol for reporting suspicious cyber threats in the library. Who should be

Figure 15.1. Secure Library Computers. *piranka/E+ via Getty Images*

contacted and how? What if that person is not available? As libraries have emergency plans for fire or suspicious intruders, so should they have an emergency plan for suspicious IT and OT events. While the hope is that these events are not attacks, they must be investigated and dealt with quickly.

A **phishing** attack that could have been easily avoided occurred when the business manager received an email that appeared to be from the superintendent of schools, requesting a spreadsheet of personal information for all district staff that included social security numbers. Rather than picking up the phone to confirm this email with the superintendent, the business manager created the file and emailed it to the sender, only to find out that the superintendent never sent the email and that it was a phishing attack. Unfortunately, the email could not be traced or retrieved, hundreds of staff had their personal information compromised, and the business manager was terminated. We should pause before we act on even a slightly unusual request.

Libraries and schools are not the only institutions that face cyber threats. They can occur in any institution or residence. Per the Commonwealth of Massachusetts[3] we should all be aware of these prevailing IT and OT cyber threats:

- Malware: malicious code or malicious software
- Spyware: malware intended to violate privacy by invading systems to track personal activities
- Ransomware: prevents or limits users from accessing their system via malware
- Denial of service (DOS) attacks: make an online service unavailable by overwhelming it with excessive traffic from many locations and sources
- Spam: unwanted, unsolicited, or undesirable messages and emails
- Phishing: a form of social engineering, including attempts to get sensitive information

What should you do about these threats if they affect library services and users? All require training, vigilance, and strong IT support. Each threat can be minimized by a combination of strategies that library and IT staff can employ. As important as the strategies, there is also the need for patron awareness and education. LSS, for example, may offer to create a set of posters and hang them around the library or short video alerts about the cybersecurity measures patrons can take to protect themselves and their computing devices. The Commonwealth of Massachusetts not only identified cyber threats, but also provides information and measures to reduce risk. The following suggestions are adapted to the library environment for LSS to consider:

Strategies LSS can do or share to protect against malware that compromises confidentiality, integrity, or availability of data:

- Be suspicious of email attachments. Scan before saving to local or removable drives.
- Do not open certain types of files (e.g., .exe files) sent in an email.
- Restrict removable media, such as CDs or flash drives, on systems that are high risk.
- Always install updates from devices' manufacturers or operating system providers.

Strategies LSS can do or share to protect against spyware that sends pop-up ads, redirects computers to unwanted websites, monitors internet surfing, or records keystrokes which could lead to identity theft:

- Always install updates from devices' manufacturers or operating system providers.
- Correct software flaws by installing updates so that hackers cannot view or steal data.
- Use antivirus software on all devices.
- Purchase and install separate antispyware software programs.
- Download software only from trustworthy sites.
- Be sure library has its firewall on, set up properly, and updated regularly.
- Use strong methods of authentication to help keep personal information secure.
- Use passwords that are hard to guess with a combination of at least eight characters.
- Choose unique passwords for each online account staff use.
- Pay attention to where you click and who you give your information to avoid data thieves.

Strategies LSS can do or share to protect against ransomware, which requires the user to pay a ransom using online payment methods to regain access to the system or data:

- Ask library administration to provide staff awareness training in protecting the library's data.

    IT manager or outsourced support should:

    - patch operating system, software, and firmware on digital devices;
    - ensure antivirus and antimalware solutions are set to automatically update and conduct regular scans;
    - manage the use of privileged accounts—no users should be assigned administrative access unless absolutely needed, and only use administrator accounts when necessary;
    - configure access controls, including file, directory, and network share permissions appropriately;
    - disable macro scripts from office files transmitted over email;
    - implement software restriction policies or other controls to prevent programs from executing from common ransomware locations.

There are strategies for LSS to protect against website response time slowdown and preventing access to opening files or the internet during an attack. Cyber criminals develop large networks of infected computers called Botnets by planting malware. Be alert to the inability of opening particular or all websites.

IT manager or outsourced support should:

- enroll library computers and networks in a DOS protection service that detects abnormal traffic flows and redirects traffic away from your network;
- create a disaster recovery plan to ensure successful and efficient communication, mitigation, and recovery in the event of an attack;

- evaluate security settings and follow good security practices in order to minimize the access other people have to your information, as well as manage unwanted traffic;
- network traffic to be monitored via a firewall or intrusion detection system.

There are strategies LSS can do or share to protect against spammers using the web to harvest email addresses.

- Do not display personal email address on blog posts, in chat rooms, on social networking sites, or in online membership directories.
- Check the privacy policy before you submit your email address to a website. Opt-out of receiving mass emails.
- Spammers troll the internet looking for computers that lack up-to-date security software.
- Spammers connect thousands of computers into "botnet" networks that send millions of emails at once.
- Disconnect library computers when not in use to prevent them from becoming part of a botnet.
- Only download free software from sites you know and trust.

There are strategies LSS can do or share to protect against phishing attempts that appear to be from a trustworthy person or business.

- Reputational businesses do not request personal information via email.
- Use a phishing filter that web browsers build in or offer as plug-ins.
- Never follow a link to a secure site from an email—always enter the URL manually.
- Be careful what you click.
- Be careful what you share.

LSS can be informed about these practical strategies and continue to discuss them at staff meetings and with IT staff and managers. Robust cybersecurity is critically important to the operation of libraries. Unfortunately, as hackers and other data thieves and malcontents become more and more sophisticated, libraries, like other institutions that rely on IT and OT, have to be aggressively defensive.

INTEGRITY AND SECURITY OF DATA

In addition to upholding patrons' privacy, confidentiality, and adhering to safe practices and methods to maintain security of information and operational technologies, LSS also strive to protect the integrity and security of library data. LSS input, use, and share library data every day at work. In many libraries, LSS are the people who are on the forefront working with data. LSS who work intensely with data might be called database managers, digital content managers, data entry assistants, or data records controllers if they worked in other industries.

LSS protect patrons' privacy. One way they do this is to keep limited patron data on file and discard information that is unnecessary or outdated. Because LSS most likely collect patrons' data at the circulation desk, work in accounting or billing, or help patrons with internet searches, they have a responsibility to follow strict protocols and methods to ensure data integrity. The term "integrity," as it relates to technology, means guarding against improper information modification or destruction, and includes ensuring **information nonrepudiation** and authenticity.[4] When working with library data, LSS should ask themselves:

1. Am I confident the modifications I am about to make are accurate and proper? If there are any doubts, seek confirmation or assistance.
2. If as part of my work I am to delete or destroy library records or data, do I have supervisor approval or authorization? If not, seek it before acting.
3. Do I have assurance that the sender of information is provided with proof of delivery and the recipient is provided with proof of the sender's identity, so neither can later deny having processed the information[5]?

In addition to asking these questions, LSS can use the following methods to help secure library data:

1. Be professional in handling of patrons' data and uphold confidentiality of all library records, including patrons' circulation and use of passwords. Close files when not in use and never share patron data with outside sources.
2. If the library is a member of a consortia, do not access other libraries' patron records.
3. Report suspicious patron or staff activity or corruption of files on any of the library computer systems or servers. Backup your work and use cloud computing properly.
4. Do not utilize library data for unauthorized purposes. Never ask to use another's password or authorization code to access files or accounts. If you know these practices are occurring, report them immediately to a supervisor.
5. Check that library computers do not store web search history, cookies, or cached files. Neither local nor external electronic systems used by the library should collect patron identifiable information through logging or tracking email, chat room use, web browsing, cookies, middleware, or other technology usage. If you suspect this is happening, discuss with a supervisor and IT manager.

Data integrity and cybersecurity occurs when all library staff are trained and committed to upholding patrons' privacy and confidentiality. LSS collect personal patron data for multiple purposes. When there is no need to retain personal data, it should be purged. Never should patron data be made accessible to outside sources or used in any other way than for the library business it was intended for when it was collected. Maintaining the integrity and security of data is both a legal and ethical responsibility of LSS.

CHAPTER SUMMARY

LSS who know basic principles and best practices discussed in this chapter have a major role in ensuring the integrity of library data and the confidentiality of user activities. LSS are on the forefront of creating, inputting, editing, and using library information and operational systems in their work and with patrons. Because of this LSS should know and practice appropriate use of technologies and share these concepts with other staff and patrons. Issues concerning the appropriate use of technology by different user groups should be discussed and policies and procedures put in place so that all staff, including LSS, can treat patrons fairly and equally when issues arise.

LSS can greatly contribute to the proper behaviors and handling of library data. If they see something that is not right, they should immediately say something because for library cybersecurity to work, it needs knowledgeable and observant LSS to be actively involved.

DISCUSSION QUESTIONS

1. What are the key issues around the cybersecurity of library IT and OT today?
2. Why is it important for libraries to have appropriate use policies? Whom do the policies protect?
3. How can LSS support the integrity of data in their workplace?

ACTIVITY

Arrange an interview with the library IT manager or administrator in the library you work at or frequent about cybersecurity issues that may occur with library IT and OT. Ask about appropriate use expectations. What is being done to avoid future threats? What can LSS do to help combat breaches in security, data integrity, and other threats or behaviors?

Write a report of your interview. At the conclusion of the report, state your own ideas about how to improve the library cybersecurity. Share your report with your library supervisor and others who are interested or responsible for library cybersecurity.

NOTES

1. Gartner, Inc., "Cybersecurity," Gartner Glossary, last modified 2020, accessed October 29, 2020, https://www.gartner.com/en/information-technology/glossary/cybersecurity.

2. American Library Association, "The Children's Internet Protection Act (CIPA)," Issues & Advocacy, last modified 2020, accessed November 2, 2020, http://www.ala.org/advocacy/advleg/federallegislation/cipa.

3. Commonwealth of Massachusetts, "Know the Types of Cyber Threats," Mass.gov, last modified 2020, accessed November 3, 2020, https://www.mass.gov/service-details/know-the-types-of-cyber-threats.

4. National Institute of Standards and Technology - US Department of Commerce, "Computer Security Resource Center," Information Technology Laboratory, last modified 2020, accessed November 4, 2020, https://csrc.nist.gov/glossary/term/integrity.

5. National Institute of Standards and Technology - US Department of Commerce, "Computer Security Resource Center," Information Technology Laboratory, last modified 2020, accessed November 4, 2020, https://csrc.nist.gov/glossary/term/non_repudiation.

REFERENCES, SUGGESTED READINGS, AND WEBSITES

American Library Association. "The Children's Internet Protection Act (CIPA)." Issues & Advocacy. Last modified 2020. Accessed November 2, 2020. http://www.ala.org/advocacy/advleg/federallegislation/cipa.

———. "Keeping Up With . . . Cybersecurity, Usability, and Privacy." ACRL. Last modified 2020. Accessed October 26, 2020. http://www.ala.org/acrl/publications/keeping_up_with/cybersecurity.

———. "Professional Ethics." Tools, Publications, and Resources. Last modified 2020. Accessed November 2, 2020. http://www.ala.org/tools/ethics.

"Awareness, Planning, Resilience: Thoughts on Libraries' Cyber Defense in 2020." *Library Policy and Advocacy Blog*. Accessed March 27, 2020. https://blogs.ifla.org/lpa/2020/03/27/awareness-planning-resilience-thoughts-on-libraries-cyber-defense-in-2020/. IFLA

Ayala, Daniel. "Security and Privacy for Libraries in 2017." *Online Searcher* 41, no. 3 (May/June 2017): 48–52. https://search.ebscohost.com/login.aspx?direct=true&AuthType=cookie,ip,cpid&custid=cs.

Briney, Kristin. "Data Management Practices in Academic Library Learning Analytics: A Critical Review." *Journal of Librarianship & Scholarly Communication* 7, no. 1 (January 2019): 1–39. https://search.ebscohost.com/login.aspx?direct=true&AuthType=cookie,ip,cpid&custid=csl&db=aph&AN=141483942&site=ehost-live&scope=site.

Commonwealth of Massachusetts. "Know the Types of Cyber Threats." Mass.gov. Last modified 2020. Accessed November 3, 2020. https://www.mass.gov/service-details/know-the-types-of-cyber-threats.

Gartner, Inc. "Cybersecurity." Gartner Glossary. Last modified 2020. Accessed October 29, 2020. https://www.gartner.com/en/information-technology/glossary/cybersecurity.

Hennig, Nicole. *Privacy and Security Online: Best Practices for Cybersecurity*. N.p.: Library Technology Reports, 2018. https://search.ebscohost.com/login.aspx?direct=true&AuthType=cookie,ip,cpid&custid=csl&db=aph&AN=128707555&site=ehost-live&scope=site.

"Is It Cybersecurity or Cyber Security?" *University of Nevada* (blog). Entry posted 2020. Accessed October 29, 2020. https://onlinedegrees.unr.edu/blog/cybersecurity-or-cyber-security/.

National Institute of Standards and Technology - US Department of Commerce. "Computer Security Resource Center." Information Technology Laboratory. Last modified 2020. Accessed November 4, 2020. https://csrc.nist.gov/glossary/term/non_repudiation.

———. "Computer Security Resource Center." Information Technology Laboratory. Last modified 2020. Accessed November 4, 2020. https://csrc.nist.gov/glossary/term/integrity.

United States Department of Justice. "Incidents of Ransomware on the Rise: Protect Your Organization." FBI News. Last modified April 29, 2016. Accessed November 4, 2020. https://www.fbi.gov/news/stories/incidents-of-ransomware-on-the-rise.

———. "Spear Phishers." FBI News. Accessed November 4, 2020. https://archives.fbi.gov/archives/news/stories/2009/april/spearphishing_040109.

CHAPTER 16

The Future of Library Technologies

Library Support Staff (LSS) know the general trends and developments in technology applications for library functions and services.
LSS demonstrate flexibility in adapting to new technology.

Topics Covered in This Chapter
Library Technology Innovations
    Broadband
    Artificial Intelligence
    Virtual Environments
    Robotics
    Service Platforms and Discovery Systems

Key Terms
Innovation: Using technology in creative ways to augment or improve upon its services.
Interoperability: The ability for two or more unlike or different network, computer, or data systems to effectively communicate with each other to provide comprehensive and seamless searching capabilities.
Machine learning: Systems that use algorithms and statistics to find patterns in massive amounts of data—numbers, words, images, clicks, etc.—to make computer-generated decisions and recommendations.
Natural language: Common, everyday words spoken to computing devices to execute a search or a command.
Personal characteristics: Individual or innate qualities that are unique to each person that spur them to learn, achieve, or perform to a high standard or level.

> *Telepresence:* Technologies that allow people to interact with a different place as if they were there.
> *Virtual reality:* An artificial environment created by a computer that, when wearing a sensory device that authenticates sights and sounds, the user experience is close to real life.
> *Virtual voice assistants:* In contrast to using a keyboard, mouse, or touchscreen, these devices let users interact with computing devices through natural spoken language speech.

Chapters 1 through 15 focus on key technologies currently used in libraries and those that will be implemented well into the future. This final chapter on the future of library technologies is not solely about more hardware and software. Rather, its dual focus is (1) how Library Support Staff (LSS) can prepare themselves to lead and support technology innovation in libraries and (2) examples of technologies LSS can expect in the next decade.

Attempting to predict the future of technology is a bold gesture. Who could have foreseen the pandemic that, in the matter of weeks, shuttered nations and economies around the globe? Yet it was the technology of virtual meetings, social media, and the internet that allowed many, including librarians, to continue to remotely meet and productively work. Technologies allowed schools, universities, health care, and other professionals to provide their critical services when buildings had to be shuttered and people socially distanced.

The key idea is that while the technology of virtual meetings existed, it had never been employed to such a useful and creative extent. It was the human approach to problem solving that fast-tracked enormous use of virtual meetings. Technology is most successful when people use it in innovative ways to solve problems or to improve lives. Similarly, LSS are in the right position to guide and support new uses of technologies to improve library services. LSS have much to contribute to its **innovation** to improve services today and well into the future.

LIBRARY TECHNOLOGY INNOVATIONS

How often do we hear the expression, "The future is now"? LSS work in a dynamic environment where change is a matter of course. LSS adapt to upgrades, new systems, and new ways to use existing technology, such as with virtual meetings, online programming, and distance learning. Our customers look to LSS to guide and support them with library technology.

Many of the technologies that are already mentioned in this book such as open source software, cloud computing, networks, robotics, digital media, and mobile devices, will be with us well into the years to come. These and many more current technologies will continue to be refined and improved upon. Smaller, lighter, faster, and cheaper are all factors that influence innovation. The more recent introductions of smart technologies with artificial intelligence, robotics, tracking, and natural language for searching will impact how LSS work and serve their customers.

Broadband

Underlying innovation is improved broadband network speed. At the time of this writing 4G is the industry standard that is being replaced by a ten-times faster speed network of 5G. The 5G network will be faster, more reliable, and able to process data at almost impossible speed and will change our use of the internet. We will be able to have it control and deliver critical services and manage devices in our daily lives. With the enhancements of the 5G network, we will move into a world of the Internet of Things (IoT) where we will connect driverless cars to global transportation networks. The next generation, 6G, is planned for 2030 and that will be, again, ten-times faster than 5G. Based on this model, anticipate that every ten years internet and network speed will increase minimally by a factor of ten.

There are real concerns about the pace and availability of broadband that favors middle- and upper-class urban and suburban areas over rural communities. Full participation in American society requires the ability to access and use digital content and technologies. However, minorities, the elderly, rural residents, and those with lower levels of education and income are less likely than others to have broadband service at home.[1] Today, libraries have a significant role, and even more so in the future, to provide digital access that impacts the health and vitality of all communities.

Artificial Intelligence

As we saw in chapters 8 and 13, 5G will support the innovation of artificial intelligence (AI) and IoT. Automated and robotic tools will "smartly" perform manual and computational work.[2] AI is packed with machine learning, or algorithms, that propose many reasonable options that computers "learn" to select from to best fit the situation. AI and **machine learning** is being used in some areas of the finance industry. Machine learning tracks how asset prices move when officials use those words in speeches and other public comments. By using AI in this way, banks have an early warning when the Fed and other central banks are preparing a policy shift that may affect financial assets.[3] AI, IoT, and machine learning will change how libraries currently perform their work. For example, circulation will change with robotic check-in, shelving, and inventory control.

Traditional reference work will also change with smarter searching that uses computer vision and **natural language**.[4] Computer vision models are currently being used by large online retailers to automate the process of assigning keyword descriptions to inventory. The systems are designed to "see" products and label them with attributes as catalogers currently do with library and museum items. While not yet perfect, future algorithms will be refined to produce more reliable search results using natural language.

Natural language are the ordinary words used by people. Keyword searching, while incredibly effective, misses the mark for many. This is because keywords have

Figure 16.1. Future Library Innovation. *Yuichiro Chino/Moment via Getty Images*

to be part of the catalog or metadata record. The keyword has to be included in the item record or the particular website metadata. Natural language works differently. AI that use algorithms will be trained to determine a user's intention. It will link natural language that aren't currently attached to items. These words have been unsuccessfully used "around" a topic. The AI computer remembers the users and their search words and will create patterns of association with what the speaker intends to find. Eventually, the computer "learns" the associations for the speaker and will point to the desired object that he describes in his natural language. The personalization of AI narrows the query to reflect the user's preferences, search habits, and personal data. Today, this is beginning to take place in the retail industry. It is within the realm of imagination that in the future AI may be how most customers search the internet and library items.

Virtual Environments

As found during the pandemic, much work can take place in remote or virtual environments away from the place of business. Currently, most people who work remotely are in white-collar professions where their work does not require the manipulation of things. Librarians were able to do some of their work remotely, such as create programs, circulate e-books, provide reference using databases, and provide other online information services. However, when the library building is closed, the collections inside remain on the shelves.

A future type of remote work being piloted is **telepresence**.[5] Telepresence includes any technology that allows a person to interact with a different place as

Figure 16.2. Learning with Virtual Reality. *FG Trade/E+ via Getty Images*

if they were there. Coupled with robotics, drones, virtual meetings, and other once unimaginable technologies, telepresence has the potential to change how almost every business, including libraries, conduct their work. For example, a type of telepresence is where a worker wears smart glasses to share what they are seeing with a remote expert who can speak to them and send images directly to the glasses to help the worker handle the problem. Remote expertise with smart glasses is like screen sharing in the real world. Google Glass Enterprise Edition 2 is a wearable device that provides hands-on workers and remote professionals voice-activated assistance.

Virtual and extended reality headsets increase user engagement. Librarians may use extended reality for in-house activities such as storytelling, virtual travel, virtual gaming, and the development of new skills. In some professions, such as medicine, extended reality provides alternatives to practicing surgery and other health training measures that once could only be done on human subjects.

Virtual reality has the potential to also be used for library instruction that would make it authentic and interesting. Replacing the traditional lectures, students could participate via virtual reality in real-life, immersive, and interesting situations that could draw on what they already know as new skills are learned.[6] Students could be presented with having to make choices about safe practices around topics they are familiar with. Once that mindset is created, they could then participate in situational choices of information from untrustworthy to peer review.

The future holds many innovative uses of virtual environments. When opportunities arise, LSS may volunteer to participate in pilot applications so that they will have a preview of future uses of these technologies.

Robotics

Robots are commonly employed in health care, manufacturing, retail, household services, and numerous other areas. Robots are computing devices that are programmed to do a specific array of complex actions, processes, and tasks. Today, many large public and academic libraries, with Radio Frequency Identification, use robotic systems to check-in, sort, organize, and perform off-site shelving. It is expected that there are many tasks in libraries that will be done robotically in the future.

LSS should not fear of being replaced by robots. Like in other industries, robotics can be used to free LSS from repetitive tasks in order to work more directly with customers. Robotics will expand in STEAM learning resources in public makerspaces, K–12 schools, and academic libraries. Social robots are a novelty, and some libraries are using them as a way to greet and engage their patrons in this new technology. Robots are beginning to be useful with simple reference requests, especially in the form of online chatbots where people can reach them 24/7. Robots can also be used to engage people in library programs, such as "reading" to children, or performing reader's advisory. As robots are programmed with advancing AI features and functions, librarians will find purposeful uses for them that, in turn, will enable the staff to engage with patrons more fully in programming, reference, and other information needs.[7]

Today, a common type of robotics is **virtual voice assistants**, which have become common in our daily lives with Alexa, Siri, Google Assistant, Cortana, and others that interact with computers with speech instead of keyboards. As they continue to evolve, virtual voice assistants will become a common tool to accomplishing most types of computer or device interaction. Future voice assistants[8] may be:

- Ubiquitous: voice assistants will be embedded in appliances and wearable gadgets.
- Proactive: voice assistants will grow smart enough to anticipate our needs.
- Stronger AI: conversational AI will learn from historical interactions and adapt to individual needs based on context and nuance.
- Available across devices: voice assistants will not be specific to one device but rather a single voice assistant will be used across appliances, IoTs, and smart devices.
- Multisensory: voice assistants will sense users' intent through voice, gesture, and touch.
- Comprehensive: voice assistants will be able to simultaneously access locally desensitized data as well as data stored centrally in a cloud.

Voice technology as we know it today will evolve in the future to combine with other platforms, such as virtual reality and Library Service Platforms and discovery systems to provide an immersive or total user experience.

Trending is a way to predict the future by describing what is currently popular or discussed online, especially in social media. Google Trends, YouTube Trends, BuzzFeed Trending, and Trending on Twitter are just a few of the places that seek our attention and input about all kinds of current and future topics. Look around to see what is trending. Are there certain trends that you follow, such as in books, music, film, clothing, food, or gaming? So, too, with today's technology. What technology do patrons use and want more of? How do they use their own devices in the library? What can the library do to give them a better experience? Based on what LSS observe happening today, they can reasonably predict how people will use technology in the near future. LSS can share their observations with IT staff and library management who do not have the opportunity to work as directly with patrons.

LSS can prepare for the future by being active technology users today who participate on their local planning teams. Teams need members who understand the need for libraries to purchase technology that is flexible and easily upgraded. Libraries need technology that will have the capacity to interoperate with other systems. LSS can ask questions about how soon any purchase may become obsolete, be it an ILS, a social robot, or a cart of mobile devices. Just as we do when purchasing an automobile, research the vendor to learn what is upcoming in their pipeline. Expect components will have to be replaced. How easy will it be to upgrade to new standards and future features?[9] Is it time to phase out a product that is no longer serving the needs of the customers and develop a timeline for replacement? Share opinions and examples of what works well and what does not about the current technology you work with. LSS have authentic experience and valuable advice about how to shape the future of library technology.

CHAPTER SUMMARY

This text concludes with observation, predictions, and encouragement for LSS to become engaged and involved in identifying general trends and future developments in technology applications for library functions and services. LSS are in pivotal positions of working directly with their customers being called upon to support and use numerous technologies. LSS are in key positions to influence the purpose of future technologies and how they can be used. When LSS have the **personal characteristics**, knowledge, and work in collaboration with others, they have the skills and flexibility to adapt to new technology.

DISCUSSION QUESTIONS

1. In what ways will artificial intelligence and robotics change library services?
2. How will virtual environments influence change in how LSS work?
3. What are your predictions for library technology in the next five years? Ten years?
4. What steps should LSS take today to be prepared to use and support library technology tomorrow?

ACTIVITY

Using the Discussion Questions plan two interviews: one with the library IT manager and the other with an LSS who has an interest in technology improvements. Ask each person the questions to obtain two differing points of view. Based on the results of the interviews, write a two-page report of the findings. Were the answers what you expected? Based on the subjects' predictions, what may the technology of this library look like and how will it change current library services in five years? Ten years?

NOTES

1. Institute of Museums and Library Services, "Priority Areas," Institute of Museums and Library Services, last modified 2020, accessed November 10, 2020, https://www.imls.gov/our-work/priority-areas.

2. Patricia Anderson and Emily Hurst, "From Enhanced Collaborations to Space Advancements: Technologies to Bring Libraries (and Librarians) Full Circle and into the Future," *Journal of the Medical Library Association* 107, no. 4 (October 2019): https://search.ebscohost.com/login.aspx?direct=true&AuthType=cookie,ip,cpid&custid=csl&db=aph&AN=138975520&site=ehost-live&scope=site.

3. J. Hookway, "Struggling to Decode the Fed?" *Wall Street Journal*, February 10, 2020, https://search.proquest.com/docview/2352538379?accountid=46995.

4. A. Loten, "In Search of Better Online Recommendations," *Wall Street Journal*, November 4, 2020, sec. R, [Page 2], https://search.proquest.com/docview/2457192065?accountid=46995.

5. C. Mims, "Remote Work Won't Be Just for White-Color Workers," *Wall Street Journal*, October 23, 2020, sec. R, https://search.proquest.com/docview/2453617645?accountid=46995.

6. "What the Future Holds," *American Libraries* 51, no. 6 (June 2020): https://search.ebscohost.com/login.aspx?direct=true&AuthType=cookie,ip,cpid&custid=csl&db=aph&AN=143591353&site=ehost-live&scope=site.

7. "What the Future Holds," *American Libraries* 51, no. 6 (June 2020): [Page 33–34], https://search.ebscohost.com/login.aspx?direct=true&AuthType=cookie,ip,cpid&custid=csl&db=aph&AN=143591353&site=ehost-live&scope=site.

8. Shih Win and Erin Rivero, "Virtual Voice Assistants," *Library Technology Reports* 56, no. 4 (May/June 2020): https://search.ebscohost.com/login.aspx?direct=true&AuthType=cookie,ip,cpid&custid=csl&db=aph&AN=143698238&site=ehost-live&scope=site.

9. Marshall Breeding, "Technology Strategies for an Uncertain Future," *Computers in Libraries* 40, no. 7 (October 2020): [Page 8–9], https://search.ebscohost.com/login.aspx?direct=true&AuthType=cookie,ip,cpid&custid=csl&db=aph&AN=146522235&site=ehost-live&scope=site.

REFERENCES, SUGGESTED READINGS, AND WEBSITES

Anderson, Patricia, and Emily Hurst. "From Enhanced Collaborations to Space Advancements: Technologies to Bring Libraries (and Librarians) Full Circle and into the Future." *Journal of the Medical Library Association* 107, no. 4 (October 2019): 595–96. https://search.ebscohost.com/login.aspx?direct=true&AuthType=cookie,ip,cpid&custid=csl&db=aph&AN=138975520&site=ehost-live&scope=site.

Association of Research Libraries. "Future Themes and Forecasts for Research Libraries and Emerging Technologies." Association of Research Libraries. Last modified 2020. Accessed November 10, 2020. https://www.arl.org/resources/future-themes-and-forecasts-for-research-libraries-and-emerging-technologies/.

Breeding, Marshall. "Library Systems Report: Cycles of Innovation." *American Libraries* 50, no. 5 (May 2019). https://search.ebscohost.com/login.aspx?direct=true&AuthType=cookie,ip,cpid&custid=cs.

———. "Technology Strategies for an Uncertain Future." *Computers in Libraries* 40, no. 7 (October 2020): 9–10. https://search.ebscohost.com/login.aspx?direct=true&AuthType=cookie,ip,cpid&custid=csl&db=aph&AN=146522235&site=ehost-live&scope=site.

Frost, Megan, Michael Goates, Sarah Cheng, and Jed Johnston. "Virtual Reality: A Survey of Use at an Academic Library." *Information Technology & Libraries* 39, no. 1 (2020): 1–12. https://search.ebscohost.com/login.aspx?direct=true&AuthType=cookie,ip,cpid&custid=csl&db=aph&AN=142453828&site=ehost-live&scope=site.

Hookway, J. "Struggling to Decode the Fed?" *Wall Street Journal*, February 10, 2020. https://search.proquest.com/docview/2352538379?accountid=46995.

Institute of Museums and Library Services. "Priority Areas." Institute of Museums and Library Services. Last modified 2020. Accessed November 10, 2020. https://www.imls.gov/our-work/priority-areas.

Loten, A. "In Search of Better Online Recommendations." *Wall Street Journal*, November 4, 2020, sec. R, 2. https://search.proquest.com/docview/2457192065?accountid=46995.

Mims, C. "Remote Work Won't Be Just for White-Color Workers." *Wall Street Journal*, October 23, 2020, sec. R, 4–5. https://search.proquest.com/docview/2453617645?accountid=46995.

"What the Future Holds." *American Libraries* 51, no. 6 (June 2020): 32–36. https://search.ebscohost.com/login.aspx?direct=true&AuthType=cookie,ip,cpid&custid=csl&db=aph&AN=143591353&site=ehost-live&scope=site.

Win, Shih, and Erin Rivero. "Virtual Voice Assistants." *Library Technology Reports* 56, no. 4 (May/June 2020): 1–40. https://search.ebscohost.com/login.aspx?direct=true&AuthType=cookie,ip,cpid&custid=csl&db=aph&AN=143698238&site=ehost-live&scope=site.

Glossary

3-D Printers: Computer driven machines used to create models and parts by layering and building up plastic or other materials to make a specific shape.

Analog: Libraries circulated these sound and film tapes for many years. Recorded in a continuous line with a beginning and end, one had to play or fast forward from the beginning of the tape to find a certain frame or location.

Analytics: The measurement of a social media and how it is used provides insight to library administrators about its success as a communication and collaboration tool for the library.

Appropriate Use Policy: Every library should have an AUP for both staff and patrons that specifies appropriate and inappropriate behaviors that are agreed to prior to using the library technologies.

Apps: An abbreviation for the word applications, this term is another name for computer programs first coined by Apple.

Assistive technology: Electronic solutions that enable people with disabilities to live independently. The term "adaptive technology" is sometimes used in a similar way.

Barcode: Often in the form of a label that represents data in a machine-readable form, these are used by libraries to keep track of items and patron information.

Bluetooth: A type of wireless service that uses short-range radio waves, it allows two devices located in close proximity to communicate with each other.

Broadband: Another term for the various technologies that provide high speed internet access.

Browser: The application or program on a computer that allows library users and staff to access and view websites from the internet.

Cellular: Technology that facilitates mobile device communications, especially with smartphones, over a specific area of coverage using transceivers on towers for sending and receiving data.

Central processing unit: Executes instructions organized in programs or software that tell the computer what to do.

Channels: Folders or unique places within the social network created around a special topic or for a particular audience or group to have better focus of conversation and collaboration.

Children's Internet Protection Act: Also known as CIPA, this federal legislation requires libraries and schools that receive internet funding to have filters on all computers being used by children under the age of eighteen.

Circuit kits: Found in library makerspaces, these are popular plastic kits that allow users to connect circuits of electricity to provide energy to lights, small motors, and other devices by snapping together appropriate parts rather than by solder.

Closed source: Software that is proprietary that has significant restrictions in the license that limits the ways the library can use it.

The Cloud: Resources such as servers and other infrastructure provided mostly offsite for users to retrieve programs and applications as well as to share and store files and data.

CNC machine: Makes parts for almost every industry out of plastics, metals, aluminum, wood, and many other hard materials. "CNC" stands for Computer Numerical Control. It is the process of using a computer-driven machine tool to produce a part out of solid material in a different shape.

Coding: The creation of taking ideas in everyday language and converting them into a specific set of forms or symbols that will be understood by either another person or interpreted by a computer or machine.

Computer language: Unique sets of codes or instructions used for communicating to the computer.

Copyright: The right given by the US government to the owner to control the sale and use of the software.

Cost-benefit: An analytical process used to compare price and value.

Cybersecurity: The combination of people, policies' processes, and technologies libraries and other institutions use to protect their information and operational technologies.

Device driver: A type of utility software application or program, a driver is necessary for printers, scanners, and other device peripherals to interact with computers to perform their functions.

Digital: This standard of today's technology uses binary code to create, store, and process data. Computers read data that is either expressed as "on" (1) or "off" (0). Alphabets and numbers are converted into binary code. Searching and other functions are much more efficient with digital than analog.

Digital Audio Workstation: Also referred to as a DAW, the station supports creating and editing digital music.

Digitization: The process of converting information and other data into bits and bytes so that it can be understood and used by computers.

Discovery: A name for systems that seamlessly allow users to search multiple databases, catalogs, websites, and other online resources simultaneously.

E-reader: Portable hardware device designed for reading digital publications.

Federated search: Also known as a metasearch, the user can find results from multiple databases and resources through a single search query.

File: A set of data created and saved with a program that needs either the program or a compatible one to open, use, or edit the data.

File extension: Three or four letters at the end of a file name that identify the type of program that was used to create the file.

Filters: Hardware, such as firewalls, or software, such as programs that reads and manipulates the input data coming into the network to compare it to what is an appropriate pattern. If it is not appropriate, it removes or blocks the data before it comes to the user.

Functionality: The name for the capability of library work the computers and software are able to perform.

Gateway: Z39.50 is a protocol developed for libraries to directly connect to other online catalogs as well as to vendor clouds of resources.

Hotspot: A small boxlike device, it is part of a cell phone data plan that converts cellular service into Wi-Fi internet. Many libraries lend hotspots to provide patrons portable Internet service.

Inclusive learning: An environment where all participants are fully respected and are open to ideas, perspectives, and ways of thinking that are distinct from their own.

Information nonrepudiation: LSS have assurance that the sender of information is provided with proof of delivery and the recipient is provided with proof of the sender's identity, so neither can later deny having processed the information.

Innovation: Libraries use technology in creative ways to augment or improve upon its services.

Instruction sets: A main category of software, these are commands that are built into the central processing unit of the computer to command routine tasks.

Integrated Library System: Known more commonly in libraries as the ILS, it is the software and hardware that manages circulation, cataloging, public online catalog, serials, acquisitions, etc.

Internet Service Provider: Also known as ISP, these are the companies that sell or provide for free internet access for library users and staff.

Interoperability: The property that allows for the unrestricted sharing of resources between different systems and computing devices or components. Libraries strive to provide internet access for all types of user devices and mobile equipment.

Library services platform: Also referred to as LSP, this is the direction libraries are moving toward where the online catalog, databases, software, and many other information services are outsourced and available in a seamless manner.

Library Support Staff: Used by the American Library Association for people who work in libraries who do not have graduate library degrees. They comprise approximately 85 percent of library workers performing a wide variety of duties and services.

License: In terms of software, it is a legally binding agreement that specifies how the software can be used by the library.

Listservs: Used by library staff these are applications that deliver email messages on a topic or theme automatically to subscribers on the electronic list.

Machine language: Also known as object code, this is the binary code made up of strings of 0s and 1s used to command computers to execute program software.

Machine learning: Systems that use algorithms and statistics to find patterns in massive amounts of data—numbers, words, images, clicks, etc. to make computer generated decisions and recommendations.

Mainframe computer: Early computers known for their large size, reliability, high level of processing power, and extensive amount of storage.

Makerspace: A designated work or lab area where library users are invited to innovate, create, solve problems, and enhance their STEAM knowledge and skills in self-paced, collaborative, hands-on ways.

Malware: Malicious software that enters a computer without the user's consent to damage files, software, and pose theft or security threats.

Mapping: Referring to a network, this is the process of creating a link to another computer, a printer, or shared devices.

Materials Safety Data Sheets: Also known as MSDS, these are safety documents required by the Occupational Safety and Health Administration that contain data about the physical properties of a particular hazardous substance.

Metrics: Statistics that measure the performance of posts, clicks, likes, etc. that help libraries understand how their social network accounts are being used.

Mobile devices: Also known as smart devices, these are handheld tablets, smartphones, or other computing equipment that are portable, lightweight, and compact.

Modules: A software package of resources with a distinct service such as circulation or cataloging.

Natural language: Common, everyday words spoken to computing devices to execute a search or a command.

Needs assessment: Staff, patrons, and community thoughtfully and systematically analyze and determine what they currently have and what would be required to improve technology services.

Network infrastructure: The equipment, wiring, software, and other resources needed to move data to and from outside providers of services like the internet or subscription databases to the patron user.

Object code: Also known as machine or binary code, source code is translated into this machine language so that computers can execute software.

Open source: Software that is freely shared or at a very low cost with libraries to manage circulation, cataloging, and other modules and functions of service.

Operating system: Software that manages the computer's memory and processes, as well as all of its software and hardware.

Participants: People who are invited and have access to a specific online meeting.

Peer collaboration: LSS work together in teams in order to accomplish tasks, using the suggestions and recommendations of others to improve the quality of their work. Likewise, LSS knowledge and skills of coding and robotics is enhanced when they learn together with others.

Peripherals: Any external devices that provide input and output for the computer.

Personal characteristics: Individual or innate qualities that are unique to each person that spurs them to learn, achieve, or perform to a high standard or level.

Phishing: Fraudulent attempts using email to get personal or sensitive information.

Platform: A hardware device, such as a desktop or laptop computer that works with a certain type of operating system and has a central processing unit.

Podcasts: The word is derived from a combination of *iPod* and *broadcast*. These are digital recordings of interviews or informative discussions about a topic or theme.

Program: One of the main categories of software, this is a set of statements or instructions to be used directly or indirectly in a computer to bring about a certain result.

Programming: Services and events that libraries plan, schedule, lead, or host that engage community involvement and learning.

Programming language: The source code written in human-readable instructions according to a particular format or configuration.

Proprietary: Closed-sourced software that libraries purchase that is copyrighted and licensed.

Public access: Cable companies are required by law to provide educational and local municipal channels for the community.

Public Access Catalogs: Also called PACs, these terminals have access to the library catalog on the main computer or server with limited functionality.

Public domain: Term given when everyone has equal rights to an item or property.

Release: New software or revisions to existing software that is meant to correct and fix a problem or add new features and enhancements to the current version.

Robotics: The result of applying computer code to instruct a device to perform a task or take an action.

Scripts: The lines of computer language that together make up a program.

Smart device: Another term for a small portable computer such as a smartphone, smart watch, etc.

Social media: Forms of electronic communication such as websites for social networking and microblogging through which users create online communities to share information, ideas, personal messages, videos, and other content.

Social networks: Dedicated website or other application that enables users to communicate with each other by posting information, comments, messages, images, etc.

Software: A set of instructions or programs that instruct computers to do a specific task.

Source code: Lists of human-readable instructions are written by a programmer when developing a computer program or software.

STEAM: In addition to the STEM areas of study, both visual and practical arts are included as essential courses of study.

STEM: The acronym for four areas of education: science, technology, engineering, and mathematics.

Strategic plan: Fundamental to the existence of the library, this type of plan states its mission, vision, values, and long-term goals.

Streamed: A method to transmit or receive audio and video data over a computer network as a steady, continuous flow that allows playback to start while the rest of the data is still being received.

Streaming video: Rather than purchasing DVDs, libraries subscribe for the rights to allow patrons to view, on their own devices, movies, programs, and documentaries via a network.

Supply chain: A process that involves a series of steps to get a product or service to the customer.

Synchronization: Through an application a device can transfer and receive data from applications on anther device or computer so that both have the same information.

Technology plan: The result of a process of determining how the library can best use technology to further its mission.

Telepresence: Technologies that allow people to interact with a different place as if they were there.

Transceiver: A device that can both transmit and receive communications, such as a combined radio transmitter and receiver.

Utilities: Programs that help and support the performance and functionality of computers for users.

Vendor host: In cloud computing this is a company or individual who contracts cloud services with libraries who access their software and content remotely.

Version: Library software or ILS modules that are significantly rewritten or revised.

Videoconferencing: Libraries conduct a meeting between two or more participants at different sites by using computer networks to transmit audio and video data.

Virtual reality: An artificial environment created by a computer that, when wearing a sensory device that authenticates sights and sounds, the user experience is close to real life.

Virtual voice assistants: In contrast to using a keyboard, mouse, or touchscreen, these devices let users interact with computing devices through natural spoken language speech.

Virtualization: The process that allows the sharing of applications to multiple customers and companies.

Webinars: Online seminars, workshops, or classes that are conducted over the internet for the purpose of instruction and new learning.

Index

3-D printer, 23, 125, 127, 131–133
4G, 112–113, 173
5G, 112–113, 173

acquisitions, 39, 40–41, 43, 67–68
adaptive technology. See assistive technology
addiction to social media, 105
Adobe, 35, 52, 131, 157
AI. See artificial intelligence
ALA. See American Library Association
Amazon, 22, 67, 116–118, 150, 153,
American Library Association, ii, xiii, xvii, 3, 25, 100, 128, 142
analog, 3–4, 76–77, 131, 157
analytics, 97, 103
Apple, 20–22, 24–26, 29–33, 68, 75, 117–118, 150, 152
Appropriate Use Policy, 161–164
apps, 29–30, 33, 111–112, 117–119
artificial intelligence, 98, 112, 171–173
assessment, 11, 14–15.
 See also needs assessment
ASGCLA. See Association of Specialized Government and Cooperative Library Agencies
assistive technology, 19, 25
Association of Specialized Government and Cooperative Library Agencies, 25
Audacity, 35, 151–153, 157
AUP. See Appropriate Use Policy
automation, 40–42, 140
avatar, 98

barcode, 41, 68
binary code, 3, 22, 51–52, 139, 153
blog, 57, 81
Bluetooth, 23–24, 73, 79, 113
broadband, 73, 75–76, 78–79, 173
browser, 21, 31, 35–36, 70, 73, 75, 162, 167
bugs, 53, 55

C++, 52, 144
cable, 24, 75–77, 149, 153, 155, 157
cellular, 111–112
central processing unit, 19, 20, 22, 30–32, 52
channel, 90, 97–100, 155
chatbox, 98
Children's Internet Protection Act, 78, 161–162, 164
CIPA. See Children's Internet Protection Act
circuit kits, 125, 131
circulation, 5–6, 22–23, 39–41, 43, 54, 64, 67–68, 111, 114–115, 162, 167, 173
clickbait, 98
closed source, xv, 51–53
cloud computing, xv, 41, 63–70, 117, 168, 172
clouds, 64, 68, 71, 118, 153
CNC machine, 125, 130
coding, xvi, 22, 35, 52, 137–144
collaboration, 35, 55–56, 97, 99, 129, 133.
 See also peer collaboration
collaborative teamwork, 171
communication, 15, 46, 52, 57, 64, 68, 79, 86, 97–99, 101, 104–105, 111, 138, 163, 166

components, 20, 22, 24, 30–31, 74, 76–77
computer language, 29–31, 75, 144
copyright, xv, 29, 36, 52–55, 101, 163
cost-benefit, 51, 53
CPU. See central processing unit
crowdsourcing, 98
customization, 51, 53, 56–58
cyber assets, 162
cyber threats, 161, 164–165
cybersecurity, xvi, 161–162, 165, 167–168

data analysis, 15
databases, 39, 41, 43, 45, 47
data migration, 57
DAW, 149, 151–152
decoding, 137–139
denial of service, 165
device driver, 29, 33
digital, 3–7
digital audio, 149–152
Digital Audio Workstation. See DAW
digital video, 149, 153–154, 156
digitization, 126, 131
discovery, 39, 46–47, 67–68, 176
DSL, 75–76

email, 21, 68, 70, 86, 92, 104, 162–163, 165–167
encoding, 137–139
e-rate, 13, 78
e-reader, 111, 113, 116
evaluation plan, 14
Evergreen, 51, 56–57
external network attack, 69

Facebook, 67, 98–99, 102–104, 154
federated, 39, 46–47
feed, 99, 103, 150
fiber, 75–77
file, 25, 29, 32–34, 65–67, 116, 118, 138
file extension, 30, 32
file format, 116, 150,
file sharing, 66–67
filter, 77–78, 161–164, 167
firewall, 77–78, 161–162, 166–167
FIRST, 140–141
fixes, 39, 45–46, 53, 55
free software movement, 54, 58
functionality, 39, 43, 45
functional teams, 171

gaming console, 113
GarageBand, 151–153, 157
gateway, 63, 67
goals, 11–14
Google, 31, 34–35, 47, 52, 67, 75, 91, 150, 175–176
graphical user interface, 70
Greenstone, 58

hacker, 78, 163, 166–167
hardware, 6, 19, 20–22, 67, 114, 156
hashtag, 99
hotspot, 73, 79, 111, 116
HTML, 25, 32, 75, 116
hubs, 77
hybrid cloud, 65
Hypertext markup language. See HTML

IaaS, 65, 67
ILS, xv, 30, 39–41, 45–46, 55–58, 67–69
ILS modules, 40, 43, 67
iMAC, 131, 152, 157
IMLS. See Institute of Museum and Library Services
inclusive learning, 126, 129
information nonrepudiation, 161, 168
information technology, 14, 162
infrastructure, 6, 65–66, 74, 76. See also network infrastructure
Infrastructure-as-a-Service. See IaaS
innovation, 53, 57, 119 , 126, 171–173
Institute of Museum and Library Services, 142
instruction sets, 30–33
Integrated Library System. See ILS
International Society for Technology in Education, 102, 142
Internet, 64, 67, 73–79, 112–113, 162, 173
Internet of Things, xvii, 173, 176
Internet Service Provider, xvi, 73, 75, 112
IoT. See Internet of Things
ISP. See Internet Service Provider
ISTE. See International Society for Technology in Education

Java, 138, 144
JavaScript, 31, 35, 70

Koha, 55–57

LANS, 76
laptop, 20, 22, 113–114, 116, 152, 157
Library of Congress, 40–41, 56, 100–101
Library Service Platform, 36, 39, 45–47, 176
license, xv, 36, 51–56, 163
licensing, 45, 51, 53–55, 59
Linux, 21, 32
listserv, xv, 3, 7–8
Local Area Networks. See LANS
LSP. See Library Service Platform

Mac OS X, 21
machine language, 22, 31, 51–52
machine learning, 171, 173
mainframe computer, 40
makerspace, xvi, 6–7, 15, 125–134, 142, 151–152, 156, 176
malware, xv, 29–30, 34, 165–166
mapping, 19, 23
MARC, 21, 44, 56, 139
materials safety data sheets (MSDS), 126, 129
metadata, 44, 56, 103, 173–174
metrics, 97–98
mission, 11–12, 14–16, 102
mobile device, 6, 22, 58, 73, 76, 111–119, 152, 172, 177
modem, 76–77
modules, xv, 40, 43, 45, 67
mouse, 24, 70, 172

natural language, 172–174
needs assessment, xv, 11, 15–16
network attack, 69
network infrastructure, xv, 74, 76–77, 79–80

object code, 51–52
OCLC, 47
online catalog, 43–44, 46–47, 53, 118
online learning, 85–86, 90–91
online meetings, xvi, 85–93
online programming, 86, 90–91, 172
open source, xv, 51–59, 172
operating system, 19–21, 24, 26, 31, 65, 165–166
OS. See operating system

P2P, 67
PaaS, 65, 67, 69
participants, 85–89, 91–92
peer collaboration, 137, 141–142

Peer-to-Peer networks. See P2P
peripherals, 6, 19–20, 22–24, 33, 76, 152
phishing, 70, 78, 161, 165, 167
platform, 19–22, 24–26, 31–33, 36, 39, 46–47, 65, 67–68, 78, 88, 97–99, 104, 176
Platform-as-a-Service. See PaaS
podcast, 149–151
port, 24
printer, 21–24, 33–34, 79
private cloud, 65
professional learning, 14, 15, 57, 81, 93, 142.
    See also training
Programming. See online programming
programming language, 52–53, 138, 143–144
proprietary, 52–55, 116, 118, 150
public access, 35, 149, 155
Public Access Catalog, 40, 44
public cloud, 65
public domain, 52–53, 101

RAM, 20, 30
random access memory. See RAM
relational database, 41
release, xv, 19, 21–22, 40, 45–47, 53, 55
reserves, 44
Robert's Rules of Order, 88
robotic competition, 140–141
robotics, xvi, 126, 131, 137, 139–140, 142–144, 172–174, 176
router, 6, 76–77, 79

SaaS. See Software-as-a-Service
safety, 129–131
satellite, 75–76, 153
school library media center, 101
Scratch, 142–145
script, 30–31, 34, 166
serial, 44–45
smart devices, 111, 113–114, 118, 176
smartphones, xv, 6, 13, 20–22, 65, 111–113
social media, xvi, 7, 57, 68, 81, 98–106
social media policy, 100–102, 106
social networks, 98–100
software, 29–36
Software-as-a-Service, xv, 36, 46, 65–66, 118
source code, 52–55
spam, 165
spammers, 167

spyware, 33, 165–166
Staff development. See professional learning
STEAM, xvi, 35, 125–129, 131, 138, 152, 176
STEM, 126
strategic plan, 11–12
streamed, 149–150
streaming video, 68, 76, 149, 153
supply chain, 126, 132
survey, 15
switch, 26, 76–77
synchronization, 111, 118

tablet, 13, 22, 78–79, 113–114, 116
Technology learning. See professional learning
technology plan, xv, 11–16
technology support, 36, 57
telepresence, 172, 174–175
TikTok, 154–155
training, 7–8, 57, 80, 128, 130, 142. See also professional learning
transceiver, 111–113
trending, 99, 176
troubleshooting, 7, 23–24, 79, 158
tutorial, 57, 142, 144, 152–155
Twitter, 68, 81, 98, 103, 106, 176

uninterrupted power supply, 77
UPS. See uninterrupted power supply

USB, 24, 157
utilities, 30, 33–34

vendor host, 63, 65–67, 69–70
version, 40, 45–47, 53, 58, 75
videoconferencing, 86, 88
viral, 99
virtual environment, 171, 174–175
virtualization, 63, 65
virtual reality, 22, 113, 172, 175–176
virtual voice assistant, 172, 176
virus, 22, 33–34, 70, 78, 163, 166
vision, 12, 14–16, 46
volunteers, 130, 133

WAN, 76
webinar, 3, 7, 57, 81, 85, 92–93, 100–101, 142
WebJunction, 7, 81, 103
wide area network. See WAN
Wi-Fi, 6, 15, 23, 64, 76, 78–79, 112–113, 116, 162–164
Windows, 21, 24, 26, 31–33, 75, 117, 152
WorldCat, 47

YouTube, 90, 128, 152, 154–155, 157, 176

Z39, 50, 40, 63, 67
Zoom, 89–90

About the Author

Marie Keen Shaw is the program coordinator for the Library Technical Assistant certificate program at Three Rivers Community College in Norwich, Connecticut, where she has also been an adjunct professor since 1999. She teaches courses in cataloging and classification, digital resources, reference services, and management strategies. She has served on the boards of the Connecticut Library Consortium and the Connecticut Digital Library. She currently serves in a leadership role on the board of the Groton Public Library in Groton, Connecticut. Marie received her doctorate of education from the University of Connecticut in educational leadership and adult learning, a Sixth-Year Degree from Southern Connecticut State University in educational leadership, and her MS from Purdue University in library and information science and educational media. A retired certified high school library media specialist and curriculum instructional leader, she has been a speaker at state library and educational media conferences in Rhode Island, Illinois, and Connecticut. Marie is coauthor of *Management and Supervision: An Introduction for Support Staff* (Rowman & Littlefield, 2019) and *Communication and Teamwork: An Introduction for Library Support Staff* (Rowman & Littlefield, 2019). She is the author of the books *Cataloging Library Resources: An Introduction* (Rowman & Littlefield, 2017), *Library Technology and Digital Resources: An Introduction for Support Staff* (Rowman & Littlefield, 2015), and *Block Scheduling and Its Impact on the School Library Media Center*. Her doctoral dissertation "Teacher's Learning of Technology: Key Factors and Process," was accepted by the University of Connecticut in 2010.

www.ingramcontent.com/pod-product-compliance
Lightning Source LLC
Chambersburg PA
CBHW060343010526
44117CB00017B/2950